G000092510

THE
INNS & PUBS
OF
NOTTINGHAMSHIRE

THE STORIES BEHIND THE NAMES

by
Gordon Wright
and
Brian J. Curtis

Nottinghamshire   County Council
Leisure Services (1995)

First published in 1995 by Nottinghamshire County Council, Leisure Services Department, Trent Bridge House, Fox Road, West Bridgford, Nottingham NG2 6BJ.

ISBN 0 900943 81 5

Typeset in 11/12 pt Gill Sans
Printed by Central Print Services, Nottinghamshire County Council.

CONTENTS

LIST OF PLATES

'This book is dedicated to our wives,

Barbara and Christine, without whose

support and encouragement it

would never have been written.'

FOREWORD

by Andrew Ludlow, Nottingham CAMRA

The concept of a book about inn names appeals to many, and especially those who have an interest in public-houses generally.

I was extremely flattered to be asked to write this introduction, but also somewhat overawed. I knew that the co-authors, Brian and Gordon, had devoted years of research into the subject before finally putting pen to paper, and that this book would eventually become a definitive reference guide.

Andrew Ludlow

However, it should not be seen merely as a reference text. There is more to it than that. This is a book full of history and tradition, interspersed with explanations for the more modern names, such as the Man In Space and the Tottle Brook. It is intended to be a fun-book, to entertain - whilst at the same time providing us with an accurate and comprehensive account of how and why our pubs came by their names.

I believe that this book achieves all these aims and more. Read it for its facts, its sense of tradition, and as an insight into the English Pub.

Enjoy the book, and on your next visit to your local, ponder fleetingly over its signboard whilst you appreciate a pint of the best!

Cheers

WHAT'S INN A NAME?

Inn-signs in general are a microcosm of the world in which we live. They reflect both our history and our heritage in a way that appeals to all.

We should always bear in mind that a pub's name - like its signboard, if it has one - requires a definite function. Sometimes it can combine tradition with a more than academic interest. Like all good advertisements, it should seek to attract custom, to be remembered, and to be spoken of between friends.

Within these pages we have explored the origins of many of our own County's inn-signia and found them to contain just such a wealth of information. Tales of the Unexpected, the Lives of Eccentric Heroes, Sporting Legends and Folklore galore - they are all here. Many of these names are unique to Nottinghamshire and cannot be found elsewhere.

'It even puts Apollo

To all his strength of art to follow

The flights, and to divine

What's meant by every sign.'

Ben Jonson

ANNESLEY WOODHOUSE

BADGER BOX - *Derby Road*

The current public house replaced an inn of the same name here in September 1962. The former pub, which was over one hundred years old, enjoyed the unique distinction of having two different names at the same time. The 'Badger Box' was painted on the front wall and the 'Robin Hood' on a side wall.

Many years ago this inn had a farmhouse attached to it and was the meeting place for the local badger hunt. In its yard there were two pits where badgers were put to fight. Though long since filled in, the positions of these pits can still be seen today.

The 'Badger Box' derives from an incident in 1938, when the then licensee, Mr James Moss, was given a badger cub by the former licensee of the 'Boot and Shoe' inn at Flintham, Sam Griffin, who had dug the animal out of a drainpipe. 'Minnie,' as she was later named, became a favourite of the patrons, and was kept in a special badger-box at the rear of the inn. Some five years later, the animal escaped and had to be shot by the Police.

In the tap room of this inn is a glass showcase containing a stuffed badger, possibly Minnie, but nobody seems to know for sure. Displayed in the Public Bar is a handsome set of large singly-framed photographs of the Nottinghamshire County Cricket team dating from the 1930s - including, of course, Harold Larwood.

GENERAL HAVELOCK - *Skegby Road*

This hostelry is named in honour of Sir Henry Havelock (1795-1857), one of the heroes of the Indian Mutiny.

Born in Bishop-Wearmouth, Sunderland, he entered the army a month after Waterloo, leaving for India in 1823. At the outbreak of the Indian Mutiny he gathered a column of 1,000 Highlanders and others at Allahabad in order to relieve Cawnpore and Lucknow. Having crossed the Ganges he fought eight glorious battles but, through sickness, his small army had to retire. When reinforcements arrived, Havelock again advanced and engaged the enemy three miles outside of Lucknow at Alum Bagh. For some two months they were besieged, until a relief column commanded by Sir Colin Campbell came to their rescue.

General Havelock, Annesley Woodhouse

A week later Havelock, now a K.C.B., was dead, killed by the disease that had plagued his army throughout, dysentery. A deeply religious man, his last words to his son were, '*See how a Christian can die!*'

LARWOOD - *Beauvale Road*

Opened on the 1st June 1965 by the then president of Mansfield Brewery, Mr C.W. Chadburn, as 'The Sir Winston,' after the famous statesman Sir Winston Churchill, this inn changed its name in 1991 to 'The Larwood' in honour of local cricketing legend Harold Larwood.

Born on the 14th November, 1904 at Nuncargate, Annesley Woodhouse, Larwood was to become the most feared and accurate fast bowler of all time.

Having spent his early days as a miner, and though only 5' 8" in height, he was extremely strong and fit, thus enabling him to sustain a spell of fast bowling for long periods, even in immense heat. A testimony to this occurred in 1932 when, in partnership with William Voce (see 'Larwood and Voce Tavern,' - West Bridgford), he bowled unchanged for Nottinghamshire throughout both Leicestershire innings, a remarkable feat.

Best remembered for his part in the so-called 'bodyline' series of 1932-33 where, under the captaincy of Douglas Jardine, both he and William Voce formed the spearhead of England's attack against the Australians. After the tour Larwood was instructed to apologise to the MCC for his aggressive bowling. As he had only been obeying his captain's instructions, not surprisingly he refused. Ignored by the selectors because of this, sadly he never played for his country again. Douglas Jardine presented Harold with a silver ashtray inscribed 'To Harold for the Ashes 1932-33. From a grateful Skipper'.

In 1950 he emigrated with his family to Australia, ironically sailing there aboard the 'Orontes,' the same ship that had carried the MCC team there in 1932. Harold Larwood died on 22nd July 1995.

ARNOLD

ARROW - *Gedling Road*

Opened by Home Brewery on the 24th July 1969, its naming is in line with this brewery's tradition of perpetuating the legend of Robin Hood and his Merry Men. The arrow here is an obvious choice, being linked with archery and therefore the famous outlaw himself.

The inn-sign depicts a warning arrow striking a mighty oak tree.

BURNT STUMP - *Burnt Stump Hill*

Up until the late 1940s this building was the home of the Millbank family. It then served as a hunting lodge until June, 1978, when it was opened as an inn by Mansfield Brewery.

It takes its name from an incident that occurred many years ago, when an old tree in its grounds was burnt to the ground. The *'Burnt Stump'* stands in 30 acres of picturesque parkland and is a real family pub.

CROSS KEYS - *Front Street*

Prior to the Reformation, the Christian heraldic emblem of the Cross Keys was a very common inn-sign, referring as it does to St Peter, to whom Jesus said, *'I will give unto thee the keys of the Kingdom of Heaven.'*

Cross Keys also feature in the arms of the old Dioceses of Exeter, York, Gloucester and Peterborough, and the new ones of Sheffield, Bradford, Ripon and Blackburn.

This inn, formerly comprising a butcher's shop and a croft and occupying a three-acre site, has stood here since at least 1801.

EAGLE - *Howbeck Road*

This inn was opened on the 11th December 1980 by the then leader of Nottinghamshire County Council, Herbert Bird. The pub's lounge is named after Richard Parkes Bonington, a 19th-century Arnold painter.

Since the 15th century the sign of the eagle has been in use as both a Christian and heraldic emblem. The symbol of St John the Evangelist, it has often been used to decorate church lecterns. The name Arnold is thought to derive from the Old English word *Ernehale* - 'place of the eagles'.

Eagle, Arnold

FLYING HORSE - *High Street*

The naming of this pub as the *'Flying Horse'* is a reference to the 'Pegasus Snooker Club' which forms part of the building.

The winged horse Pegasus, ridden by Bellerophon in Greek mythology, has also been used as an heraldic device by the Knights Templar.

The former *'Flying Horse'* inn which stood in the Poultry at Nottingham, is believed to have derived its name from an ancient swinging horse which entertained the crowds at medieval fairs. A rider, having mounted the horse, would be swung to and fro as he attempted to take a ring from a quintain using a sword.

The Arnold pub can be traced back to 1850 when it was called the *'Friendly Tavern.'*

FRIAR TUCK - *Gedling Road*

Opened in December 1958 on the site of old farm buildings, this inn commemorates the legendary fat and jovial chaplain who was a member of Robin Hood's band of Merry Men.

It is said that Tuck was a renegade friar from the Greyfriars Order in Nottingham, thought to have sought sanctuary at Fountain Dale, Blidworth, where he was allowed to live in a cell (Friar Tuck's well can still be seen within its precincts).

Friar Tuck is first mentioned, as being part of the Robin Hood legend, in a medieval ballad *'The Ballad of Robin Hood and Sir Guy of Gisbourne.'*

Interestingly, a Friar Tuck certainly did exist. Robert Stafford, a chaplain in the Parish of Lindfield (Sussex) assumed the name 'Frère (brother) Tuck' when he led an outlaw band during the early part of the 15th century.

GREYHOUND - *Nottingham Road*

A pub of this name has stood on this site for at least one hundred and fifty years.

The *'Greyhound'* has been used as an inn-sign since the Tudor period. Until the late 18th century a silver greyhound was worn on the sleeve of the King's Messengers who, when carrying royal and state mail, would use it as a means of recognition. In the days of coaching, this led to several public houses taking up the name.

This inn's name though, is most likely a reference to the Dukes of Newcastle whose heraldic emblem is the greyhound and who were major landowners

Greyhound, Arnold

throughout the county. Other pubs of this name can be found at Aslockton, Beeston, Pinxton, Skegby and Nottingham.

Interestingly, due to its reliance more on sight than smell, the greyhound is often referred to as the 'gazehound.' The dogs themselves were originally used in the chase, but are now used mainly for greyhound racing or 'greycing.'

HORSE AND JOCKEY - *Front Street*

There is a plaque on the wall of this pub that gives an insight into its history and explains the reason for its name. It reads:

'This building was established in 1802 and was originally called The Horse and Groom because it had stables at the rear and was sited on half an acre of grazing land. The original owner of the Horse and Groom, Daniel Simpkins, a butcher by trade, ran three businesses from this building - a butchers shop, a pub and of course the stables at the rear. Daniel died in 1827 and the new owner George Phipps discontinued the butchers shop and after a few years leased the pub and the stables to his sister Ann for the sum of 5 shillings a year. During the next 30 years the pub changed hands four times and in 1891 was purchased by John Robinson who renamed it the Horse and Jockey because of his love for racehorses. During the next 100 years the grazing land at the rear was sold to Arnold Health Centre to develop, and the stables converted to a furniture warehouse. One thing remains intact, this is still one of Arnold's favourite ale houses!'

LONGBOW - *Calverton Road*

This inn opened in spectacular fashion in April 1968, when three lady members of the Sherwood Archers, led by Mrs Joyce Matthewson, the then County Champion, made their entry. Dressed in Lincoln green, they demanded admission in the name of Robin Hood and aimed three arrows through the open doorway at a full size target in the lounge.

From the remotest times archery has been practised by many nations. The longbow was used by the Normans with deadly effect at the Battle of Hastings and, under the Plantagenets and Tudors, legislation decreed that every man under the age of 60 years must practise his skill with this weapon - the only exceptions being clerics and lawyers. Butts were provided to the south of Park Row in Nottingham and also in many villages throughout the county to facilitate this activity during holiday periods and Sunday afternoons.

LORD NELSON - *Front Street*

There are more hostelries throughout England named after Horatio Nelson (1758-1805) than any other person.

Born at Burnham Thorpe in Norfolk, Nelson began his naval career at the age of twelve in 1770 and by the time he had reached 21 he was promoted to post-captain. At the outbreak of the French Revolutionary Wars (1792-1802), he commanded the 'Agamemnon' under Lord Hood in the Pacific. During the reduction of Bastia and Calvi (in Corsica) gravel, scattered by a shot, destroyed the sight in his right eye. Soon after returning to duty he was promoted to the rank of rear-admiral and charged with seizing a richly-laden Spanish ship at Santa Cruz (in Tenerife). It was during this battle that he lost his right arm.

In 1798, his destruction of the French fleet at the Battle of the Nile, off Aboukir Bay, ended Napoleon Bonaparte's planned conquest of the East and led to Nelson being raised to the peerage as Baron Nelson of the Nile. He later became a Viscount.

In October 1805, Nelson recorded his greatest victory, the destruction of the combined French and Spanish fleets off Cape Trafalgar. Before the battle he hoisted the famous signal, *'England expects that every man will do his duty.'* Sadly, whilst directing the engagement from the deck of his flagship the 'Victory,' he was mortally wounded by a sniper's bullet. His body was later brought home and buried in St. Paul's Cathedral.

There has been an inn of this name on this site since at least 1842.

MAID MARIAN - *Coppice Road*

Opened on 26th July 1956 by Home Brewery, the sign here (not put up until 1992) features the outlaw's beloved Maid Marian.

Evidence of Marian's association with the legend is first made in a 17th-century broadsheet called *'Robin Hood and Maid Marian.'* Reputedly, fair Marian was led from Blidworth to the church at Edwinstowe where Robin made her his bride.

MAJOR OAK - *Rolleston Drive*

Opened on 9th September 1965, the name features the legendary home of Robin Hood and his outlaws in Sherwood Forest.

This magnificent oak still stands in the Birklands area of Sherwood Forest Country Park, a mile north of Edwinstowe. Originally called the Queen Oak, this hollow tree, with a girth of some thirty feet, was reputedly used by the outlaw and his merry men as both a hiding place and a meeting place.

It is believed that it acquired its name of the 'Major Oak' from Major Hayman Rooke, a soldier, antiquarian and meteorologist, who lived in Mansfield Woodhouse in the 18th century. Rooke surveyed and catalogued many of the Sherwood oaks. In 1791, this tree was marked on an estate map as a *'tree called Major Rooke.'*

Major Oak, Arnold

The Major Oak has witnessed many events over the years. During the 19th century, beneath its leafy boughs, cock fighting took place, and for a while it became known locally as Cock Pen Oak. During the August Bank Holiday of 1982, this sole surviving massive oak of Sherwood Forest was set ablaze. Fortunately, the fire was confined to the hollow trunk of the tree and it survived. Off-cuts of a bough severed from it by the fire were later inlaid into wooden caskets in 1992, and presented to the film star Kevin Costner as part of an award for his role in the film 'Robin Hood - Prince of Thieves.'

The old oak tree has been 'cloned' and genetically identical 'Major Oaks' are now growing in a number of different countries including Japan and America!

Nell Gwynn, Arnold

NELL GWYNN - *Oxclose Lane*

Opened on the 14th December 1961 by the Vicar of St. Paul's, Daybrook, the Reverend Norman Keen, this pub recalls Eleanor (Nell) Gwynn (1650-87).

The planners made sure that Nell had a proven association with the district before they went ahead with the naming of this inn and found it in the fact that the first Duke of St Albans - a title long associated with nearby Bestwood Park - was one of her sons by Charles II.

Born in Hereford, Nell worked as an orange-seller at the Drury Lane Theatre in London. At the age of fifteen she became an actress, performing her first role in a play, *'The Indian Emperor'* by Dryden, at this very same theatre. She was an excellent dancer and comic. When she laughed, it was said that her eyes almost disappeared, so abandoned did she become.

Nell became extremely popular, especially with men. Her most notable admirer was Charles II who took her as his mistress and by whom she had two children. During her acting career she withdrew from the stage for indefinite periods, quite often at Royal request, before finally leaving it for good in 1682.

It is thought that Nell often visited Bestwood Lodge (a Royal Hunting Lodge which once stood on the site of the present Bestwood Lodge Hotel), with King Charles II when he came to hunt in Sherwood Forest which, in those days, stretched from Worksop in the north to Nottingham in the south.

Within two years of the death of her King, Nelly died of a sudden apoplexy at the age of 37.

The inn-sign displayed outside this house depicts a young Nell, selling oranges.

OXCLOSE - *Oxclose Lane*

Opened in 1980, the name of this inn and its sign, depicting a magnificent ox, is an obvious reference to the road on which it stands.

Many public houses have been named after a particular prize-winning animal or a special breed (see 'The Durham Ox' at Beeston).

ROBIN HOOD AND LITTLE JOHN - *Church Street*

The popularity of the title 'Robin Hood and Little John' is believed to stem from an old rhyme:

> *'You gentlemen and yeomen good*
> *Come in and drink with Robin Hood.*
> *If Robin Hood be not at home,*
> *Come in and drink with Little John.'*

An inn of this name has stood here for over 150 years. (See also the *'Little John'* at Ravenshead).

ASKHAM

DUKE WILLIAM - *Town Street*

The little known village of Askham has a pub with a name unique in Nottinghamshire. Duke William later became King William IV. He was the third son of George III and in 1789 was created Duke of Clarence. He became the heir presumptive to the throne in 1827, and then King in 1830 on the death of his eldest brother George IV.

The deeds of this pub are in the possession of the landlord. They date back to the 1820s, the time when the Duke married Adelaide, and it may well have been to honour this event that the pub was so named. (see also *'King William IV'* and *'Queen Adelaide'*, both at Sneinton).

There used to be extensive hop-fields to the east of this village and at picking times the *'Duke William'* would have been crowded with people, many having walked from Worksop or Retford to earn money helping with the harvest. The hops were taken by horse drawn carts to Tuxford where they were sold at the annual September Hop Fairs.

Duke William, Askham

ASLOCKTON

Cranmer Arms, Aslockton

CRANMER ARMS - *Main Street*

An inn of this name has stood on this site for over 140 years and is first recorded in White's Directory of Nottinghamshire in 1853.

The inn takes its name from Thomas Cranmer (1489-1556), the first Protestant Archbishop of Canterbury, who was born in Aslockton. At the age of fourteen he was sent by his mother to Jesus College, Cambridge where, in 1510, he obtained a fellowship. In 1523 Cranmer took holy orders and some six years later, when an epidemic of the plague spread throughout Cambridge, he left there for nearby Waltham.

It was whilst there that he found favour with King Henry VIII and was subsequently appointed Royal Chaplain and Archdeacon of Taunton. Shortly after his appointment Cranmer was sent on two embassies, to Italy in 1530, and to Germany in 1532.

Upon his return from Germany in May 1532, and on being consecrated Archbishop of Canterbury, he pronounced Henry VIII's marriage to Catherine of Aragon null and void *ab initio* (void from the beginning) and the king's marriage to Anne Boleyn valid. Cranmer was soon to preside over Henry's subsequent actions regarding his wives, annulling the king's marriage to Anne in 1536 and divorcing him from Anne of Cleves in 1540. Upon the king's new marriage to Catherine Howard, Cranmer began to meddle in affairs of state and informed Henry that his wife was guilty of premarital affairs. Catherine was subsequently executed for infidelity and the king took his sixth wife, Catherine Parr.

Despite all this, Cranmer was at his happiest when engaged in literary pursuits, promoting the translation of the Bible. Upon Henry VIII's death in 1547, Edward VI ascended the throne and Cranmer compiled the new king's First Prayer Book.

When it became apparent that Edward's reign was to be short-lived due to his continuing ill-health, Cranmer supported the claim of Lady Jane Grey to the English throne and was doomed when Mary I succeeded in 1553.

On the 14th September 1553, guilty of conscious perjury, Cranmer was sent to the Tower of London and arraigned for treason. In 1556, having been taken to the stake, he displayed one final act of courage before he died, bravely thrusting his right hand into the flames and keeping it there crying *'This hath offended! Oh this unworthy hand!'*

OLD GREYHOUND - *Main Street*

This, the oldest inn in the village, is first recorded in White's Directory of Nottinghamshire in 1832. Its name derives from the heraldic coat of arms of the Barons Clinton and Pelham Clinton (Dukes of Newcastle) who were major landowners in the county (see pubs of the same name at Arnold and Beeston).

At one time this hostelry had a small room set aside for dominoes where, up until 1968, ale was served straight from the cask into jugs and shoved to the players through a serving-hatch.

Old Greyhound, Aslockton

ASPLEY

BEACON - *Aspley Lane*

Opened on the 3rd November 1936, the name here just possibly refers to the well-known Belisha Beacon, itself named after the Minister of Transport who introduced this safety regulation in 1934. However, the signboard picture shows a group of patriots lighting the type of signal fire which in various times of danger in our island's history (when invasion was threatened with the approach of the Spanish Armada - or later, Napoleon) was used as part of a chain of bonfires set up on strategic hill-tops by local vigilantes.

A similarly dramatic picture is presented by the sign of the *'Beacon,'* in Bluebell Hill Road, St Anns.

COCKED HAT - *Broxtowe Lane*

The original sign had the rare distinction of being painted by a member of the Royal Academy, Ralph Ellis, shortly after the pub's opening in 1933. It belongs in one of those happily-selective categories of 'pairings' in which the artist paints a different interpretation of the name on each side of the signboard. In this case two different aspects of the 'tricorn,' the three-sided hat often adorned with ostrich plumes which has the brim permanently turned up. On one side, it is being worn by an admiral, on the other side by a general - both being in former full-dress or ceremonial uniform.

Those of us who remember the once-vivid colours of this superb sign can only reflect, sadly, that the gradual pollution of the atmosphere down the passing years has done successive re-paintings no favours at all. The look of the present sign - as similarly, say, with the *'Happy Man'* (qv), another splendid 'pairing' - gives it a curiously washed-out aspect - the original arresting imagery has somehow disappeared.

WHITEMOOR - *Nuthall Road*

The name here is most likely a reference to its close proximity to the Whitemoor Estate.

Built around 1936, this pub's splendid sign depicts a herd of sheep grazing on a snow covered moor.

ATTENBOROUGH

BLUE BELL - *Nottingham Road*

This pub, mentioned in White's Directory of Nottinghamshire in 1832, was rebuilt in 1938.

A bell is a simplistic sign and easily recognisable. It was often used as the sign of hostelries with religious connections, or those (like this one) that were within earshot of local church bells.

The name may also have derived from the flower the bluebell (many of which are shown on the signboard growing around a large blue bell with a church in the background). Other *'Blue Bell'* inns are to be found at Sutton-cum-Lound, Gringley-on-the-Hill, East Drayton, Carlton-in-Lindrick and Ranskill.

AWSWORTH

HOG'S HEAD - *Giltbriggs Farm*

Opened in December 1986, this pub's name conjures up images of a pig's head on a plate - nothing though could be further from the truth. In fact a hogshead is a beer barrel containing 54 gallons of ale.

This pub was converted from a farmhouse and barn known as Giltbriggs Farm. The buildings, dating back to the early 18th century, had been derelict for at least forty years before the conversion.

BAKERSFIELD

GREENWOOD TREE - *Greenwood Road*

Mr James Shipstone, former chairman of Shipstone's Brewery, officially opened this pub on 30th December 1960 with a quotation from Shakespeare's 'As You Like It', a play set in the Forest of Arden, about the Greenwood Tree:

'Come hither, come hither,
come hither, here shall you
see no enemy but winter and
rough weather.'

Tally Ho sign, Bakersfield

OAKDALE - *Oakdale Road*

Named after the road on which it stands, this inn was opened on the 27th October 1933.

TALLY HO - *Oakdale Road*

Opened on the 12th October 1962 by the Reverend Peter H. Boulton, the then Vicar of St John's, Oakdale Road, Carlton, this pub's sign has no significance with the area - its name being thought up by the brewery directors.

The pub stands on a site once occupied by Harriman's Nurseries, and known locally as 'the Onion Patch' - where, prior to the building of the pub, folk used to buy their produce.

'Tally-ho' is the modern equivalent of the Norman hunting cry *'taillir au,'* which means 'to the coppice.' Nowadays the cry is used to signify that a fox has broken cover.

BALDERTON

CHESTERS - *Main Street*

Formerly the *'Cock Inn,'* this house was refurbished and underwent a change of sign to its current title in December 1984.

One feature of its new image as a Victorian-style pub, was the inclusion of six leather Chesterfield sofas in its decor. It is from these sofas that the pub takes its name.

TURK'S HEAD - *London Road*

Occupying a prime site on what was once the Great North Road, this pub replaced a former coaching inn of the same name that once stood here. The previous house, which used to have stabling for horses, had been demolished as part of a road widening project.

Since it opened in 1970, the new *'Turk's Head'* has played host to a nefarious presence which rearranges paintings in the Lounge, refusing to allow them to be hung straight!

Turks were a common topic of conversation in the 15th, 16th and 17th centuries. The scourge of the European nations, they often held Christians captive for huge ransoms. The interest in them led invariably to the popularity of this sign.

BARNBY MOOR

Ye Olde Bell, Barnby Moor (c.1920)

YE OLDE BELL - *North Road*

The symbol of the bell has been in common use as an inn-sign since the early part of the 14th century and its popularity led Chaucer to say that *'the gentil hostelrie that heighte the Tabard,'* was *'faste by the Belle.'* Possibly the sign of the bell, an easy visual symbol for people to relate to, became popular due to our national fondness for bell-ringing, an occupation that led to our country being described by the composer Handel as the 'ringing island.'

For over three hundred years, travellers along the Great North Road have called at the 'Olde Bell.' Originally it was called the *'Blue Bell Inn'* and in its heyday, soon after 1635 (when it served as a posting house on the route between London and Edinburgh), it had bed-accommodation for sixty postboys and stabling for twice that number of horses, as well as numerous rooms for its patrons.

From 1727 until the advent of the Great Northern Railway, the *Bell* maintained its high esteem. But with the rise of the railway came a decline in its popularity and the *Bell* was forced to close. After the surrender of its licence the building was purchased by a Mr Beevor and used as a private dwelling-house for over sixty years, during which time part of it was occasionally employed as a chapel. When it eventually reopened as a hotel in order to capture the thriving trade now being provided by travellers using motor cars, it soon regained the popularity it had enjoyed in former days.

Over the years this inn has witnessed many noteworthy events. In 1695 Ralph Thoresby, the famous antiquary and historian of Leeds stayed here on his journey from London. The prize-fighter 'Game Chicken' Pearce, before his battle with Jim Belcher at Blyth, used the place as his headquarters, and in 1830 the inn gained further notoriety locally, when followers of the 'Captain Swing' movement (a group opposed to farmers using threshing machines) arrived and set fire to haystacks nearby. The Bell's landlord, George Clarke, mounted some fifty men to scour the district for these arsonists, two of whom were later apprehended and upon their conviction sentenced to deportation.

During his sojourn in England during the Second World War, the King of Norway stayed here, no doubt noting the panelling to be found in this hotel's splendid dining room, all of which came from Bradgate House near Leicester, the former home of Lady Jane Grey.

Curiously enough, this inn is reputedly haunted by 'a lady dressed in grey' who, from time to time, frequents its ballroom.

BASFORD

BARLEY MOW - *Basford Road*

A 'Mow' is a stack, and a barley-mow sign - especially in farming areas - was meant to be a simple indication that beer was sold, barley being one of its main ingredients. The sign here shows the stack only, but the rural scene is capable of several variations - sometimes showing farm-labourers busy on top of the stack, or sharing their lunch in the shade of a tree nearby, their pitchforks propped alongside them. One of the best we have seen, pictured a group of children dancing in a ring around the base of the stack, to the lively accompaniment of a penny-whistle played by the farmer.

The pub itself is about 200 years old.

There is another pub with this name in the North Nottinghamshire village of Mattersey.

CATCHEM'S CORNER - *Vernon Road*

The junction of Vernon Road and Bulwell Lane has been known as *Catchem's Corner* for as long as anyone can remember, and in fact the football field which used to be situated across the road in pre-War days was always referred to as *Catchem's*. It was here that Basford United, one of the best teams in the area, won so many victories.

When Vernon Road was made, to accommodate the tramway traffic, two more entrance doors were provided on the west and north sides of the *'Station Hotel'* (as it was then), the existing east-side doorway being for entrance from Bulwell Lane. At that time, the distance from the backyard to the local station (closed in September 1964) was only a stone's-throw. The trams, which stopped running about 1929 had their terminus right outside the *'Station Hotel,'* so it was the common expression in those days to say 'I'll catch 'em all ways' - i.e. one's connection either by tram, or by train on the line going through from Daybrook to Ilkeston.

It is by no means certain, however, that the new name for the pub (adopted in October 1969) was decided upon for this

Catchem's Corner, Basford

reason. Local legend says that an old chap named Catchem kept a shop on this same corner before the pub was built (which was around 1886), and there are those who claim it got its present name from the custom of miners' wives congregating outside the pub on Friday pay-nights in order to waylay their husbands before they were tempted to spend all the house-keeping money inside - this being the first place of refreshment available to them after coming off shift at the former Gedling Colliery and taking the train home. So if your shovel isn't handy, take your pick ... although it did seem from the humorous aspect of the previous signboard that hung outside this pub (showing a city gent sprinting madly out of the premises to catch the waiting train) that the first-mentioned theory is the most *expressive!*

Fox and Crown, Basford

FOX AND CROWN - *Church Street*

Originally known as the *'Fox,'* the history of this old pub can be traced back to 1707 when it was kept as both an inn and a Debtors' Prison by James Pearson, a butcher, innkeeper and gaoler, together with his wife, Isabella. An inventory of their possessions records, amongst other things, pigs, dung, gaol bed, a twiggen chair, shovels, tongues, a pair of frogs and all the apparatus of innkeeping.

Between 1776 and 1779, the premises were visited by John Howard, the prison reformer, who was shown the parts of the inn used as a gaol. These comprised one main room with three beds, and a further small room for women prisoners - though at the time of the inspections the latter was in use as a servants quarters only.

The cells once fulfilling this purpose are nowadays used as cellars (see similar Note as regards the *'White Hart'* at Lenton).

In 1791, the gaoler, having no allowance to buy food for his prisoners, and fearing that he would be accused of murder if he allowed them to starve, let them all escape.

Locally this pub has also been known as the *'Bowling Green'* because at one time there existed a rink at the rear of the premises as well as a skittle alley. On New Year's Day 1806, 17 year old Lieutenant Browne, having been inveigled into a pistol duel, was killed near to where this green once stood - his body later being removed to Basford Church, and finally to St. Mary's churchyard in Nottingham.

HAVEN - *Nottingham Road*

Opened in September 1971, the unpretentious title of this pub readily suggests that it constitutes a safe and comfortable refuge for all sections of the community. So, indeed, might a hospital - but this establishment has ale on sale as well!

LORD NELSON - *Percy Street*

Opened on the 6th February 1969 by Hardys and Hansons, this pub replaced an older house of the same name that had once stood some 100 yards away before being demolished under the Basford Redevelopment scheme.

An explanation for the name here can be found by referring to the *'Lord Nelson'* pub at Arnold.

MILL - *Bagnall Road*

A large framed photograph is on view here, showing a map of the area and, beneath it, the century-old flour mill which was in use until 1950 in nearby Mill Street. An accompanying caption reads:

> *'This old mill is shown on the Ordnance Survey of 1885, as is the site of these premises.'*

The pub itself was opened in November 1964, its attractive sign depicting both the mill-wheel and the mill-stream.

OLD PEAR TREE - *Bulwell Lane*

As well as displaying the more traditional signboard, the whole of one of this old inn's side walls is covered with a 'fruitful' mural of (naturally) a pear tree - a reminder of the orchard that once grew at the back of the premises.

It is a listed building, dating back to 1645 in the time of the Civil War between the Cavaliers and the Roundheads (or, if you prefer, between the Royalist forces of King Charles I and the Parliamentary army of 'Old Ironsides' himself, Oliver Cromwell). A former post-house, it was also a staging-point for small carriages known as post-chaises passing by on their journeys to and from Nottingham. The stable-boys used to sleep in the top storey of the inn, on a floor made out of old millstones - no sprung beds in those days, of course, for these likely lads ...

Downstairs there is a set of framed photographs from the days when the *'Old Pear Tree'* was the headquarters of the so-called 'Enthusiasts' Club' - a convivial group of men (with now and then a few adventurous young ladies, too) whose specialist interests focused mainly on trains, boats and planes. Also available for inspection is an old document specifying that the land on which this building stands was sold by its owner, John Hutchinson to Richard Pickstone (labourer) for the princely sum of Two pounds, seventeen shillings and sixpence. (!)

In 1985, builders undertaking renovation work knocked down a brick wall at the pub and by chance discovered an extra room. Hanging from its rafters they found a noose, and on the floor beneath it, a packet of Woodbines (cigarettes) dating back to the 1930s ...

PALM TREE - *Gladstone Street*

This pub opened just before Christmas, 1966. There are others in Nottingham named after trees, of course - including the *'Elm Tree'* not far away in Beech Avenue - but these are all English trees (even the rarefied *'Peach Tree,'* now *'Langtry's'*) whereas the *'Palm Tree'* sign suggests the mysterious Middle East, along with its surrounding street names of Cairo, Delta, Egypt, Ekowe, and Suez. Why, we can even throw in Isandula and Zulu Road for good measure - this last name reminding historians (or anyone who saw that spectacular film 'Zulu') why Chard Street nearby is named after Lieutenant Chard of the Royal Engineers, the senior British officer at Rorke's Drift who was one of several who gained his Victoria Cross in that immortal defending action against a vastly superior foe.

The palm tree is actually one of the oldest symbols known. It was used as such by the Assyrians, the Greeks, and the Romans, and by them transmitted to the early Christians. Saint Ambrose, in a very forcible image, compares the life of an early and faithful Christian to the palm tree - *'rough and rugged below, like its stem, but increasing in beauty upwards where it bears heavenly fruit.'*

The proliferation of Egyptian place-names in the local topography lies in the fact that this was the era of colonial development and military campaigning in that part of the Middle East. The Zulu War had been fought two years earlier, Britain and France had assumed dual control in Egypt about the same time and the revolt of 'the mad Mahdi' had prompted Gladstone to despatch the Nile Expedition under Sir Garnet Wolseley (qv) which so tragically failed to reach Khartoum in time to save General Gordon.

PARK TAVERN - *Arnold Road*

In 1869 a small farmhouse (where ale was sold) and an adjacent building (formerly a textile business) were knocked into one to form this pub. It takes its name from the nearby park on Vernon Road.

RAVEN - *Rawson Street*

This ancient pub - known locally, and not surprisingly, as the *'Dickybird'* - is so close to Shipstone's brewery (acquired by Greenalls in 1978) that it comes as rather a shock to find its beer supplied by a rival concern. Mentioned in the 1844 County Directory, it was open for business as an alehouse a good thirty years before Home Brewery (acquired by Scottish and Newcastle in 1986) was established in 1875.

The really outstanding feature of the pub is its acid-embossed glass panels, five each in both the 'Public' and the Lounge - wherein the Raven is represented in place of the customary clear-glass windows. These display a very fine piece of craftsmanship and as such they are insured for a considerable sum. Almost needless to say, the window-cleaner has to be extremely careful!

Despite strenuous efforts we never did find out why the *'Raven'* was so named. It is certainly an unusual ornithological choice - although one can find numerous pubs named after birds. The raven itself was considered sacred to the ancient Danes, possibly because it has been a symbol of death from time immemorial. No doubt Edgar Allan Poe had this in mind when he immortalised the raven in his long poem of that name, whereas the bird described by Dickens in *'Barnaby Rudge'* was much more domesticated!

Those familiar with heraldry will know that the black raven was an emblem used by the old Scottish kings - so it happened that this sign (as with the *'Royal Oak,'* *'Black Boy'* and others) was, in Jacobite times, an indication of political allegiance on the part of a defiant landlord who favoured the House of Stuart.

STANDARD OF ENGLAND - *Park Lane*

The sign here is suitably patriotic in showing the flag of St George - the white one quartered by broad red stripes. This should not be confused by name with the Royal Standard, the present one of which dates from the accession of Queen Victoria. The latter is flown from any (royal) building when the queen is in residence, and likewise, a much smaller flag (a pennant) from the roof or bonnet of a limousine carrying her Majesty to and from one of her official engagements. This Royal Standard is quartered twice by the three heraldic lions of England, and once each by the heraldic red lion of Scotland and the heraldic harp of Ireland. The pub itself is about 100 years old.

STAR - *Nottingham Road*

The sign here is a large gilt star on the facade of the building - but it does not refer (as might be supposed) to the Star Brewery of Shipstones nearby - these premises belong in fact to the Scottish and Newcastle group of companies which acquired Home Brewery in 1986.

Originally a religious sign (referring either to the Star of Bethlehem or the Virgin Mary), the *'Star'* as a pub-name dates from the 15th century.

There are a number of pubs with this name throughout Nottinghamshire. This one was licensed in the 1930s.

VERNON - *Vernon Road*

The reference here is to George John Warren, the fifth Baron Vernon (1803-1866). His mother was the only daughter of Admiral Sir John Borlase Warren (qv), who was born at Stapleford Hall. George Warren himself belonged to the branch of the Vernon family which owned Sudbury Hall, Derbyshire.

The pub itself dates from 1888.

Vernon, Basford

WHITE SWAN -
Church Street

Appearing in Pigot's 1822 Directory as the *'Swan,'* this was for years a Home Brewery pub, being rebuilt in 1928. In 1993 it was purchased by Mansfield Brewery, thus acquiring for its new 'logo', one of those unusual circular-shaped pictorial signs by which this company is rapidly becoming better-known. The original sign depicting an elegant, realistic looking swan forms part of a nice ceramic architectural feature on one of the side walls.

In heraldry, the white swan appears on the coat of arms of both Edward III and Edward IV - and of course the swan itself is a royal bird.

White Swan, Basford

Boat and Horses, Beeston

BOAT AND HORSES - *Trent Road*

The *'Boat and Horses'* appears in White's 1832 Directory of Nottinghamshire. In its former days it was regularly frequented by bargees, who used the stables at its rear for dossing-down overnight with their horses. These horses would have been in need of the rest, having spent their day pounding the towpaths of the nearby Nottingham and Beeston Canal hauling barges, a scene reflected in this inn's sign.

Interestingly, in 1968, the landlord used to throw halfpennies into a bucket at the side of the till. When full it contained the princely sum of £18 and weighed 108lb. He offered the bucket and its contents to the first person who could carry it from the pub to a corner shop some two hundred yards away.

Many folk, including wrestlers, weightlifters and blacksmiths, came from far and wide to try. All were able to lift it, but the metal handle soon bit into their fingers and they were forced to set the bucket down.

It was six or seven months before the bucket was eventually carried by a Clifton labourer called Ron. When he arrived at the shop he was so tired that he dropped the bucket and spilled some of the halfpennies onto the floor. These were soon pocketed by local children.

COMMERCIAL INN - *Wollaton Road*

Purchased by Hardys and Hansons in 1896, this pub stands at the edge of what was once called Markham's Field - the site of Beeston Wakes Fair from 1871 to 1947.

At one time it used to provide accommodation for commercial travellers commuting between Nottingham and Derby, hence its name.

In March 1984 a tremendous fire occurred at what was once the Swiss Mills premises opposite. So intense was the blaze that it melted the double glazing in this pub's windows.

CROWN INN - *Church Street*

Originally a 16th century cottage, it was later sold for the princely sum of five shillings (an indenture marking this sale can be viewed within). The 'confessional,' one of the smallest and oldest serving bars in England, dating back to when the pub was still a cottage, is still in use today.

In 1830 the pub was purchased by a captain in the Queen's regiment who named it the *'Crown Inn.'*

The sign of the crown, the third most popular pub name in the country, shows allegiance to the monarchy and is also an easily recognised visual symbol.

Reputedly, the premises are haunted by the ghost of a Cavalier.

Crown Inn, Beeston

DURHAM OX - *High Road*

This inn, mentioned in White's 1832 Directory of Nottinghamshire, takes its name from a famous beast bred by Charles Collings of Ketton, near Darlington, a man who vastly improved the breed of Durham Shorthorns. In 1795 his famous bull 'Hubback' had a grandson, a roan calf which grew into the celebrated 'Durham Ox.' By the time it was six years old, this ox weighed 3,024 pounds, and was something to marvel at. It was soon sold for the hefty sum of £250 and its new owner was offered over ten times this amount for his newly-acquired animal, but refused. Between 1801 and 1810 he recouped his investment by touring the country with the beast, conveying it in a specially-built vehicle. During a visit to London, the exhibition took as much as £100 in one day. The great impression made by this animal is apparent from the many pubs that have been named after it, especially those to be found in towns visited by the tour.

Other pubs with this name can be found at Orston and Wellow.

GREYHOUND - *High Road*

Built in 1741, one of the earliest owners were the Stone family who actually brewed on the premises. The present building was modernized in 1984.

In the early 19th century days of the industrial revolution, it is said that Luddites called here and, after raising the landlord from his bed to serve them refreshments, marched on into Nottingham to wreak their havoc. This inn, and also the *Durham Ox,* were visited by Reform Act rioters in 1831. Having burnt down Nottingham Castle, they marched to Beeston and caused the silk mill there to suffer a similar fate.

The name here is taken from the heraldic coat of arms of the Barons Clinton and Pelham Clinton (Dukes of Newcastle) who were major landowners in these parts. *'Greyhound'* pubs can also be found at Arnold, Aslockton, Pinxton, Skegby and Nottingham.

The *'Boke of St. Albans,'* dated 1486, gives a useful piece of doggerel listing the shape of a good greyhound:

'A head like a snake, a neck like a drake;
A back like a beam, a belly like a bream;
A foot like a cat, a tail like a rat.'

JOLLY ANGLERS - *Meadow Road*

The original *'Jolly Anglers'* stood for over a century on the banks of the nearby canal until it was pulled down in 1937 as part of a housing development.

This pub, a replacement for the former house, is named after its association with the sport of fishing and is still extremely popular with anglers frequenting the nearby River Trent.

NURSERYMAN - *Derby Road*

Opened in November 1956, this pub occupies a position directly opposite what was once the site of William Lowe and Son's Nurseries.

The choice of name is therefore self-evident, especially as the area of land round about was also previously taken up with allotments.

Star, Beeston

STAR - *Middle Street*

This pub dates from the turn of the 19th century when it was known as the *'Queen's Head.'* A former coaching inn, it was rebuilt in 1914.

Originally the sign of the star was a religious sign, referring either to the star of Bethlehem or to the Virgin Mary. In heraldry a star on a coat of arms informs us that the bearer is of knightly rank. Since 1634 a star with sixteen-points has also appeared on the arms of the Worshipful Company of Innholders.

Interestingly, this pub had a brief change of name during the 1990s when it appeared as the *'Drum'* in an episode of Central Television's programme *'Boon.'*

THREE HORSESHOES -
Middle Street

This pub opened on the 9th December 1965 as a replacement for a former house of the same name which had been demolished to make way for a ring road.

In heraldry, the sign of the *'Three Horseshoes'* represents the arms of the Smiths, the Worshipful Company of Farriers (1673).

Three Horseshoes, Beeston

VICTORIA - *Dovecote Lane*

Built around 1899 and originally called the *'Victoria Hotel,'* there has been a pub on this site since 1837. It is named after Queen Victoria (1819-1901) - a popular monarch who is often featured on signboards.

In 1971 an eccentric landlord used to keep a small zoo at the rear of this pub, as well as a python inside. The collection included a puma, a lion, a bear, a leopard and a baboon. A number of incidents occurred involving these animals - the puma bounded into the public bar and frightened regulars and the leopard bit the landlord, to name but two. Often he would be seen about town, taking the bear for a walk at the end of a rope.

The zoo was eventually closed when a terrified elderly couple complained to the police after the baboon escaped, shinned up a drainpipe and tried to break into their bedroom window.

Purchased in 1994 by Tynemill Ltd, the 'Victoria' has been refurbished and restored to its former glory.

WHITE LION - *Middle Street*

This 250 year old pub's name stems from heraldry and is a reference to the badge of either Edward IV, or the Duke of Norfolk.

The house is reputed to be haunted by the occasional apparition of a female ghost. There are at least eight other pubs in the county named the 'White Lion', including those at Bingham, Rempstone, Southwell, Calverton and Worksop.

BESTWOOD

GREEN BARREL - *Arnold Road*

Opened on 30th July 1965 by the Lord Mayor of Nottingham, Alderman William Derbyshire. He also unveiled the sign outside this pub - a large green barrel suspended between two white posts. This barrel has since been replaced by the brewery with a more traditional sign showing coopers at work.

Though superseded in modern times by metal kegs, many inns feature a barrel in their names. The word 'green' (as in this pub's name), symbolises freshness, hence 'fresh barrel.'

Following the end of World War II, the 'Green Barrel' was the fiftieth pub to be built by Home Brewery - and the twelfth in Nottingham.

POTTERS - *Beckhampton Road*

Opened on the 26th August 1964 by Home Brewery as the 'Cavalier,' named after the 17th century Royalists who fought for King Charles I against the Roundheads.

When it changed hands to Bass in December 1984, it also underwent a change of name to 'Potters.'

This new name, reflected in its sign's pictorial depiction of a pool player 'potting' balls, was chosen as an indication that it now contains a room dedicated to the pursuit of this particular sport.

SPORTSMAN - *Southglade Road*

This pub was opened in December 1956 by Mitchells and Butlers as the 'Deerstalker.' Deer-stalking was very much a royal pursuit in the Bestwood Park area during the reign of Charles II, who had a hunting lodge there.

Built in a paddock that used to belong to Southglade Farm, this inn changed hands in 1993 when it was acquired by Hardys and Hansons Brewery. Later that year, on May 5th, it was reopened by Notts. County FC star Paul Cox under its new sign the 'Sportsman,' a name selected because of the pub's close proximity to Southglade Sports Complex.

Sportsman, Bestwood

BILBOROUGH

BEECHDALE - *Beechdale Road*

Opened on the 19th December 1955 by Councillor A.E. Morley, the then vice-chairman of Nottingham City Housing Committee, this pub takes its name from the road on which it stands.

EARLY BIRD - *Beechdale Road*

Opened in 1968, three years after the communications satellite of this name was launched (from Goonhilly Downs near Helston, Cornwall) to provide a regular Transatlantic TV satellite programme transmission between America and Western Europe. A much more proverbial interpretation is given on the other side of the signboard, where the inspired 'pairing' depicts another early bird busily digging out a juicy worm.

PELICAN - *Bracebridge Drive*

This pub, opened in October 1962, replaced the old pub of this name which used to stand in Pelican Street (off Alfreton Road) Nottingham until it was closed in March 1958, the licence of which was transferred to the new building.

The rarity of a pelican being chosen as a pub name derives in this instance from the bird's appearance on the family coat of arms of the Pelham Clintons (Dukes of Newcastle) who have been extensive landowners in the area.

POACHER'S POCKET - *Glaisdale Drive*

When opened on the 12th December 1986, this pub was called the *'Milestone'* - it indeed represented one for Banks's Brewery, as it was their first purpose-built house to be established in the Nottingham area.

In November 1994 it became the *'Tottle Brook'*, named after a watercourse that runs across the industrial estate on which the pub is built. The derivation of the word *Tottle* (according to the researches of that learned local body the Thoroton Society) is as a corruption of *Tothill* - a tumulus or conical hill dedicated in centuries past by those ancient Celts to their god *Taute* (meaning Mercury). There is some evidence that the local Tothill in this area was the Hemlock Stone (qv) - not far from which is the source of the Tottle Brook on Trowell Moor - where the Druids celebrated their worship and brought their sacrifices. Flowing underground through a culvert, the brook re-emerges on the Riverside Business Park site, before finally entering the River Trent opposite Wilford Church. On 2nd October 1995, another unique inn-name was lost when the pub acquired its current title the *'Poacher's Pocket'*.

BILSTHORPE

COPPER BEECH - *Kirklington Road*

This pub, a former farmhouse, Home Farm, takes its name from a large copper beech tree that stands sentry over its entrance.

The building itself is over 150 years old.

BINGHAM

CHESTERFIELD ARMS - *Church Street*

Recorded as an inn in White's 1832 Directory of Nottinghamshire, it takes its name from the Earls of Chesterfield, once lords of the manor of Bingham. A former posthouse, people used to group here to hear the news of the day being read from broadsheets, and later, the local magistrates used it to hold court before the present court house was built.

In 1843 Queen Victoria stayed here on her way to Belvoir Castle - her only visit to Nottinghamshire.

Chesterfield Arms, Bingham

CROWN - *Market Place*

In 1966 this large new building replaced a small and cramped pub of the same name that had stood on this site for centuries.

The sign of the crown, an easy-to-relate-to visual symbol, has been used by pubs for well over six hundred years and shows allegiance to the reigning monarch. There are other inns with this name at Bathley (near Newark), East Markham and North Muskham.

MOOT HOUSE - *Bowland Road*

This pub was opened in 1983. The name here was suggested by the Crown Commissioners on whose land it is built. It refers to the "Moot-house pit", the former meeting place of the Court of Bingham Hundred, which is situated about half a mile away by the side of the A46 Fosse Way.

A *'moot'* to the Anglo Saxons was a meeting, especially one which had to make a judgement of some kind - such as a court of law. Later it came to mean a legal action. The word survives in the English language today and is most often associated with the phrase 'a moot point,' meaning one that can be argued about.

WHEATSHEAF - *Long Acre*

Throughout Britain, the *'Wheatsheaf'* has been in common use as an inn-sign since the 17th century. Nottinghamshire contains a number of such hostelries by this name (see Burton Joyce).

A sheaf of wheat appears in several coats of arms, including those of the Worshipful Company of Bakers (1486). It is also one of the devices on the arms of the Brewers' Company. At one time brewing and baking were often performed under the one roof, and by the same person. This was not surprising as both of these trades share a common ingredient - yeast.

This particular building is dated 1779 on the brickwork.

WHITE LION - *Nottingham Road*

The *'White Lion'* as a sign is usually a heraldic reference to Edward IV, the Earls of March or the Duke of Norfolk. This old pub was, at one time, called the *'Stingo Tap'*, no doubt because of the strength of the beer which the landlord brewed on the premises.

BLEASBY

WAGGON AND HORSES - *Gypsy Lane*

A late 18th Century inn owned at one time by the variety artist Bradley Truman (see also the *'Red Lion'* at Costock). Waggons and horses were a familiar sight before the advent of railways, as they carried goods and farm produce for short distances.

BLIDWORTH

BIRD IN HAND - *Main Street*

The sign of this pub, owned by Mansfield Brewery since 1892, may have been suggested by the saying, *'A bird in the hand is worth two in the bush.'* This proverb is of great antiquity. It means 'possession is better than expectation.'

It is also possible that the name may be a reference to the once popular sport of falconry - the bird being held by a gloved hand.

BLACK BULL - *Main Street*

Parts of this impressive Tudor-style pub are considered to be 400 years old. It is thought that some "black" names date from the Gin Act of 1736 which caused tavern owners to drape their signs in black velvet, or add "black" to the pub name.

FOREST FOLK - *Mansfield Road*

Opened in 1926 as a residential hotel, it was built on pillars to avoid the dangers of subsidence from the nearby colliery workings.

It takes its name from a book called *'The Forest Folk'* written by James Prior Kirk, which he reputedly conceived whilst out rambling in the area around Blidworth. The story is set in, and around, Blidworth in the early 19th Century days of the machine-smashing Luddites, when the wild wastes of Sherwood still stretched from Nottingham to Mansfield. The book is full of Nottingham dialect, while the countryside around Blidworth is vividly described. Much of it remains today, with Haywood Oaks as the home of the Skrenes, and Sykebreck Farm at Blidworth Bottoms as the home of the Rideouts - the two contrasting families around which the story is written.

A unique feature of this pub is an impressive stained glass window to Kirk's memory. The window once formed part of the Memorial Room which, at one time, contained a large collection of momentoes of Kirk's life. He was an unashamed teetotaller who lived for many years in Bingham, and is buried in Bingham cemetery.

Forest Folk window, Blidworth

JOLLY FRIAR - *Dale Lane*

Opened in 1966 as a replacement for the *'New Inn,'* it stands on a spot not too distant from Friar Tuck's Well, which is situated in the precincts of the one-time Fountain Dale Abbey. It was here, according to legend, that Friar Tuck christened local children.

The village of Blidworth itself is steeped in the history of Robin Hood. Maid Marian was reputedly born here and Will Scarlet buried here.

BLYTH

ANGEL INN - *Bawtry Road*

Records show that this old coaching inn was in existence in 1274. When returning from an audience with the king in London, Robert de Insula, the newly elected Bishop of Durham, in company with the Prior of Durham, Richard Claxton, stayed here with their retinue. Their Bill of Fare at the *'Angel'* was as follows:

'In pane (bread) 10s.,
in cervisia et vino (ale and wine) 33s. 5d.,
in conquina (kitchen food) 27s. 5½d.,
in prebenda, feno et litera (provender, hay & litter
for their horses) 18s. 9d.'

Until Blyth Hall was demolished in 1972, it was widely believed that a tunnel linked the *'Angel'* with the old Priory, and was used by monks to go to the inn unseen. The tunnel, in fact, only led to the house next door which had, at one time, been part of the inn.

The Angel, as a sign, has been in use since the Middle Ages reflecting the early connection between religious establishments and travellers' hostels. Other *'Angel'* inns can be found at Kneesall and Misson.

WHITE SWAN - *High Street*

In 1635, the Mellish family purchased much of the village, including the remains of Blyth Priory. Edward Mellish built Blyth Hall after making his fortune as a wine merchant. Not all the Mellishes were as scrupulous with money. Henry Mellish, a member of the Prince Regent's court, was an infamous gambler, losing £40,000 on one occasion with a single throw of the dice. He is also reputed to have lost Blyth Hall in a gambling session in 1805. At the end of Long Row, creeper covered cottages with unusual cast iron window frames, built by Robert Mellish in 1780, stands the *'White Swan'* which takes its name from the heraldic crest of the Mellish family.

Another *'White Swan'* can be found at Dunham-on-Trent.

White Swan, Blyth

BOUGHTON

BLUE TIT - *Tuxford Road*

When this pub opened in 1957, the wooded area round about contained several allotments which were frequently visited by many different species of wild birds - in particular the blue tits.

Originally owned by Samuel Smith's Tadcaster Brewery, it was acquired in the mid-1960s by Shipstones and refurbished in 1985.

BRAMCOTE HILLS

ROSE GROWER - *Sandringham Drive*

Opened in December 1971, this pub (like its Brewery partner the *'Nurseryman'*) is just within the Beeston boundary, although in fact its postal address is Bramcote Hills. There are numerous pubs named in connection with roses, of course, but this one is unique in being called the *'Rose Grower'* and the circumstances leading up to this choice by the present writer are quite interesting.

Initially the Kimberley brewery of Hardys and Hansons held a public competition to find a suitable name, but when this proved unsuccessful the chairman at that time (Col. R.G. Hanson) asked me if I could do any better. In response, and after due thought, I suggested that as the Nottingham area was nationally-known for rose-growing (with such as Bardill's and Gregory's nearby and Wheatcroft's at Ruddington not far away) the new name should focus on this aspect of horticulture - especially since there was no other *'Rose Grower'* in the Inn-signia catalogue!

Happily, my suggestion was adopted, and framed photographs of 'classic' roses were put up to accompany the interior decor. However, a follow-up idea on my part that celebrity Harry Wheatcroft should be invited to perform the opening ceremony didn't materialise. I was really hoping that his famous whiskers would feature on the signboard, too, but even today, a pictorial sign here - to partner the *'Nurseryman,'* at least - is still (more than twenty years on) disappointingly absent.

BRINSLEY

YEW TREE - *Cordy Lane*

Brinsley is a former mining village, and the old wooden headstocks can be seen at the picnic site nearby. D. H. Lawrence's father worked at Brinsley Pit. The inn once had a number of very small rooms, but these have now been converted into one large room. It lost its cellars in 1989 when the building's foundations needed to be strengthened because of mining subsidence. The *'Yew Tree'* won the Nottinghamshire County Council's 'Best Pub Food' award in 1994.

See the *'Yew Tree'* at Hucknall for further information about the name.

Yew Tree, Brinsley

BULWELL

APOLLO - *Hucknall Lane*

Opened in January, 1956, there is only one other instance of this sign in Nottinghamshire (at Sutton-in-Ashfield) and it is quite rare elsewhere.

It relates to Greek mythology, in which Apollo is represented as the perfection of youthful manhood - being the god of music, poetry, archery, prophecy and the healing art. The sign here shows him playing his lyre (a musical instrument like a small harp, anciently used as an accompaniment to poetry) - though some signs of this name have focused on the American Space programmes, especially with Apollo XI which landed on the moon in 1969. Bulwell (Hempshill Vale) also has the distinction of having a number of roads named after various astronauts.

BLENHEIM - *Snape Wood Road*

Opened in June 1980, taking its name from the neighbouring Blenheim Industrial Estate.

The original reference is to the village of this name in Bavaria, near which an important battle took place in 1704 resulting in a victory for Marlborough and Prince Eugene, leaders of the English and Austrian troops over the French and Bavarians. Blenheim Palace was later given to the Duke of Marlborough (hitherto General John Churchill) by his sovereign Queen Anne and a grateful nation, in token of winning the War of the Spanish Succession.

COCK 'N' BULL - *Main Street*

Until July 1989 this pub had been named the *'Star.'* Its present name may possibly relate to the long, rambling and frankly incredible yarns perpetuated by some of the 'regulars' who patronise the place. Otherwise the reference is to two rival coaching inns which stood opposite one another at Stony Stratford (Bucks) called the *'Cock'* and *'Bull'* respectively. In times past, garbled versions of recent events in the Napoleonic wars were invariably 'improved upon' in the gossip among coach arrivals, so much so that they came to be known throughout the land as *Cock and Bull* stories.

Again, possibly, the title here was 'borrowed' from a pub of the same name situated in Sinfin, near Derby, which was built in 1982.

COOPERS ARMS - *Bardney Drive*

This former alehouse is known locally as the *'Top House,'* due to the remote position it once held at the 'top' of Bulwell at a time when no other buildings or houses stood in its locality. In its entrance is an old stone dated 1830, which indicates that the premises were once known as *'The Lime Kiln'* - the proprietor at the time being a T. Marshall.

This pub, like so many others throughout the County, is named after a particular trade (in this case barrel making) that was flourishing at one time in the area. Associations of tradesmen were in the habit of meeting on licensed premises, and trade unions in their early days often held their meetings in the local inn.

Forest, Bulwell

FOREST - *Hucknall Lane*

The sight of a tram on the sign here is quite mystifying until one remembers that hereabouts (in the area known as Bulwell Forest) was the terminus of the old Route 44, the longest in Nottingham. On an outer wall of the pub is a plaque. It reads:

"Built in the early 1900s, 'The Forest' became known locally as the 'Swinger' due to its position near the tram terminus where the overhead pick up pole was swung to allow the trams to travel in the opposite direction."

The tram depicted on the sign is unusual in that it is of the type which does not run on tram lines.

Framesmiths Arms, Bulwell

FRAMESMITHS ARMS - *Main Street*

A unique name, this, recalling that the frames made by these local craftsmen were used in the hosiery and lace industries, still of importance in the Nottingham area today.

In common with so many pubs, this one had a special nickname of its own, i.e. *'The Monkeys'* - referring to the tale told since long ago when the premises consisted of a small cottage and an alehouse. Apparently there was then a tame but rhythmically-minded monkey which was kept tethered in the garden. It spent most of its captivity perched up an apple tree banging a drum.

Above the door of this pub, a small sign reflects these events - depicting a small black monkey playing a drum.

GOLDEN BALL - *St Albans Road*

This inn, opened on the 7th February 1964, replaced a house of the same name which had stood for over a century on Main Street, Bulwell before it was demolished.

The sign of the golden ball was used by numerous tradesmen in the past, not just innkeepers. It arose from the Royal Orb of Constantine the Great who adopted a golden globe as his symbol, later adding a cross to it when he was converted to Christianity.

Golden balls became extremely common when the early silk mercers adopted it as their sign - perhaps because, in the Middle Ages, all silk was bought from the East, and more particularly from Byzantium. It continued as a silk mercer's sign until the end of the last century. In the 18th century the golden ball became the symbol of quacks and fortune-tellers. The Compleat Vintner in 1720 had this to say about golden balls:

'If in Moorfields, a lady stroles
Among the globes and golden balls
Where ere they hang she may be certain
Of knowing what shall be her fortune.
Her husband too, I dare to say,
But that she better knows than they.'

GOOSE FAIR - *Hucknall Road*

Yet another unique pub-name, this one relating to the ancient annual fair of the same name for which Nottingham has achieved fame far and wide.

The fair itself was first mentioned in a Royal Charter granted to the town by King Edward I in the year 1284, and its present title began to be used about the middle of the 16th century - notably in 1542, when a man named John Trussell, steward to the Willoughby family of Wollaton Hall, left a record in his accounts of the purchase of a pair of trousers at 'the goose fayre'. They cost him the remarkable sum of eightpence!

The fair continues to be held each October on The Forest since its transfer from the Old Market Square in 1928.

The site on which this pub stands had been owned by Shipstones since 1955. Their fourth application to build on it having been successful, the premises opened for business on the 17th December 1982.

Goose Fair sign, Bulwell

HORSESHOE - *Station Road*

Shown in the 1844 Directory, the sign or name of a single horseshoe is quite rare, and the only instance of this in Nottinghamshire appears to be in Bulwell, only a short distance from the Leen Bridge.

Before the building became a pub, there were stables at the rear where horses, en route from Bulwell to Nottingham, were shoed before commencing their journey. A funeral parlour that once stood next door, used to store its coffins at the pub when it ran short of space.

Iron has always been regarded as a protective charm against the wiles of evil spirits, sorcerers and witches. The horseshoe itself was supposed to indicate the crescent moon, and from time immemorial has been the symbol of good luck. In ancient times the blacksmith or farrier was credited with supernatural powers and regarded as a magician, his forge, anvil and hammer appearing on many inn-signs to symbolize the shoeing of a horse.

The horseshoe nailed up over a doorway must be the right way up, so says tradition, otherwise the luck, instead of being 'held in' will 'run out'. Also, it must be found or stolen - a given or bought one would be useless.

No reference to horseshoes would be complete without mention of the biggest pile in Britain which can be seen at Scarrington, just north east of Bingham. It was built over a period of 20 years (between 1945 and 1965) by Mr George Flinders, the village blacksmith. It is 17 feet high, solid throughout with no supporting column, has a base circumference of almost 20 feet, weighs about 10 tons, and contains approximately 50,000 horseshoes.

LIME KILN - *Camberley Road*

The opening of this pub in December 1991, was marked with the arrival of a 1912 Lancia Simplex vintage car belonging to the former owner of the site Mr John Brydon.

The name here, arrived at via a newspaper competition, celebrates the area's links with the limestone quarry industry. It was the fourth Banks's public house to be opened in Nottingham.

LION REVIVED - *Robinsons Hill*

This 19th century pub started life as the *'White Lion,'* a name it retained until its closure in 1931 when the Licensing Justices deemed it 'redundant.' That same year, it reopened as a social club (The Robinson Hill Club), closing in 1976.

In September 1978, it was again restored to its former glory as a pub by Hardy and Hansons, who named it the *'Lion Revived,'* an ingenious name, reminding locals that a resuscitation job (in a practical as well as a poetical sense) had been performed in restoring to life the former *'White Lion.'* Considering the old title of the pub to be too common, the brewery preferred this new name.

Lion Revived, Bulwell

LORD NELSON - *Hempshill Lane*

Opened in May 1971, this pub is named after the hero of Trafalgar, Horatio Nelson (see pub of this name at Arnold).

NEWSTEAD ABBEY - *St. Albans Road*

There seems to be no special reason why this pub (built shortly before the First World War) should be so-named, except perhaps that it is situated 'as the crow flies' not far from the real Abbey - which was actually built not as an abbey but a priory. However, it has no connection as such with the county's other ecclesiastically-named pub, the *'Westminster Abbey'* in St. Ann's, Nottingham.

Newstead Abbey itself, formerly the home of one of England's most famous poets, Lord George Gordon Byron, once stood in the heart of Sherwood Forest, having been founded about 1170 by King Henry II. After the Reformation it became one of the nation's great country houses, and Byron (after whom pubs have been named in neighbouring Hucknall, Mansfield and Nottingham) was the last of his line to possess it. When the Abbey was dedicated to the City in 1931 as the gift of Sir Julian Cahn, Prime Minister Venizelos of Greece was present to pay tribute to the memory of the English poet who had died in 1824 at Missolonghi in his personal crusade to aid the Greeks in their battle for independence.

SCOTS GREY - *Main Street*

The Royal Scots Greys were raised in 1678 - during the reign of Charles II - and it is uncertain whether the regiment's name originated from the colour of its uniforms or its horses. They re-formed as the Royal Scots Dragoon Guards, a 'dragoon' in those days being a mounted infantryman armed with a musket. Their Home HQ was then, as now, at Edinburgh Castle.

The front of the pub is the newer part and was built in 1884 for the benefit of railway employees who had arrived in the district and were set to work on current projects. At that time, as many as 16 rooms were in full use as accommodation. The old stone part at the rear is of considerable age, and there is ample evidence that in former days a large number of horses could be stabled in the yard.

The Nottingham Borough Records mention the Royal Scots Greys as follows:

Vol. VI, page 229 per City Chamberlain's accounts dated 17th January 1748: item from the Quarterly bill of John Gunthorpe, Carrier . . .

Warrant to impress Scots Grey to Loughborough = 3 shillings.

Vol. VII, page 188 per City Chamberlain's accounts dated 17th May 1748:

Carriage of baggage to Mansfield with Scots Greys = 7 shillings.

Vol. IX, page 103, dated 10th July 1854:

Departure of Scots Greys for Crimea - Civic send-off.

Surprisingly enough, there is no true regimental tartan belonging to the Scots Greys, so the Royal Stewart dress tartan has been used in the pub for both the bar panelling and the lounge curtains. Behind the bar is framed the regimental crest, and also a set of buttons and cap-badges.

We have no wish to confuse anyone with singulars and plurals, but it so happens that the regimental magazine has the same title as this Bulwell pub - whereas until its closure in December 1970 there was in St Anns Well Road, Nottingham, another ancient pub called the *'Scots Greys.'* It is worthy of note at this point that troops from this famous cavalry regiment were used by general Sir Charles Napier (qv) to quell the uprisings staged on The Forest at Nottingham in 1839, in support of the People's Charter presented by Parliament the previous year.

Finally, a graphic account from the Nottingham Date Book of 3rd July 1854:

"A company of the Scots Greys, numbering about 120 men, marched into the Great Market-place to meet the Mayor and Corporation, before leaving Nottingham for the Crimean War. The troops formed an impressive square, in the centre of which the Corporation were met by Colonel Griffiths and officers of the Regiment.

Toasts were drunk from an ancient gold drinking-cup presented by the Duke of Newcastle to the Guild of Nottingham in 1681. While the cup was being passed round and the soldiers served with Nottingham Ale, the band played 'The girl I left behind me,' 'Scots wha hae' etc. The Mayor then proposed the health of the Regiment in a well-timed speech, the Colonel responded, and after other toasts and speeches the soldiers fell into marching order, waving their swords in acknowledgement of the waving of the ladies' handkerchiefs from nearly every window and the cheering of the multitude, the market-place being literally crowded - and proceeded along the road to Derby . . ."

TUT 'N' SHIVE - *Coventry Road*

The name of this old pub (mentioned in the 1832 County Directory) was, until February 1986, the *'Bull and Butcher'*. It was then reduced to merely the *'Bull'* for a short while, but then it was transmogrified into its present technical description - having a distinct affinity, one supposes, with the ever-growing chain of pubs in the northern counties all rejoicing in the term *'Tap and Spile.'*

The 'shive' is a circular wooden plug, partly bored in the centre which is hammered into the bush (i.e. belly) of the cask when it has been filled. The 'tut' is a bung, smaller in diameter and with a counter-sunk centre, which is used to seal the tap hole.

BUNNY

RANCLIFFE ARMS - *Loughborough Road*

The *'Rancliffe Arms'* appears in White's 1844 Directory of Nottinghamshire.

Its name honours the Parkyns family who used to live in nearby Bunny Hall. A later member of this family, Lord Rancliffe, planted Rancliffe Wood, whilst the second baronet, Sir Thomas Parkyns (1663-1741), became known as *'The Wrestling Baronet.'*

Sir Thomas was such a fanatic about the sport of wrestling that he called himself 'Sir Thomas Luctator' and employed professionals to wrestle with him. In 1712 he established an annual wrestling tournament in the village and even wrote a book on the finer points of the sport called *'The Cornish-Hugg Wrestler.'*

Until 1811, these yearly bouts took place in what are now the grounds of this inn.

BURTON JOYCE

CROSS KEYS - *Main Street*

There are many hostelries throughout the county with this name. It is a common sign in Christian heraldry, referring as it does to St Peter, to whom Jesus said, *'I will give unto thee the keys of the Kingdom of Heaven.'*

A *'Cross Keys'* inn has stood on this site for at least three hundred years. In 1860, the landlord was John Hogg, a butcher by trade, who also kept wicket for the Nottinghamshire cricket team.

The building itself was formerly a series of small bars which were knocked into one room around 1985. Its car park was once the site of *'The Wheatsheaf'* public house, which was demolished in 1938 and rebuilt a short distance away on Church Road.

Cross Keys, Burton Joyce (c.1910)

22

LORD NELSON - *Chestnut Grove*

Named after Horatio Nelson (1758-1805), hero of the Battle of Trafalgar in 1805 (see pub of the same name at Arnold).

Over 200 years old, this inn was modernized in 1933. Throughout its history it has undergone a number of changes of name. In 1809 it was known as *'The Swan and Salmon,'* in 1811 as *'The White Swan,'* and in 1826 it was referred to as *'The Swan.'*

It is a popular headquarters for fishing match draws relating to competitions that take place along the banks of the nearby River Trent. During the 1890s the landlord was Alfred Shaw, an outstanding spin bowler who captained both the Nottinghamshire and England cricket teams.

WHEATSHEAF - *Church Road*

The former pub of this name used to occupy a position next door to the *Cross Keys* public house in the village, a site now occupied by the latter house's car park.

The current building dates from 1938 when major development work occurred in Burton Joyce. The architect was Cecil Howitt who designed the 'Council House' in Nottingham's Old Market Square.

A common sign since the 17th century, a sheaf of wheat appears in several coats of arms, including those of the Worshipful Company of Bakers (1486). It is also one of the devices on the arms of Brewers' Company.

There are numerous inns throughout the county with this sign.

CALVERTON

ADMIRAL RODNEY -
Main Street

One of the oldest buildings in the village, this pub is first mentioned in White's Directory of Nottinghamshire in 1832.

It is named after George Brydges Rodney (1719-92), remembered for his victory over the French in 1782 at the 'Battle of the Saintes' in the West Indies - a victory that hastened the Peace of Versailles in the following year. He was raised to the peerage as the 1st Baron Rodney.

Other pubs with this name can be found at Wollaton and Southwell.

Admiral Rodney, Calverton

CHERRY TREE - *Collyer Road*

Opened in December 1959 by Samuel Smith's of Tadcaster, this pub is now owned by Greenalls. It is the newest of the pubs in the village.

There seems to be no special reason why it should have been called *'The Cherry Tree'* - the area has never been noted for its cherry-growing. It would appear however, that at the time this pub was christened, the brewery chose this particular title as it fitted in with their policy of naming their houses after aspects of the countryside - be it birds, beasts or whatever.

GLEANERS - *Bonner Lane*

The original pub, which first appears in Wright's Directory of 1874, was called *'The Gleaner'* (singular), but the building existed before that date as an unnamed beerhouse. It was replaced by the current house around the 1930s, and has the distinction of being the only pub in the country with this name.

Gleaners were farm labourers who gathered up the ears of corn left by the reapers. Their work was immortalised by the French artist Jean François Millet, whose painting entitled *'The Gleaners'* and dated 1857, hangs in the Louvre in Paris.

The name of this inn relates to a once local pastoral pursuit in the village where, many years ago, it was the custom at harvest-time, for the women and children to be employed as gleaners by the farmers. Their gleanings were then taken to the old water-mill at Lowdham and ground into flour.

CAR COLSTON

ROYAL OAK - *The Green*

This pub overlooks the wide open spaces of the enormous village green in Car Colston, the 17th century home of Dr Robert Thoroton, who wrote the first major history of Nottinghamshire. In 1832, the village had at least three beerhouses. Twelve years later only one remained - the 'Royal Oak' beerhouse. This was run by Richard Cragg, who later combined the roles of innkeeper and village joiner. The *'Royal Oak Inn'* developed further - by 1922 it had become the *'Royal Oak Hotel'* and six years later even had a refreshment room. The building is about two hundred years old and some think it may have been a hosiery factory but documentary evidence does not bear this out. The arched brick ceiling in the lounge is certainly a very unusual feature. The *'Royal Oak'* has two ghosts - one a Roman centurion who haunts the cellars (the pub is said to be on the site of a Roman villa, and the Roman Road - the Fosse Way - is only a stone's throw away), the other is an old man dressed in late Victorian clothes, who occasionally helps serve behind the bar! This popular pub name is explained under the entry for East Bridgford. There is another *'Royal Oak'* in the neighbouring village of Screveton.

Royal Oak, Car Colston

CARLTON

BLACK'S HEAD - *Burton Road*

A pub of this name has stood on this site for at least one hundred and sixty years, and probably longer.

Originally the sign of the *'Black's Head'* or *'Black Boy'* (see pub of this name at Retford) was used by tobacconists. Ben Jonson in 'Bartholomew Fair' says, 'I thought he would have run mad o' the Black Boy that takes the scurvy, rogey tobacco there.'

The *'Black Boy'* in particular is often taken to refer to Charles II, who was so nicknamed due to his very swarthy complexion. It was first adapted as an inn-sign during the period of the Commonwealth (1649-1659), when tavern-keepers of Royalist sympathies displayed defiance to Cromwell by referring in this oblique way to their exiled leader.

Perhaps the sign of the *'Black's Head'* or the *'Black Boy'* is a reference to the little Negro pages who became very fashionable in Queen Anne's time, during the era of the coffee-houses. Lavishly dressed, they became known as 'tigers' - their elaborate and expensive uniforms often being striped. The nobility and gentry carried these personal-servants on their carriages and cabriolets so that they could hold the horses, lower the steps, ring door bells, and so on . . .

Black's Head, Carlton

Still another possibility is that the sign of the *'Black's Head'* is, in fact, as old as the Crusades, and is thus a variant of the *'Saracen's Head'* (as at Southwell). The pub's sign has recently been changed, and now has a picture of a black horse to avoid any racist overtones.

CAVENDISH - *Cavendish Road*

The signboard here portrays William Cavendish (1592-1676), the 1st Duke of Newcastle-upon-Tyne, an ancestor of the Duke of Portland who lived at Welbeck Abbey. A dedicated Royalist, he became known as 'The Loyal Duke of Newcastle' and commanded the Royalist forces in the north at the outbreak of the Civil War.

EARL OF CHESTERFIELD - *Carlton Hill*

An Earl of Chesterfield pub has occupied this site for over three hundred years and is thought to have been the haunt of highwaymen at one time. It appears in the 1853 directory as the *'Earl of Chesterfield Arms'* - the word 'Arms' most likely disappearing when the present building was constructed on the old site about 1905.

To this day though, the pub is still known by its nickname the *'Bruno.'* The story goes that the second Earl of Chesterfield was very fond of bear-baiting and that during Carlton Wakes week he spent much of his time here drinking with friends, leaving his favourite bear tethered in the stables outside. On occasions he would bring the animal into the bar, where it soon acquired a taste for the landlord's fine ale - downing it by the quart.

ELWES ARMS - *Oakdale Road*

Opened on the 8th June 1962 by the late Sir Richard Elwes, a former High Court judge - this pub was named after his family to commemorate their long connections with Nottinghamshire.

Known as the 'lawyer poet,' Sir Richard, the son of an opera singer, the late Gervase Elwes, and a brother of the portrait painter Simon Elwes, was called to the Bar of the Inner Temple in 1925. He became a Bencher in 1948 and took silk two years later. In 1958 he was appointed a judge of the Queen's Bench Division - retiring in 1965 due to ill-health. His daughter, Polly Elwes, once a BBC television personality, is married to Peter Dimmock and was voted TV woman personality of the year in 1959.

The coat of arms of the Elwes family, whose motto is *'Deo non fortun'* (Through God, not by chance), are reproduced on the signboard outside this pub.

In June 1983 the *'Elwes Arms'* temporarily changed its name to *'The Lodge,'* before reverting back to its present sign in 1992.

INN FOR A PENNY - *Burton Road*

Appearing in White's Directory of 1832 as the *'Royal Oak,'* it changed its name to the *'Inn For A Penny'* in 1984.

Some locals would have you believe that this unusual new name derives from the fact that visitors to nearby playing-fields often drop into the pub just to 'spend a penny!' According to a brewery spokesman though, the name was thought up in their office when they decided to make it a 'fun-pub' and has no significant meaning.

OLD VOLUNTEER - *Burton Road*

The existence of this pub is recorded in White's Directory of 1832 as the *'Volunteer.'*

During the English Civil War many inns served as recruiting offices. The premises were visited by mostly local men, eager to volunteer their services to whichever cause they supported.

The name here may be a reference to the 'Old Contemptibles,' a nickname of the British Expeditionary Force which fought at Mons (France) in 1914. The name was adapted by the soldiers themselves after they learned that the German Kaiser had supposedly referred to them as *'General French's contemptible little army.'* The sign outside this pub now depicts a soldier in full battledress, but the original one showed an 'Old Contemptible' wearing a chest-full of medals and looking remarkably like Lance-Corporal Jones of the television comedy-series 'Dad's Army.'

Another pub of this name can be found within the county at Caythorpe.

PUNCH BOWL - *Porchester Road*

Converted from a private house (later known as the Deccan Club), this pub opened in October 1961.

The word 'punch' may derive from the Hindi word 'pac,' meaning 'five' - suggesting five ingredients are used to make up this alcoholic beverage (water, sugar, lemon-juice, spice and spirits). It may also be a shortened form of 'puncheon,' a large cask containing over one hundred gallons. Either way, punch is usually ladled from a bowl - hence the name.

THORN BUSH - *Old Brickyard, Porchester Lodge*

When it opened in December 1969 as the *'Engine House,'* this pub had one of the most unusual inn-signs of all time - a full-sized horizontal steam engine.

The engine, made by 'Tangyes' of Birmingham in 1850, was first used at a colliery in Nottingham before being purchased by the Nottingham Patent Brick Company in 1867 for £659. Near to what is now the site of this pub, it used to drive mills and agitators, processing and working raw clay into a suitable consistency to make bricks - helping to produce 450 million of them (using 225,000 tons of coal in the process), before it was retired in 1966 and donated to Shipstones Brewery. The engine was incorporated in the design of the pub and housed in a long glass-fronted lounge.

When the premises were refurbished in June 1982, the brewery decided to donate the engine to the City of Nottingham Industrial Museum at Wollaton Park and, due to its immense size and weight, the lounge roof had to be removed to allow it to be hoisted out. It was at this time that the pub changed its name to the *'Steam Engine.'*

In 1989 the brewery decided to rename the pub, yet again, and ran a 'name-a-pub competition.' The winning selection was the *'Thorn Bush'* - after the plant that once grew profusely round about this area.

TOBY JUG - *Carlton Hill*

Opened in June 1958, this pub is probably named after the jug of the same name.

The jugs, also known as 'Toby fill-pots,' are traditionally formed in the shape of a stout old man wearing 18th-century costume, comprising a long, full-skirted coat and a three-cornered hat - an example of which is portrayed on this pub's colourful sign. The name of the jug itself derives from a poem written in 1761 about a certain Toby Philpot upon whom a popular drinking-song was based:

> *'a thirsty old soul*
> *as e'er drank a bottle*
> *or fathom'd a bowl ...'*

WINDSOR CASTLE - *Carlton Hill*

A pub of this name has stood on this site since at least 24th May 1806. The current house (nicknamed *'The Lantern'*) was opened on the 18th July 1992 by the Mayor of Gedling, Councillor Roland Spencer.

The name here originates from the royal residence founded by William the Conqueror on the site of an earlier fortress in Windsor, Berkshire.

Interestingly, the official name of the British royal family prior to 1917 was Saxe-Coburg-Gotha - they changed it to Windsor in deference to anti-German sentiment - choosing Windsor because of its specific association with Windsor Castle.

CARLTON-ON-TRENT

GREAT NORTHERN INN - *Ossington Road*

This inn takes its name from its location close to the Great Northern railway line. The inn was once owned by the London and North Eastern Railway Company (LNER), whose great locomotives of the steam era, including the

legendary *'Flying Scotsman'*, *'Mallard'*, *'Cock o' the North'* and countless others, thundered past its doors. At one time, the inn was also at the busy centre of agricultural activity with the home of the world famous Forshaw shire horses nearby. Dealers from all over the world who came to buy these beautiful animals, used this inn for refreshment. It even had a weighbridge on which the mighty stallions were weighed.

The present inn sign shows GNR engine no. 1414.

Great Northern Inn, Carlton-on-Trent

CAUNTON

PLOUGH - *Main Street*

Glance at the wall of this typical village pub and you may find the date 1774. This represents additions to a much older, 17th century building. *'The Plough'* has been modernised and today draws attention to itself by its super floral displays in summer and fabulous food and drink all year round.

In the last century, Caunton had a tradition known as "Rangtannings" - punishment meted out to disgraced locals, whereby noisy villagers would assemble outside the victim's house and chant and sing derisively. Effigies of the 'victim' would be burnt, the church bell rung and, after several days of such constant harassment, the subject of this attention would, no doubt, be left suitably chastened. The last of these 'Rangtannings' is thought to have taken place at the *'Plough'*.

Plough, Caunton

Royalty and the Peerage

King William IV, Sneinton

Royal Children, Nottingham

Queen Adelaide, Sneinton

Magna Charta, Lowdham

Duke of Wellington, Kirkby-in-Ashfield

Sir Charles Napier, Nottingham

Earl Howe, Nottingham

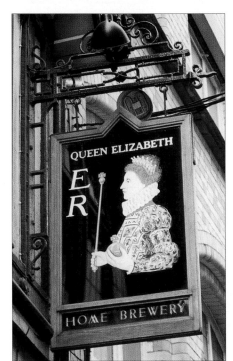
Queen Elizabeth, Nottingham

Lord Roberts, Nottingham

King's Head, Mansfield

Plate I

Robin Hood & Sherwood Forest

Robin Hood, Sherwood

Major Oak, Arnold

Little John, Ravenshead

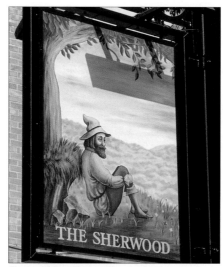

Will Scarlet, Hucknall

Sherwood Inn, Sherwood

Robin Hood, Elkesley

Greendale Oak, Worksop

Maid Marian, Arnold

Friar Tuck, Arnold

Plate II

CAYTHORPE

BLACK HORSE - *Main Street*

This pub, dating from the early part of the 18th century, was kept for many generations by the Branston family until purchased by Shipstones Brewery in the 1950s.

One of its former owners, Mrs Florence Branston, became better known as 'Mother Duck' on account of the large number of ducks she used to keep on the Dover Beck across the road from the pub.

Once the meeting place and favourite haunt of many of Nottinghamshire's famous cricketers - great names like Mordecai Sherwin, Wilfred Flowers and William Gunn often used to visit here - the pub is also noted for its association with the notorious highwayman Dick Turpin.

Turpin reputedly visited here regularly, and on occasions is said to have stayed for several days in a small secret cupboard. This cupboard, still in existence today, was in fact a very carefully-constructed hideout. It had two rooms, one in either of the inn's bars, and a window from which he could have made his escape if discovered. Reputedly, Turpin would leave the Fosse Way near East Bridgford and after fording the river there, 'lie low' at the *'Black Horse.'* Upon leaving the comfort of the pub, he would then ride his equally-famous horse 'Black Bess' cross country to the Dukeries area in order to rob the wealthy travellers using the Great North Road.

The pub takes its name from its association with this infamous outlaw and his faithful black horse.

Black Horse, Caythorpe

OLD VOLUNTEER - *Caythorpe Road*

The earliest mention of this pub is recorded in the County Directory of 1853.

It is thought that at one time it was briefly called the *'Stand-Up Man'* and had a signboard which bore a picture of a uniformed volunteer - sadly this has disappeared and the house no longer displays a pictorial sign.

An explanation of the origin of the name *'Old Volunteer'* as an inn-sign can be found by referring to the pub of the same name at Carlton.

CHILWELL

CADLAND - *High Road*

As the signboard shows, this inn (listed in the County Directory of 1832) takes its name from a famous racehorse, which not only won the Derby in 1828 but the 2,000 Guineas as well.

This noble creature was owned by the Duke of Rutland and trained by his friend Sir James Borlase Warren on the open country known as 'The Flats' which then existed between Chilwell and Sir John's home at Stapleford Hall.

There is a pub in Surrey at Mickleham (near Dorking) called the *'Running Horses'* which depicts the exciting dead-heat finish between 'Cadland' and his rival 'The Colonel' in that famous Derby. This is on one side of the signboard, on the other, 'Cadland' is shown winning the re-run by a clear neck, thus justifying the Duke's confident challenge. By the way, it should be said that there are more than sixty pubs bearing the names of racehorses to be found throughout the country - most of them winners either of the Derby or the Grand National, sometimes dating back (like the pubs themselves) considerably more than a century.

The famous pugilist, Bendigo (qv), was a regular at the *'Cadland.'* On one occasion here, under the influence of drink, he fought an unscheduled three-cornered fight in the furniture-cluttered room with William Bailey, the Champion of Nottingham, and a local woodsman called Joseph Wall, the latter surprisingly emerging victorious.

Cadland, Chilwell

CHARLTON ARMS - *High Road*

Evidence of this pub's existence is recorded in the 1844 Directory.

From 1620, Chilwell was the home of the Charlton family, who lived at nearby Chilwell Hall. That same year, Nicholas Charlton, son of Thomas Charlton of Sandiacre, bought the mansion from Christopher Pymme.

This family have an interesting history, Sir Richard Charlton was killed at the Battle of Bosworth, John Charlton was MP for London in 1318, and Sir Thomas Charlton was Speaker of the Commons in 1453.

The pub takes its name from this family - the signboard displaying their coat of arms.

Chequers Inn sign, Chilwell

CHEQUERS - *High Road*

An ancient tavern sign this, which was probably brought to Britain by the Romans. Evidence from Pompeii suggests that it was already in use there, perhaps referring to a game such as Draughts played on the premises. The sign was later associated with a money-table (and indeed the word 'exchequer' originally meant a kind of chessboard). This money-table, divided into squares, was used by money-changers, accountants and judges, who arranged matters of Revenue. They sat on a bench covered by a chequered cloth which was referred to as a 'banc' - a word of Germanic origin which gave us our familiar 'bank' - and indeed the earliest inns may have used the *'Chequers'* sign to indicate that they were always ready to change money or act as bankers in some way.

Pubs named as such can also be found within the County at Cropwell Bishop, Elston (near Newark), Hucknall, Ranby (near Retford) and Stapleford - but not, strangely enough, in Nottingham itself. The *'Chequers'* at Chilwell is an old inn, listed in the 1832 Directory.

CORN MILL - *Swiney Way*

Opened in November 1993, this pub stands on a site near to which an old corn mill once stood - hence the name.

DOUBLE TOP - *Bramcote Lane*

Opened in February 1969, the sign of this pub was most unusual, consisting of a pair of double-sized dartboards. The present signboard shows a different interpretation, a most attractive picture of a double-sized 'Big Top' of a travelling circus, in front of which are paraded some of the performers, both animal and human.

HOP POLE - *High Road*

The sign of the hop is well-known around Nottingham as an advertising medium for its last independent brewery (Hardys and Hansons at Kimberley). The only other pubs named the *'Hop Pole'* are in the north of the county at Ollerton and Retford. This area was, in times past, noted for its hop-growing, and mentioned as such in a report of Robert Lowe (local historian) in 1794.

Hop-growing started in Kent in the early 1400s, following the importing from Flanders in 1390 of beer that had been made with hops. It was intended for Dutch merchants then working in England, but no doubt some samples were nobbled on being landed. Until this time, English ale had been made of malt, yeast and water. This produced a strong, sweet drink but having poor keeping qualities (four to five days, usually) - the hop changed all this. The new-style ale could be safely stored, the quality of the product was improved, and the taste greatly enhanced. Beer, as it soon became known, came into its own a century later, and has reigned supreme ever since.

This pub was opened in March 1956.

Headstocks, Cinderhill

CINDERHILL

HEADSTOCKS - *Bagnall Road*

Opened in December 1975 - the name here refers to machinery used in support of the winding-gear at the former Babbington Colliery which stood directly opposite this pub. The colliery itself closed down in 1986, not long after the now-defunct *'Colliers Arms'* nearby.

JOHN BARLEYCORN - *Nuthall Road*

This pub dates from the early years of the 20th century, with more recent additions. The original inn, listed in the 1832 Directory, once stood at the back of the present day building, where the car park is now. In fact the cellars of the pub are now under the car park! The pub was called the *'Sir John Barleycorn'* until the late 1980s when he lost his knighthood!

The title represents the personification of malt liquor - a jocular name in both English and Scottish literature, and referred to by writers such as Robert Burns and Sir Walter Scott, as well as the American novelist Nathaniel Hawthorne. There is an old ballad about this fictitious (Sir) John Barleycorn in which he is described as 'of noble blood, well beloved in England, a great supporter of the Crown, and a maintainer of both rich and poor.'

As *John Bull* is the legendary name for a typical English squire in times past, so is *John Barleycorn* the successful, hearty 'Mine Host' of the old coaching days, when he would combine the life of a country gentleman with that of a farmer and an important businessman. The writer who is said to have popularised the term is Scotland's famous poet Rabbie Burns. He was himself very partial to malt liquor, as exemplified in these lines from one of his own favourite ballads :

John Barleycorn sign, Cinderhill

> *'John Barleycorn was a hero bold,*
> *Of noble enterprise,*
> *For if you do but taste his blood*
> *'Twill make your courage rise!'*

RED LION - *Nuthall Road*

Opened in September 1938, this house has the most popular of all inn names (an explanation for this can be found by referring to the pub of the same name at Costock).

CLARBOROUGH

GATE - *Smeath Lane*

The *'Gate'* has stood adjacent to the Chesterfield Canal, for over 200 years and is possibly contemporary with the canal itself. It had a wharf where goods could be unloaded from the barges. In 1832 John Sherrat is listed in the directory as 'victualler and coal dealer', and no doubt subsequent landlords had a similar dual role.

There is another *'Gate'* inn at Sutton-cum-Lound.

KING'S ARMS - *Main Street*

The *'King's Arms'* has been serving ale in the village since about 1860, and may well have been a farmhouse before that. The sign board outside is a particularly fine one depicting an armour-clad King Richard I on his white charger, the coat of arms on his shield.

Gate Inn, Clarborough

CLAYWORTH

BLACKSMITH'S ARMS - *Town Street*

In 1869, Thomas Parkinson was the village blacksmith and farrier, as well as a "shopkeeper and beer retailer". This three hundred year old smithy developed into *'The Blacksmiths Arms'* in the 1870s when the blacksmith became the landlord. Thomas Parkinson used his skills to create an attractive, and unique, wrought iron inn sign depicting the tools of his trade – hammer and pincers – along with some horseshoes. This still hangs outside the inn, alongside a more conventional sign. Jane Parkinson took over both the inn and the shop after her husband's death.

Old photographs show that the front door once opened on to the main street but this has now been replaced by a window. A curious item to be found in the 'Wiseton Room', part of the restaurant, is a very large brass bell some 18 inches in diameter, suspended from the ceiling and frequently rung by inquisitive visitors! It is thought that in early Victorian times, part of the building may have been used as a schoolroom, with the bell being run to tell the children of Clayworth that it was time for lessons.

Blacksmith's Arms, Clayworth

BREWER'S ARMS - *Town Street*

The *'Brewer's Arms'* was originally a farmhouse, in fact one of the old cowsheds has been converted into a shop selling country clothes. Around 1890 the enterprising owner used farm outbuildings as a brewery, and opened the farmhouse as an inn appropriately called the *'Brewery Arms'*. Although the name has undergone a subtle change, the inn remains very traditional. Every April the old custom of 'blessing the plough' takes place at the church. After the service, the villagers meet up at the *'Brewer's'* for lunch, real ale and singing.

CLIFTON

CLIFTON BRIDGE - *Brookthorpe Way*

Known locally as the *'Ponderosa'* (from the TV western series 'Bonanza'), a reference to its first landlord whose surname happened to be Cartwright. This pub was opened on the 16th March 1962 by one-time Nottingham South MP, Mr William Clarke - its licence having been transferred from the former *'Rising Sun Inn'* on Hornbuckle Street, Radford.

It takes its name from the nearby Clifton Bridge which spans the River Trent at Wilford (opened to take vehicular traffic on the 18th February 1958).

CRUSADER - *Hartness Road*

Opened in October 1984, this pub honours by its name Sir Gervase Clifton, who was killed whilst fighting in the Third Crusade (1189-1192). He was a member of that illustrious local family who lived at Clifton Hall and who had figured prominently both at Court and on the battlefield. Many of them had the name Gervase, the English form of the martyred Saint Gervasius. Centuries later another member of this family, in the person of Sir Arthur Clifton, commanded a regiment at Waterloo.

The 'crusading' theme inside the pub is emphasised with Saracen-style wallpaper and mock stained-glass windows ... but more appealing is the legend that the heart of the valiant knight who fell in battle was brought home in a leaden casket and rests in peace within the village church.

GREY MARE - *Farnborough Road*

This pub was opened in March 1961, and its name inevitably reminds one of the beast of burden which belonged to Tom Pearce in that celebrated folk-song. Certainly the handsome shire horse shown on the sign looks sturdy enough to carry any intending passengers to Widecombe-in-the-Moor and back again, if need be! However, this particular Grey Mare is by no means apocryphal - her name was *Rose*, and at that time she had been one of Shipstone's famous drayhorses for eleven years and was due to be sent into retirement at Home Farm, Barton-in-Fabis.

At the pub's opening, Rose and her recently-born foal Jane, were conveyed to Clifton in a cattle-lorry by the brewery's head ostler so they could be present at the official proceedings (you know how daft the British can be with animals, but this was good publicity). A large portrait of the pair can be seen inside the pub, and another was hung in the entrance hall of the brewery's head office.

MAN OF TRENT - *Gotham Lane*

Opened in October 1957, the name here was inspired by the pub's proximity to the River Trent - a fact reflected by its signboard, which depicts an angler standing on the riverbank landing his catch.

PEACOCK - *Southchurch Drive*

The name of this pub, opened on the 28th April 1961, derives from the coat of arms of the Clifton family who used to live at Clifton Hall, now part of Nottingham Trent University. The traditional sign outside the pub depicts a splendid peacock standing on a balustrade, with Clifton Hall in the background.

The licence for this house was transferred from the former *'Lumley Castle Hotel,'* Radford Road, which was demolished in the early 1960s under the Hyson Green Clearance Scheme.

WINNING POST - *Farnborough Road*

Opened in December 1956, this pub's name refers to the sporting interests of the Farr family, then owners of Home Brewery, who for many years have been successful in breeding racehorses.

CLIPSTONE

DOG AND DUCK - *Main Road*

A pub of this name has stood here for at least 150 years. At one time it served as both a farm and a hostelry - neither facility alone being capable of providing its owner with a living.

It takes its name from a rather cruel sport which used to be popular between 1665 and the early 19th century called the 'Royal Diversion of Duck Hunting,' a pastime much favoured by Charles II. It involved ducks with pinioned wings being thrown into a pond and spaniels sent in to hunt them. The only way that the duck could escape from the dogs was by diving under the water.

Reputedly, this pub is haunted by a mischievous ghost that from time to time turns on taps or rattles pots and pans in the kitchen.

SQUINTING CAT - *Mansfield Road*

This unusual name is derived indirectly from the researches of the German professor Dr Leyhausen at the University of Gottingen into cat behaviour. It is from one of his feline films that the pub's sign, a first-prize winner in a 1980 'paint-a-pub-sign' competition organised by Shipstone's Brewery, has been copied. The artist was John Burton.

COLSTON BASSETT

MARTINS ARMS - *School Lane*

This 300 year old pub, a Grade II listed building, was once a farmhouse. The origin of its name is linked with the history of the village itself.

The Domesday Book, compiled in 1086, refers to a place known as Newbold, from which developed the Manors of Kinoulton and Colston Bassett. The latter has passed through many hands including those of the 15th century Dukes of Buckingham, and the Kitson, Golding, Hacker and Wentworth families.

The last of the Wentworths, the 3rd Earl of Strafford, died without an heir - the Manor being left to his sister, Augusta Ann. Through a series of leases and indentures the Colston Bassett estate passed to Mr Henry Martin, a former military man and Member of Parliament. Upon his death in 1839, it was inherited by his second son, Mr Henry Burgess Martin.

The 1832 Directory is the first to mention the existence of this pub in the village - recording it as an unnamed beerhouse. Later, in the Directory of 1844, the pub is recorded by its current sign for the first time - a Mr William Herrick junior being named as victualler and farmer - no doubt naming the hostelry in honour of his landlord, Mr Martin, whose permission he must have sought.

Since 1257, a weekly market used to be held each Wednesday on the site (outside the pub) marked by the old Market Cross, now owned by the National Trust. The village expanded considerably during the 1840s, a period of great agricultural prosperity.

More recently, in 1990, the pub was featured in an episode of Central Television's drama series *'Boon.'*

Martins Arms, Colston Bassett

COLWICK

STARTING GATE - *Colwick Road*

This pub, opened in May 1973 on part of the Candlemeadow Estate, is admirably named because it was built on the site of the former 'Straight Mile' starting-post belonging to Nottingham Racecourse. Like that of the *'Winning Post'* at Clifton, its name echoes the racing interests of the Farr family who once owned Home Brewery.

Starting Gate, Colwick

COSSALL

GARDENERS - *Awsworth Lane*

This pub, opened in May 1959, is built on land formerly occupied by allotments - hence its name.

The signboard here depicts an amusing interpretation of the pub's name - an old gardener resting on his spade whilst rubbing his aching back.

COSTOCK

GENEROUS BRITON - *Main Street*

The existence of this pub is recorded in White's 1844 Directory of Nottinghamshire. The only other example of this name in the county can be found in Alfreton Road, Nottingham.

Despite the obvious meaning suggested by the name here, it is in fact a political reference. During the 19th century it was common to see the word 'Briton' (prefixed by varying adjectives) as a nom-de-plume for political letters addressed to the Press. The Scottish biographer James Boswell, in one of his letters to Dr Samuel Johnson, signed his name as *'Ancient Briton,'* indicating that he was a true Tory patriot.

Generous Briton, Costock

RED LION - *Old Main Road*

The *'Red Lion'* is the most popular pub name in Britain. Its early use as an inn-sign is attributed to John of Gaunt (1340-99), the most powerful man in England for most of the 14th century. The fourth son of Edward III, John of Gaunt was married to Constance of Leon and Castile and bore the 'gules of Leon' (the lion rampant) as his cognizance to signify his claim to the throne of Castile.

Its popularity as a choice of pub name was further assured when James I of England (James VI of Scotland) ascended to the throne in 1603. He ordered that the heraldic Scottish red lion should be widely displayed in public places.

A converted farmhouse, this pub is at least 150 years old. At the turn of the century former variety artist Bradley Truman, after his comparative success on the stage, retired here. He was so popular with his fellow entertainers that whenever they played in Nottingham they would search him out, spending at least one night in this hostelry. To record his guests, Truman kept a visitors' book. Between 1905 and 1910 this must have read like a veritable 'Who's Who' of music-hall personalities - Harry Lauder, Hamilton Hill (the Australian baritone), Sam Poluski (one of the famous Poluski brothers), Vasco the 'Mad Magician,' Ernest Rommel (a 34" tall comedian), Jack Lane, Frank Benson, Dan Leno, Marie Lloyd and George Formby - all of whom stayed here at one time or another whilst on a visit to see their old friend Bradley Truman.

Red Lion, Costock

COTGRAVE

BLACK DIAMOND - *Owthorpe Road*

Opened on the 27th September 1978, this pub's name is a reference to the coal that used to be mined from nearby Cotgrave Colliery before its closure in 1993.

The signboard here displays a miner holding a bag of coal that sparkles like a diamond (both coal and diamonds being carbon based).

At one time the phrase 'a black diamond' referred to what would be called 'a rough diamond' today - someone of good moral quality, but of unpolished manners.

Manvers Arms, Cotgrave

MANVERS ARMS - *The Cross*

Built about 1725, this former coaching inn was once called the *'Black Lion.'*

Its current sign is a reference to the Earl Manvers, whose earldom dates from 1807 when Baron Pierrepont of Thoresby Hall married Annora de Manvers. In 1955, on the death of the 6th and last Earl Manvers, the title became extinct - though it is still remembered by the sign of this pub and by another of the same name at Radcliffe-on-Trent where the family owned considerable estates. Until the 18th century, their main residence had been at Holme Pierrepont, which relates to their family name.

During the Napoleonic Wars, White's Dragoons were stationed at this hostelry - the soldiers enjoying their last drink before going off to fight. Reputedly, the building is haunted by a male ghost wrapped in a cloak or blanket, which walks about supping ale from a stone jug.

COTTAM

MOTH AND LANTERN - *Outgang Road*

Dominated by the massive cooling towers and chimney of the very close-by Cottam power station built in 1968, the old village pub, the *'Grenville Arms'* acquired its current title in 1981. The pub's new owner of the time ran a competition to find a more appealing name, the Moth and Lantern being symbolic of its attraction, drawing customers as a moth is drawn to a bright light. The inn dates from about 1850 when it was known as the *'Railway Inn'*. By 1890 it was the *'Railway Hotel'*, changing to the *'Grenville Arms'* after World War II.

Moth and Lantern, Cottam

CROPWELL BISHOP

Lime Kiln Inn, Cropwell Bishop

LIME KILN INN - *Kinoulton Road*

The date on a side wall shows that this inn was built in 1840. Standing in splendid isolation at the crossroads, ³/₄ mile south of the village, it became a beerhouse in 1844, when the licensee was William Smith, 'victualler and lime burner'. He would have burned limestone quarried locally, in his kilns nearby, to produce lime. The gypsum quarries provided work for over half the men in the village, at one time.

WHEATSHEAF - *Nottingham Road*

This former coaching inn (which at one time had many stables at the rear) is thought to tbe at least 400 years old. It might well have been used by highwayman Dick Turpin when carrying out his unlawful business on the Fosse Way nearby. (See also pub of same name at Burton Joyce).

Wheatsheaf, Cropwell Bishop (c. 1920)

CROPWELL BUTLER

PLOUGH - *Main Street*

The village once boasted 3 inns but only the 19th century *'Plough'* survives today. The oldest part of the pub, furthest from the road, once had a thatched roof. It is one of a number of *'Ploughs'* to be found in the south of Nottinghamshire.

In 1846, a group of tradesmen and labourers from the village, including the publican, William Smith, formed a branch of the Independent Order of Oddfellows. As their meetings were held in a room at the *'Plough'*, the lodge became known as the *"God Speed the Plough Lodge"*. Every Whit Sunday, lodge members, led by a brass band, would march behind the lodge banner, to Tithby Church for their annual service before returning to the *'Plough'* for dinner. The Lodge was disbanded in the early 1900s.

CUCKNEY

GREENDALE OAK - *Budby Road*

It is claimed that this pub was serving liquor at a time when Charles II was still wooing Nell Gwynn. Originally it was owned by the Duke of Portland, who sold it to Home Brewery in the late 1920s.

The name here commemorates a famous giant oak tree that once stood on the Welbeck Estate, the *'Greendale Oak.'* This tree, which is said by some to have been the big brother of the *'Major Oak,'* was the subject of a wager made between the Earl of Oxford and a number of his associates in 1724. The Earl bet them that a hole could be cut through its girth, large enough for him to drive a carriage-and-pair between.

The bet was taken up, and an archway ten feet high and six feet wide was formed through the centre of the tree trunk, which was 35 feet in circumference. The wood that was removed was later given to the Countess of Oxford, who had a writing-cabinet constructed from it. This cabinet, known as the 'Greendale Cabinet,' passed into the possession of the Portland family and is kept at their ancestral home, Welbeck Abbey.

As for the bet, well, the Earl won. Sadly though, this venture proved to be the downfall of the giant tree, which later died. When its remains were removed there was found to be more than nine tons of wood still left in the trunk.

The signboard outside this pub - constructed itself of solid beaten copper that once formed part of an old tombstone in the nearby churchyard - recalls this famous tree and the Earl's wager.

In a lounge of this pub hangs a framed statement which enlightens us to the origin of the word 'Cockney:'

'In the reign of Edward III, a knight held some land at Cuckney in Nottinghamshire free of rent during the reign of the king on condition of shoeing the king's palfrey (saddle-horse) on each foot with the king's nails and materials - but if he lamed the palfrey he was to give the king another, worth 4 marks. The knight of Cuckney attended at the king's stables to perform his duty when one of the monarch's farriers offered to instruct him how to do it - but in order to save his purse he declined the offer. Consequently, by his ignorance, he lamed the horse. This was repeated until he had to forfeit more marks than the value of the land, by which act of folly the word Cuckney became proverbial, even at Court: and every stupid, untutored citizen was called a Cuckney Knight - afterwards changed to Cockney.'

Another pub of this name can be found at Norfolk Street in Worksop.

DAYBROOK

GROVE - *Mansfield Road*

A plaque on the wall of this pub records its history. It reads: *'Purchased by Home Brewery in 1897 for £7,000, 'The Grove' has refreshed travellers for over a century. The inn originally stood on farm land adjoining the 'sand track,' now Mansfield Road, and served textile traders on their way to the Nottingham Lace Market. Its double cellars, carved from solid rock, were once home for poor farm workers, then a cock-fighting pit, and later used to store the wares of visiting textile merchants. Today, The Grove maintains its tradition of welcoming everyone to sample its superb real ales and atmosphere.'*

OLD SPOT - *Mansfield Road*

As the signboard outside this late 18th century pub clearly indicates, it was named after a racehorse.

This noble creature by the *Selaby Turk* (also known as the *Marshall Turk*, and owned by Mr Marshall, stud-master to William of Orange, Queen Anne and George I), was the property of the Duke of Newcastle and ran at Newmarket in 1698. Throughout its racing career it was variously known as *Spot, Curwen Old Spot, Marshall's Spot* and *Pelham Spot*.

Old Spot later became the maternal grandsire of Partner (foaled 1718) - the grandsire of the famous stallion Herod.

Old Spot, Daybrook

VALE - *Mansfield Road*

Opened in 1938, this pub takes its name from nearby Arno Vale (originally Arnot Vale). The building was designed by Cecil Howitt (cf 'The Wheatsheaf' at Burton Joyce), and many of its '30s style features remain. The sign is different on each side — one depicting a valley at sunrise, the other at sunset.

DRAKEHOLES

GRIFF INN - *Eel Pool Road*

Set high on a hill, the distinctive outline of this popular pub is an easily recognisable landmark to those travelling on the old Roman Road from Clayworth.

In the late 18th century, Squire Jonathan Acklom, of nearby Wiseton Hall, built the *'White Swan'*. This overlooks a wharf on the Chesterfield Canal, and is also adjacent to the Drakeholes Tunnel, where horse drawn barges had to be 'legged' through by the bargees while the horses were led to the other end of the tunnel.

The name of this pub changed in recent years when the licensee was J. D. Griffiths. This unique variation on the more common *'Griffin'* is therefore particularly apt.

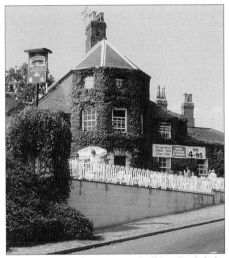

Griff Inn, Drakeholes

EAKRING

SAVILE ARMS - *Bilsthorpe Road*

The Savile family were wealthy, long-established Yorkshire gentry. In 1626, Sir George Savile inherited the Rufford estate, 3 miles from Eakring, and now a Country Park run by Nottinghamshire County Council. The estate remained in the Savile family until it was sold in 1938.

A number of Saviles made their mark. Sir William Savile fought and died in the Civil War, while his son Sir George Savile became the 1st Marquis of Halifax and one of the great statesmen of the 17th century. He is buried in Westminster Abbey. Later Saviles included Captain Henry Savile, successful owner and breeder of racehorses

Savile Arms, Eakring

including Derby winner Cremorne, (who has a pub in the Meadows, Nottingham named after him) and Sir John Savile, British Ambassador to Rome. He was also an archaeologist who brought back many items from the Temple of Diana at Nemi.

The '*Savile Arms*', has served the village of Eakring since the early 17th century when it was known under the sign of the '*Horse and Trumpet*', symbols of the stage coach days. The name changed to the '*Savile Arms*' in the 1860s when the Rufford Estate acquired a controlling interest in Eakring. In 1639 we find that Henry Gillan, the "ale man" was presented at the Manor Court for "*keeping company in his house in evening prayers time*". The landlady of 1719, Sarah Johnson sounds quite a character. She was charged at Newark Quarter Sessions with being "*a barrator and common scold, and a sower of strife and discord in her neighbourhood*" (The case was dismissed!).

In 1800, Eakring had a second inn other than the '*Horse and Trumpet*' and later, seven more came and went. Today the '*Savile Arms*' is the oldest of them all, and the only survivor.

EAST BRIDGFORD

REINDEER - *Kneeton Road*

The '*Reindeer*' was first used as a signboard for an inn in 1630 at Lincoln. The name derives from the reins used when the animal is drawing a sledge. When the Reindeer first came to the notice of the public they were so confused by it, they spelt its name in a variety of different ways, such as Ranged Deer, Rain Deer and Rained Deer. The Reindeer, like the boar, lion, bear and other animals, was a medieval heraldic charge and may in fact represent an alternative form of the stag in heraldry.

Reindeer, East Bridgford

Nowadays, as can be gleaned from the colourful sign that hangs outside this late 18th century pub, the reindeer has developed a very sentimental Father Christmas image.

ROYAL OAK - *Main Street*

In 1651, after his defeat at the Battle of Worcester, Charles II was forced to seek refuge from the Roundhead soldiers who were hunting for him. Together with his aide Colonel Carlos, he climbed an oak tree known as the Boscobel Oak near Shifnal in Shropshire, hiding in its branches from noon until dusk, thus eluding his pursuers.

Upon the King's Restoration to the throne (on May 29th, 1660) it was declared that this day would henceforth be celebrated as 'Royal Oak Day' or 'Oak-apple Day' - a tradition that was followed until the Special Service inserted in the Book of Common Prayer was removed in 1859, almost two centuries later.

The popularity of the pub sign may thus be attributed to genuine rejoicing that the monarchy had been restored, following a decade of comparative austerity imposed since the declaration of the 'Commonwealth' period under Cromwell's rule as 'Lord Protector.' It is an extremely common name, second only in popularity to that of the '*Red Lion*.'

This old pub has an escape story of its own. Centuries ago, the landlord John Spurs helped a fleeing Cavalier to elude troops searching the village and aided him in his escape down river to Newark.

Other inns with this name can be found at West Markham and North Leverton.

EAST LEAKE

BULL'S HEAD - *Main Street*

Recorded in the 1844 Directory, this pub has an ancient and widespread sign.

The name '*Bull's Head*' is sometimes a reference to a papal bull (Latin - *Bulla*) - the leaden seal attached to the Pope's edicts. Most often though, the sign originates from the heraldic badge of Henry VIII, who introduced a bull's head into his coat of arms after he had defied the papal bull of 1538 by abolishing the 'annates' paid to the Pope and declaring himself supreme head of the Church of England.

NAG'S HEAD - *Main Street*

The existence of this pub is recorded in the 1844 Directory of Nottinghamshire.

At one time a traveller could probably have hired a small horse or riding pony (a nag) from an inn bearing this sign. A previous sign here conveyed a less-conventional interpretation of this fairly-common pub name by showing the nag itself with a wholesome grin and a large cigar between its teeth.

THREE HORSESHOES - *Main Street*

The current house was built in the 1960s and is the second to bear this name. The former pub occupied the old Smithy which once stood on the nearby village green, hence the name.

An explanation for the origin of the name the '*Three Horseshoes*' as an inn-sign can be found by referring to the pub of the same name at Beeston. There is another pub of this name at Willoughby-on-the-Wolds, which has an amusing sign depicting a clown juggling 3 horseshoes, one of which he has dropped onto his toe!

Three Horseshoes, East Leake

EAST STOKE

PAUNCEFOTE ARMS - *Fosse Road*

This pub first appears in the 1853 Directory as the '*Pensez Forte Arms.*' It is named after the Pauncefote family whose home was nearby Stoke Hall.

In 1889, Lord Pauncefote became the first British Ambassador to the United States, when he was sent there to restore relations between the two countries after a former minister had been dismissed for interfering in a Presidential election. Having won back the confidence of the American Government, he went on to become a very popular figure. Upon his death at the British Embassy in Washington in 1902, the Union Jack which flew above the building was draped over his coffin, and his body was sent home aboard an American warship. The flag is now in the church.

Before he died, Lord Pauncefote had secured a major treaty between America and Great Britain - both countries pledging never to war with one another again (as they had done between 1812-1814).

He is buried in the village churchyard at East Stoke, with a beautiful bronze angel watching over this much-respected Statesman's grave.

EASTWOOD

GREASLEY CASTLE - *Castle Street*

Greasley Castle was, in reality, a fortified manor house belonging to the Cantilupe family, one member of which, Nicholas Cantilupe (a close friend of Edward III) founded Beauvale Priory nearby. Manor houses were often fortified in the 14th century, when there was general lawlessness in the country, and threats of invasion by the Scots were real.

The castle is shown on Mary Eyre's 1632 tapestry map in Nottingham's Costume Museum, and was probably a square enclosure, with towers on the four corners and surrounded by a moat. Some of the old remains survive around Greasley Castle Farm, and to the south east of Greasley Church.

The pub bearing this name is on Castle Street in Eastwood.

MAN IN SPACE - *Nottingham Road*

This pub, opened on the 15th December 1966 by Councillor Colin Dyson, chairman of Eastwood Urban Council, replaced an old inn called the '*Coach and Horses*' which used to stand on an adjacent site.

The name here commemorates Alan Shepard, the first American in space, aboard the '*Friendship 7*' space capsule on the 5th May 1961. The signboard depicts an astronaut walking in space at the end of his safety cord.

Man in Space, Eastwood

MOON AND STARS - *Brookhill Leys Road*

This is one of Eastwood's oldest pubs, a three storey Georgian building of around 1760. Arthur Coleman in his book *"Eastwood, Through Bygone Ages"* indicates that Solomon Shelton built the house, probably as a farmhouse, as early records show him to be a farmer by occupation. When he died in 1797, he is described as an inn holder. His inn was known as the *'Seven Stars'*. It then became the *'Moon and Seven Stars'* but today is simply the *'Moon and Stars'*. The stars are a reference to the constellation *"Ursa Major"*, commonly known as the Plough.

The name will be familiar to readers of 'Sons and Lovers' by D. H. Lawrence, as there is a *"Moon and Stars"* described there. This is, in reality, the fictional name of the *'Three Tuns'* (qv). When D. H. Lawrence was a boy, the Brookhill Leys Road area used to be called New Eastwood, and was close to the canal and the railway, (the A610 bypass now follows the line of this former railway). The Newthorpe and Greasley Station was behind the *'Moon and Stars'* and Lawrence would have known it well, as he caught the train daily to Nottingham, where he was a pupil at the High School.

Born in Eastwood's Victoria Street (now the Birthplace Museum), Lawrence (1885-1930) became a writer whose work expressed his belief in emotion and the sexual impulse, as creative and true to human nature. In a letter to Lady Cynthia Asquith (in November 1913) he wrote, *"I like to write when I feel spiteful - it's like having a good sneeze"*.

The sign of this pub is an ancient one and was used as a convenient visual symbol. The moon is often featured in the name of a public house, eg the *'Full Moon'* at Morton (qv).

OLD WINE VAULTS - *Church Street*

According to a board on the side of the building, this pub was established in 1779 and is one of the three oldest in Eastwood. Arthur Coleman describes the *'Old Wine Vaults'* as a "typical Georgian building in the same style of architecture as the Sun Inn". Possibly the Sun is the older of the two. Vaults are the cellars where wine and other liquors are stored.

PALMERSTON ARMS - *Greenhills Road*

Opened in 1959, this pub is built on the site of a former inn of the same name. Standing at the front of the premises is a pear tree of some considerable age which is subject to a Preservation Order. In the lounge of the pub hangs a portrait of Henry John Temple Palmerston (1784-1865), from whom it takes its name. Lord Palmerston's wife was a Cowper who lived at Beauvale and owned land in the Eastwood and Greasley area.

Prime Minister on two occasions (1855-1858 and 1859-1865), Lord Palmerston became known as 'Firebrand Palmerston' due to his self-assertiveness and brusque manner of speech. During his premiership many notable events occurred - the American Civil War, Napoleon III's war with Austria, and the Austro-Prussian war with Denmark.

On his death-bed, Lord Palmerston's last words were, *"Die, my dear Doctor? That's the last thing I shall do!"*

SUN INN - *Market Place*

This pub was built about 1754 by the Lords of the Manor, who used to hold court in an upstairs room of the premises. As the property belonged to the Plumptre estate, no deeds exist to verify the exact date of building.

A plaque on a wall outside records that the premises were also the venue for a very important meeting which took place on the 16th August 1832. Here, a group of local colliery owners met in response to the worrying threat posed by a nearby railway company and decided to form their own coal line from Eastwood to Leicester. This historic decision was to lead to the birth of the Midland Counties Railway. In 1838, four thousand men were employed in the construction of the line, opened on the 30th May, 1839. For many years, a Friday evening market, described by Lawrence in 'Sons and Lovers', was held outside the *Sun Inn*.

Considered to be of pagan origin, the sign of the Sun ranks among the oldest and most common of pub names.

Sun Inn, Eastwood

Three Tuns, Eastwood

THREE TUNS - *Three Tuns Road*

The first reference in the directory to this pub, at Hill Top, is in 1844, when the landlord was Joseph Savery, victualler. The *'Three Tuns'* was one of Arthur Lawrence's favourite locals (he lived for a time just round the corner in Walker Street) and his son D. H. Lawrence used the pub as one of his locations in *Sons and Lovers,* where it became the *"Moon and Stars"*. *Sons and Lovers* is generally regarded as an autobiographical novel. In it, the author talks of his father working at this inn (Walter Morel is the character Lawrence based on his own father): *"He's helping to wait at the Moon and Stars. I see him through that black tin stuff wi' holes in, on the window, wi' his sleeves rolld up"*. Walter Morel is depicted as being a heavy drinker, although Lawrence's own father is unlikely to have drunk to such excess.

In Lawrence's day, the 'Hill Top Wakes', a travelling fair, used to be held annually, on land in front of the pub. In *Sons and Lovers,* Walter Morel stayed to "'elp Anthony" during the Wakes.

A tun is a large cask, used for wholesale distribution of wine and ale. Three tuns appear in the arms of the Worshipful Company of Vintners as well as the Worshipful Company of Brewers.

This pub has the sign on the front wall, a large picture showing tuns being unloaded from the dray, and rolled towards the inn itself.

EDINGLEY

OLD REINDEER - *Edingley Village*

Shown in the 1853 Directory, this pub was purchased from Courage Brewery in March 1992 by Mansfield Brewery.

The circular signboard depicts (as might be expected) a large reindeer standing on a snow-covered hill.

An explanation for the origin of the name *'Reindeer'* as an inn-sign can be found by referring to the pub of the same name at East Bridgford.

EDWALTON

MEADOW COVERT - *Alford Road*

The sign outside this pub depicts two men in Norfolk jackets trying to wing a high-flying pheasant - an indication that certain species of wild life used to be plentiful in these parts.

The name here was chosen by the brewery after reference to an early Ordnance Survey map, which simply named the countryside in proximity to the pub as *Meadow Covert.*

EDWINSTOWE

BLACK SWAN - *High Street*

This is the oldest public house in the village. Inside, it has Sherwood Forest oak beams which were hewn from the woods shortly after Robin Hood and his Merry Men inhabited the area.

Despite its almost 600 years existence as an inn, it was nearly forced to close 1970 when a cash shortage meant it couldn't be brought up to 20th century standards - despite a preservation order for historic buildings at Edwinstowe. In 1987 the necessary modernization was completed and the sign of the *'Black Swan'* remained in the village.

The name here first appeared as an inn name in the 16th century, and may have meant to signal what a rara avis, (a remarkable 'old bird') the landlord was. Later references may well be to Australia (discovered in 1770), since a black swan is the emblem of Western Australia.

There is an interesting story about a former local vicar who used to patronize this pub. It is said that he was often so drunk upon leaving here, that back at his church he used to confuse the wedding service with the funeral service.

DUKERIES - High Street

Built in 1897 by Mansfield Brewery, its name is a reference to the ducal estates in nearby Sherwood Forest - Welbeck, Clumber and Thoresby.

ROBIN HOOD - Rufford Crossroads

Mentioned in the 1832 Directory, this pub was originally called the 'New Inn.' It was purchased by Mansfield Brewery from Hornbys (mineral water manufacturers) in 1955, and rebuilt in 1957.

Situated close to Rufford Abbey, the original house witnessed many notable events. During the Civil War a close watch was kept on the Abbey by the local Parliamentarians who suspected it was being used as a meeting place by Royalist supporters plotting to seize York for the King. On one occasion three mysterious strangers put up at the New Inn, and received from the Abbey a supply of sack and claret. It is rumoured that the strangers were Prince Charles, the Duke of York and the Duke of Gloucester, but no one can be sure.

The name here is a reminder of Nottinghamshire's association with the legendary outlaw.

Robin Hood, Edwinstowe

ROYAL OAK - High Street

Shown in the 1832 Directory, the sign outside this pub portrays King Charles hiding from the searching Roundhead troops in the Boscobel Oak.

A full explanation of the origin of this house's name can be found by referring to the pub of the same name at East Bridgford.

Old Plough, Egmanton

EGMANTON

OLD PLOUGH - Main Street

The 'Old Plough' is over 200 years old and, until the early 1980s incorporated the village shop. Innkeepers here have often combined two jobs - Sandys Jackson in 1832 was victualler and blacksmith, Elizabeth Stafford in 1864 was victualler and baker whilst John Gale in 1881 was victualler and grocer. Egmanton originally had two other inns but by 1880 both the 'New Plough' and the 'Rose and Crown' were no more.

Several times each year there are pilgrimages to the famous local church nearby and the inn is blessed as the pilgrims pass by.

ELKESLEY

ROBIN HOOD - High Street

Elkesley once stood in the heart of Sherwood Forest so what better name for this extremely popular and busy inn, than local legend Robin Hood. The pub was first established around 1840 (although parts of the building may well be considerably older) when, strangely enough, Elkesley also had another 'Green Man'. (See also the 'Robin Hood' at Sherwood, Nottingham).

Robin Hood, Elkesley

Chequers Inn, Elston

ELSTON

CHEQUERS INN - *Toad Lane*

The *'Chequers Inn'* is over 250 years old and a former coaching inn. It is the only one remaining of five that once served this village, the one-time home of the Darwin family, the most famous member of which was Charles Darwin, author of *"The Origin of Species"*. Photographs of the village hang on the walls inside the pub which also has a collection of items associated with village life.

See the *'Chequers'* at Chilwell for the origin of this pub name.

ELTON

MANOR ARMS - *Main Road*

This very attractive old brick building on the A52 road once belonged to the Manor of Elton. Lord of the Manor in the 1840s was William Fletcher Norton Norton, and with so much emphasis on the surname, it is no surprise to find that the inn was named the *'Norton Arms'* then, and throughout the remainder of the century. After World War I, it became the *'Elton Arms'*. The old Manor house was demolished in 1935 and no doubt to enable the name to live on, just as the old gardens, including a topiary garden and orchard, have done, the inn became the *'Manor Arms'* that we know today.

EPPERSTONE

CROSS KEYS - *Main Street*

At the turn of the century Epperstone used to boast two pubs, this one and the *'King's Head.'* The latter pub (which stood close to Epperstone Manor) closed around the time of the First World War.

The *'Cross Keys'* itself is some 200 years old and was purchased by Shipstones in 1912 but later sold to Hardys and Hansons in 1940. The *'Cross Keys'* was the winner in 1993 of a Nottinghamshire County Council Tourism Award for the "Best Pub Food".

An explanation for the origin of this house's sign can be found by referring to the pub of the same name in Nottingham's Byard Lane.

Cross Keys, Epperstone

EVERTON

BLACKSMITHS ARMS - *Chapel Street*

This pub is probably 300 years old, and was originally the Smithy, hence the name. The low ceilings and oak beams help to create the atmosphere of the traditional village pub.

Many pubs are named after trades which flourished at the time and other examples include:

Brewers Arms   - Clayworth
Bricklayers Arms - Ruddington
Butchers Arms   - Laneham
Carpenters Arms - Walesby and Boughton
Masons Arms   - Retford and Sutton in Ashfield.

There are also other *'Blacksmiths Arms'* at Clayworth (qv) and Mattersey.

Blacksmiths Arms, Everton

FARNDON

LAZY OTTER - *Wyke Road*

This late 17th century pub was originally called the *'Britannia Inn.'* Situated close to the River Trent, it was frequented by bargees who would bed-down their horses in the stables which used to stand at the rear of the building, or alternatively put them out to graze in one of the two fields nearby. Though the fields still adjoin this pub, the stables are long gone.

In 1989, the house underwent a change of sign to the *'Lazy Otter.'* Chosen as a result of a competition, the name reflects the pub's proximity to a 'willow holt' which is teeming with wild life - though no otters themselves have as yet been spotted here as the water is too dirty.

Outside the pub, a humorous signboard depicts an otter lying on a log whilst fishing in the river.

Lazy Otter, Farndon

FARNSFIELD

PLOUGH - *Main Street*

Though the *'Plough'* displays a plaque on an outer wall dated 1742, according to records, evidence of its existence as an hostelry can be traced back much further to 1451. It is likely that the date on this plaque refers to an occasion when an extra wing was added to the building.

In 1955 the pub was purchased by Mansfield Brewery from Hornbys (mineral water manufacturers), and furnished with a colourful new signboard depicting two powerful shire-horses pulling a plough.

In use since at least the 16th century, the sign of the *'Plough'* is extremely common, especially in rural areas.

White Post, Farnsfield

RED LION - *Main Street*

Recorded in White's 1832 Directory, this pub was acquired by Mansfield Brewery in 1883.

In 1976 builders uncovered an 18ft deep, 3ft wide well, dating back to at least 1791, whilst working on an extension to the inn's lounge.

An explanation for the origin of the name *'Red Lion'* as an inn-sign can be found by referring to the pub of the same name at Costock.

WHITE POST - *Ollerton Road*

The original old coaching house (recorded in the 1832 Directory) which used to stand on this site was demolished in 1926 by Chesterfield Brewery to make way for the current building.

Now owned by Mansfield Brewery, this pub takes its name from its glory days as a 'White' staging post on the Great North Road.

FISKERTON

BROMLEY ARMS - *Main Street*

This old 17th century pub stands on the west bank of the River Trent overlooking the site of the famous battle of East Stoke which finally ended the Wars of the Roses, begun in 1455.

In 1486, Henry VII made his throne more secure by marrying Elizabeth of York, so ending the long struggle between the Yorkists (the White Rose) and Lancastrians (the Red Rose). Despite the

Bromley Arms, Fiskerton

marriage there was still unrest among supporters of the White Rose, who were duped into accepting Lambert Simnel, the son of an Oxford joiner, as the rightful heir to the throne. Simnel was crowned king in Dublin and, together with an army of Irishmen and 1,500 German mercenaries, invaded England. After travelling to York they marched south, and on the 16th June 1487 forded the River Trent at Fiskerton across to East Stoke, on their way to take Newark. Here they were met by the King's army which had marched out from Nottingham, and for three hours a fearsome battle ensued. Finally, the rebels were beaten back and in their attempt to escape ran into a meadow near to the river (known today as Red Gutter) where many of them were slaughtered.

At the time when horse-drawn barges plied the river, this pub was one of the many stations used for changing horses. It is said that, at times, there used to be so many barges moored outside this pub during the evenings, that it was possible to walk across their decks to East Stoke.

The inn takes its name from Lord Bromley who lived at East Stoke Hall. Apparently, his Lordship wanted to hunt on both sides of the river, so he bought this pub at Fiskerton and named it the 'Bromley Arms.' It was purchased around 1933 by Hardys and Hansons Brewery.

FLINTHAM

BOOT AND SHOE - *Main Street*

Recorded in the 1832 Directory, this former coaching inn's name indicates a welcome to all visitors - irrespective of whether they wear the horseman's jackboot or the labourer's shoe.

During the Second World War this pub was enormously popular with aircrews from the nearby airfields of Syerston and Newton. One of its former patrons, Wing Commander Guy Gibson VC, led the famous 'Dambusters' raid on the Mohne and Eder dams in 1943.

Another inn with this name can be found at Granby.

FOREST TOWN

PRINCE CHARLES - *Clipstone Road*

The unusual name of this pub, opened in 1952 reminds us that protocol forbids the use of any name as a signboard title which belongs to a royal personage *still living*. However, the then brewery (Holes of Newark) neatly evaded this stricture, issued by Buckingham Palace, by presenting their hero as 'Bonnie Prince Charlie' instead - and in fact the pub is still referred to by its regulars simply as *The Charlie.'*

The signboard itself portrays a kilted piper amid a nostalgic Highland setting.

WHITE GATES - *Clipstone Road East*

Opened on the 4th April 1963, this pub takes its name from a pair of white gates that used to fasten across a private road leading to nearby Cavendish Lodge. Though these gates have long since been removed, their name is perpetuated with the opening of these licensed premises.

GEDLING

CHESTERFIELD ARMS - *Main Road*

Most of the land in both Gedling and Carlton was at one time owned by the Earl of Chesterfield - hence the name of this old pub (mentioned in the 1832 Directory). See also the *'Earl of Chesterfield Arms'* at Shelford.

GREY GOOSE - *Arnold Lane*

Opened in December 1956, this pub's name was chosen by its former owners, Samuel Smiths Brewery of Tadcaster. The sign of the 'Grey Goose,' was in line with their policy, at the time, of naming their new pubs after birds and animals. Now owned by Greenalls, it was refurbished in 1990.

The pub's signboard portrays a picture of a goose flapping its wings, while a model of a goose in a glass case stands near the entrance.

PHOENIX - *Shelford Road*

Opened on the 2nd December 1965, the sign here displays the phoenix, the fabulous bird which every one hundred years or so sets fire to itself, only to later rise from its own ashes with renewed youth to commence a new life.

A symbol of our Lord and an emblem of immortality, this mythical bird of the Arabian Desert inspired Lord Byron to write:

> *'Glory, like the phoenix*
> *'midst her fires,*
> *exhales her odours,*
> *blazes and expires.'*

The pub in fact takes its name because it was built on land which was formerly part of Phoenix Farm. The estate which it serves is often referred to as the Phoenix Estate.

GILTBROOK

Hayloft, Giltbrook

HAYLOFT - *Nottingham Road*

Formerly a tiny century-old pub called the *'Old White Bull,'* this house, opened in December 1983, was completely rebuilt by Shipstones and transformed into the *'Hayloft.'* In order to enlarge the former house, three cottages that once stood adjacent to it (one at the side and two at the back) were incorporated into its new design, making it three times its original size.

Its current sign derives from the extraordinary range of farming implements and equipment that hang from its ceilings or form set-piece displays inside the building. Some, such as scythes, ploughs and rakes, are well known, but others, including a cheese press and a potato cleaner, are less obvious.

GOTHAM

CUCKOO BUSH - *Leake Road*

The earliest reference to the existence of this old pub can be found in the Nottingham Journal. Dated the 14th January 1826, it refers to a sale *'at the House of Mr Woolley, the Sign of the Cuckoo Bush, Gotham'* of *'339 valuable timber-trees now standing at Gotham Wood.'* The current house was rebuilt on the site of the original pub in 1858.

Its name is a reference to the antics of the 'Wise Men of Gotham' who feigned madness to avoid paying taxes to King John in the 13th century.

The story goes, that when the good folk of Gotham learned of the imminent visit of their king to the village, they began to fear for their livelihood. Believing that the king would assess their prosperous meadow for tax or possibly even build a royal hunting lodge in the area, they devised a clever trick to keep him away.

Cuckoo Bush Inn, Gotham

Aware that the one thing that all men of this period were afraid of was madness, there being no cure for insanity in those days, they decided to play the harmless fools.

When the king's advance party approached the village, they discovered a number of men trying to rake the reflection of the moon out of a pond, swearing it was a cheese. Others were rolling real cheeses down a hill towards Nottingham, leaving them, so they said, to wend their own way to market. The so-called village genius tied two bushels of wheat round his own neck and rode after the fast-disappearing dairy produce, explaining that his horse wouldn't have to bear the load.

The king's equerries must have looked on with amazement at the bizarre scenes that unfolded before their eyes, especially when villagers began to build a fence around a tree where a cuckoo had chosen to roost for the night.

When asked what they were about, they explained that if they could keep the cuckoo trapped in the tree, it would always be Spring in Gotham.

Needless to say the king and his men, deciding that the men of Gotham were fools to be avoided at all costs, rode away from the village.

From that time, whenever the villagers became aware of royal representatives in the area, they always acted strangely. And so, Gotham's reputation for stupidity grew, leading to many stories, such as that recounted by the following nursery-rhyme:

'Three wise men of Gotham,
Went to sea in a bowl.
If the bowl had been stronger,
My story would have been longer.'

The pub takes its name from these legendary stories - in particular that concerning the cuckoo in the tree.

Sun Inn, Gotham

SUN - *The Square*

A pub of this name has stood here since the 1840s. The sign of the Sun is fairly common throughout the country, being used as an inn-sign due to its simple visual form.

WINDMILL - *Nottingham Road*

The 'Windmill' built around 1860, is one of the main pubs in the area. It recently made the news after it was decided to replace the old pub sign with a new one. The Lowe family (also landlords of the nearby 'Cuckoo Bush') asked one of their 'regulars' at the 'Windmill', artist Rob Brown, to create an eye-catching new design. The various members of the family take their cartoon-style place, by the windmill, along with the barmaid and the cleaner for good measure!

GRANBY

MARQUIS OF GRANBY - *Dragon Street*

John Manners, eldest son of the 3rd Duke of Rutland (whose ancestors had purchased the estate), took his title from this little Vale of Belvoir village which once, was more important as a small market town. The pub bearing his name is a very old one, probably dating back to the reign of Charles II, and was kept by the Watson family for more than two centuries until the retirement, in 1947, of Alfred Watson. The inn, often nicknamed the 'Dragon' (from the road on which it stands), had its own brewhouse for many years.

For more information about the benevolent Marquis, please refer to the pub of the same name at Hoveringham.

GUNTHORPE

ANCHOR - *Main Street*

A simple emblem, the anchor is an extremely common inn-sign, especially for those pubs situated close to the sea or near to waterways like this house (mentioned in the 1844 Directory). In earlier days it was used as a religious symbol - St. Ambrose said of the anchor, *'It is this which keeps the Christian from being carried away by the storm of life.'*

TOM BROWN'S BAR - *Main Street*

Until 1974, the village school stood between the 'Anchor' and the 'Unicorn' near Gunthorpe Bridge. An imaginative conversion has transformed the old place of learning into a lively bar, with restaurant, flanked by the two older hostelries - where else can such a threesome be found? On the walls inside hang sepia photographs of pupils, teachers and the building itself, as a school. It is interesting to speculate as to how many regulars who now drink here, were also taught here!

The pub's name appropriately provides a link between schooldays and the eponymous hero of Thomas Hughes' famous novel, although before that the pub had the equally suitable title 'The Upper Sixth'.

Tom Brown's Bar, Gunthorpe

Unicorn, Gunthorpe

UNICORN - *Main Street*

Recorded in the 1832 Directory as the *'Ferry House,'* parts of this pub are considerably older than this, dating back to 1664 when it was in use as a row of cottages.

In 1855 it was renamed the *'Unicorn Ferry House Inn,'* and is believed to have been used as a ferry-point by travellers crossing the River Trent by boat, well before the first bridge was built at Gunthorpe in 1875. By the time the pub was purchased by Mansfield Brewery in 1937, its name had already been shortened to its current form.

The single long horn on the forehead of a unicorn (the legendary animal with the body of a horse), is said to possess magical properties. Its use as a pub name is an heraldic reference. Two unicorns support the Royal Arms of Scotland. A unicorn also features in the coats of arms of the Worshipful Company of Goldsmiths (1327), the Worshipful Company of Wax Chandlers (1483) and the Worshipful Society of Apothecaries (1617).

HALAM

PLOUGH - *The Turnpike*

As well as being a brewhouse, this pub (mentioned in the 1844 Directory) once housed a blacksmith's shop and a bakery as well.

An explanation for the origin of the name the *'Plough'* as an inn-sign can be found by referring to the pub of the same name at Farnsfield.

WAGGON AND HORSES - *Mansfield Road*

A former brewhouse, this old pub (dating back to 1752) used to have a stable and a blacksmith's shop attached to it, a former landlord combining both of these businesses. Upstairs, a number of its old oak beams are believed to have come from Humber boats which had been dismantled during the early part of the 17th century, their wood being salvaged and used for building work. In 1984 the old village shop and general store which used to stand adjacent to the pub were incorporated into its bar.

The origin of this pub's name quite possibly lies in its earlier use as both a brewhouse and a blacksmith's shop - no doubt its former owner had plenty of customers for both his trades - waggon and horses being a common feature of village life in those days, being used to carry all manner of things, including goods and farm produce.

HARBY

BOTTLE AND GLASS - *High Street*

Nottinghamshire's most easterly village is Harby, remote and lonely, and almost in Lincolnshire. It was here that Queen Eleanor of Castile, wife of Edward I, died in 1290, with 'Eleanor' crosses later erected to mark the stopping places where her body lay, en route to burial in Westminster Abbey.

The history of this pub dates back to the late 17th century, and it was at this time that beer in bottles was very much a novelty. Innkeepers, anxious to show that they were up to date, liked to advertise their possession of such articles.

HAYTON

BOAT INN - *Main Street*

Hayton stands adjacent to the Chesterfield Canal, and at one time had two inns. The *'Anchor'* was the older of the two and may well have been built at the same time as the canal, in the 1770s. It closed in 1924. However the *'Boat'*, dating from around 1840 (with subsequent additions and extensions) survives. The inn stands close to Townend Bridge, one of the many quaint old bridges to be found along this canal.

Throughout the country there are countless *'Boat'* inns situated beside canals, rivers or the sea. A saying connected with boats and pubs occurs in naval slang - 'to push the boat out' means to pay for a round of drinks.

HICKLING

Plough Inn, Hickling

PLOUGH - *Hickling Road*

The 33 mile long Grantham to Nottingham canal passes through Hickling on its way to join the Trent. In the last century, barges carrying coal, gypsum, timber and a host of other goods, used the canal which, at Hickling Basin, had wharves and a storage barn which still stands. Today the Basin is a quiet haven for fishermen, but it was once a hive of activity, with several pubs to serve the thirsty navigators ('navvies') who toiled there. *'The Navigator'*, *'The Wheel'* and the *'Old Bowling Green'* are now gone, leaving the quaint little *'Plough'* (complete of course, with old plough fixed to the wall) as Hickling's only pub.

HOCKERTON

SPREAD EAGLE - *Caunton Road*

This small village inn was probably a blacksmith's forge before it became a pub in the early 1840s. The landlord James May had, ten years previously, been known merely as a 'beerseller', probably conducting his business from the same premises. It is not known why the inn adopted the sign of an eagle with its wings spread out, established as a national emblem by the Romans.

HOVERINGHAM

MARQUIS OF GRANBY - *Main Street*

Hoveringham once possessed four inns. One, the *'Elm Tree'* closed in 1989. Another, the *'Duke of Wellington'* later became the *'Calf-Jobbers Arms'* (an amazing name for an inn!) and is now a private residence. In 1881, Hugh Silverwood was the landlord, but by 1888 he had moved to the *'Marquis of Granby'*, the first time an inn of this name is found in the village, although the building itself is much older.

The sign honours John Manners, Marquis of Granby (1721-1770). The eldest son of the 3rd Duke of Rutland, whose family seat is Belvoir Castle, Leicesterhire, John Manners became the Colonel of the Royal Regiment of Horse Guards (known as 'The Blues') in 1758 and Commander-in-Chief of the British Army in 1766. Known universally as 'The Soldiers' Friend', he set up numerous of his NCOs as tavern-keepers on their retirement, and this no doubt is the reason for the high number of pubs with this name throughout England. He died at the early age of 49 leaving personal debts of almost £40,000 - said to result from his reckless spirit of generosity.

After his death in 1770 the following lines appeared in a national newspaper:

'What conquest now will Britain boast,
Or where display her banners?
Alas, in Granby she has lost
True courage and good Manners!'

His courage was amply displayed when leading a cavalry attack against the French in the Battle of Warburg during the Seven Years' War. He lost his hat and then his wig in the charge, revealing his bald pate - on which the sun shone, according to legend, to such dramatic effect that it focused the attention of his men on the sight of their leader riding furiously onwards, sword held aloft, until they responded in kind and put the enemy to flight. This episode is said to reflect the origin of the phrase, *'Going at it bald-headed.'*

There is another pub of this name in the village of Granby itself (from which the Marquis took his title).

REINDEER - *Main Street*

In the 1770s, the owners of Vine Cottage, which stands close by, built a dwelling house as a 21st birthday present for their son. Today it is the *'Reindeer Inn'*. In the 19th century it became an unnamed beerhouse, run for nearly 50 years by John Kirk (who was described as a 'beer-retailer' after 1848) and then for a further 40 years by Martha Woodsend. It wasn't until the 1930s that the name *'Reindeer'* first appeared in the Directories, the landlord then being Jack Derry, who was also a "threshing machine proprietor".

In the 1940s, the *'Reindeer'* was run by Bessie and Josie Wilson, a very formidable pair, as older residents of Hoveringham still remember. The two ladies, as sitting tenants, were able to purchase the inn "for a song" from Newark brewers Warwick & Richardson. Josie Wilson continued to run the Reindeer until the 1970s. Then the pub had just two small rooms for the regulars, and drinks were served through a hatch in Josie's kitchen, she having brought the beer up from the cellar by jug! In those days, the car park was a lawn and a skittle alley ran its full length up to the ivy covered inn.

In the past few years, the *'Reindeer'* has seen changes. Gone is Josie's kitchen and serving hatch, and the inn now has a proper bar. A large dining area has been added, and a long 'corridor' built out at the front in 1981, the year Prince Charles married Diana, as the commemorative brick by the door indicates.

For its 'back garden', the *'Reindeer'* has the village cricket pitch - an idyllic setting on Saturday afternoons in summer.

They say the inn has no ghosts, but the living presence of the friendly Oscar, said to be the oldest pub dog in Nottinghamshire, more than makes up for this. With the colourful flowers in baskets on the red brick walls outside, and old beams, brasses and beermats inside, this is a most typical example of the friendly English village local.

Why this inn was called the *'Reindeer'*, no-one seems to know. For further explanation of the name, see the *'Reindeer'* at East Bridgford.

HUCKNALL

CHEQUERS - *High Street*

The origin of this old pub's name (mentioned in the 1832 Directory), can be found by referring to the hostelry of the same name at Chilwell.

FLYING BEDSTEAD - *Watnall Road*

This pub opened on the 8th June 1967 as a replacement for the former *'Crown Inn'* which used to stand on Byron Street.

In line with Hardys and Hansons general policy of naming their new hostelries after some local association with the area in which they stand, and also due to its close proximity to a tiny corner of Hucknall aerodrome, this pub was named the *'Flying Bedstead.'*

It was in 1941 that the late Dr. A.A. Griffith, Rolls-Royce's chief scientist, first envisaged the idea of vertical take-off using jet engines for lift. A number of years later his notion was developed by the company, who built a contraption not unlike an old-fashioned bedstead.

Built without wings and powered by two Rolls-Royce Nene engines, it was nicknamed *'The Thing,'* - its main features being four huge legs complete with castors. In August 1954 at Hucknall aerodrome, under its official title as the RB 108, this aircraft made its maiden flight - hovering for almost ten minutes at heights varying from five to ten feet. At that time, it was piloted by the late Captain Ronald Shepherd.

Capable of a thrust equal to eight times its own weight, it had its share of tragedy, too, for Wing Commander Henry Francis Larsen was killed when the aircraft overturned during tests.

One of the guests at the opening of this pub was Mr H.C. Rodgers, former chief test pilot for Rolls-Royce, who was very much concerned with the pioneering work carried out on this experimental aircraft.

The forerunner of the now famous Harrier aircraft, the prototype RB 108, now occupies a place of honour in the Science Museum at South Kensington in London.

GREEN DRAGON - *Watnall Road*

This pub is first recorded in the will of framesmith William Truman of Hucknall, dated 1845.

The humorous sign that hangs outside, a whimsical green dragon sampling a pint of ale, was designed and painted by artist Bill Cole, and was the winning inspiration for the first of two Paint-a-Pub Sign Competitions organised by Shipstones Brewery during 1980/1982.

The sign of the *'Green Dragon'* itself can be traced to heraldry - appearing on the coat of arms of the Earls of Pembroke. A popular sign for centuries, it is one of the oldest heraldic symbols. In the Bayeux Tapestry, a winged dragon on a pole is constantly represented near to the person of King Harold. It is also possible that the name has its origins in the 18th century when pilgrims returning from the Holy Land had seen crocodiles on the banks of the River Nile.

Green Dragon sign, Hucknall

HARRIER - *Christchurch Road*

This pub opened on the 7th December 1979 and, like the nearby *'Flying Bedstead'* (qv), reflects the town's connections (via Rolls-Royce) with pioneering experiments into the creation of an aircraft capable of vertical take-off and landing. This eventually lead to the development of a useful combat aircraft - the Hawker Siddeley Harrier. This aircraft, powered by a single Rolls-Royce Pegasus engine, first saw squadron service on the 1st April 1969.

MALT SHOVEL - *Annesley Road*

This pub, opened on the 4th August 1966, has a name closely linked with centuries of brewing - the malt shovel being an essential tool of the trade.

Malt is grain (usually barley), which is steeped in water and fermented, before being dried over a kiln and shovelled into the brewing vat using a malt shovel.

The malt supplies the brew's strength, whilst hops provide it with its bitter flavour. The ale of the Saxons was brewed from barley alone. Hops were eventually added by Flemish brewers in London who called the drink 'biere.' On average six hop flowers provide the flavour of one pint.

A genuine two-handed malt shovel, at least a century old, stands in the entrance to the Lounge of this pub.

MASONS ARMS - *Watnall Road*

Red Lion, Hucknall

Opened on the 16th December 1959, this house replaced an old inn of the same name that used to stand on High Street.

A popular sign for a pub - it relates to the Company of Masons, who cut stone into shape for building purposes and were granted a coat of arms in 1473.

RED LION - *High Street*

This pub has been in existence since 1749 and was once the property of the Byron family of Newstead. Tenants used to pay their dues to them, in one of the rooms here.

An explanation for the origin of the name here can be found by referring to the *'Red Lion'* at Costock.

SEVEN STARS - *West Street*

The sign of this old pub (mentioned in the 1832 Directory), may have once been used as a Masonic emblem - a circle of six stars, with one in the centre. It is also possible that the seven stars may represent the *Plough* or the ancient seven planets.

WAGGON AND HORSES - *Broomhill Road*

This pub opened in September 1964 as a replacement for the former *'Fox and Hounds'* (known locally as the *'Top House'*), which used to stand in Annesley Road.

The opening ceremony was attended by two of Shipstone's famous Clydesdale horses, which were closely associated with this brewery for many years.

WILL SCARLET - *Watnall Road*

Formerly the Westville Social Club, this building was converted into a pub on the 3rd July 1982. The opening ceremony was attended by the Robin Hood Society, who no doubt ensured the occasion was a 'merry' one.

The name here leaves no doubt as to its origin - Will Scarlet being a well-known member of the legendary outlaw's so-called 'Merrie Men.' An original character, he appears in all of the early ballads of Robin Hood, including *'The Little Geste,'* where he is called both Scarlock and Scathelocke.

It is said that Will Scarlet lies buried in St Mary's Churchyard, Blidworth.

Yew Tree, Hucknall

YEW TREE - *Beardall Street*

Mentioned in the 1832 Directory, the *'Yew Tree'* was one of the oldest pubs in the parish. It was replaced by a pub of the same name and situated about 150 yards further along Beardall Street. The present *'Yew Tree'* was built in 1877 by Joseph Beardall who was also the first landlord.

Its location, near to a church, may provide a clue to the origin of its name. In medieval England, the yew tree was of great importance because its wood was used to make the English longbow. Under the Plantagenets and Tudors, legislation required every man under the age of 60 to practise with the longbow, unless he was a cleric or a lawyer - and Edward IV (1461-1483) ordained that every Englishman should have a bow his own height.

Butts were provided to the south of Park Row in Nottingham (also in many villages of the county) which were required usage at holiday times and on Sunday afternoons.

A living symbol of 'life after death,' the yew trees were often planted in churchyards (where you can still find some very ancient specimens), as they were less likely to suffer damage in such a place.

HUTHWAITE

PORTLAND ARMS - *Sutton Road*

At one time, most of the land in Huthwaite was owned by the Duke of Portland - in fact, this pub is first recorded in the 1832 Directory at a time when the 4th Duke was Lord of the Manor. The family seat of the Dukes of Portland was Welbeck Abbey, and they are the descendants of William Cavendish, the 1st Duke of Newcastle, and Royalist leader during the Civil War.

SHOULDER OF MUTTON - *Blackwell Road*

Mentioned in the 1853 Directory, the pub's name reflects the popularity of this particular dish at inns in former times. Occasionally, the sign indicated that the licensee was also the local butcher and meat could be obtained from the house as well as ale.

WHITE HART - *Main Street*

This pub was acquired by Mansfield Brewery in 1893. The sign here is a popular one, appearing as the emblem for many pubs throughout the county, and indeed, throughout Britain.

An explanation for the origin of this sign can be found by referring to the pub of the same name at Lenton.

HYSON GREEN

ALBANY - *Birkin Avenue*

Although mentioned as a brewhouse in Kelly's Trade Directory of 1853, this pub was built in its present form in 1881, the year in which the youngest son of Queen Victoria came to Nottingham in order to officially open the old University College buildings in Shakespeare Street. The royal visitor was Prince Leopold (otherwise the Duke of Albany), after whom a pub was named in Moffatt Street (both the street and the pub were demolished in 1971, under the St. Anns Redevelopment Scheme). The word *Albany* itself is a poetic name for Britain, similar to *Albion*, and is also an ancient ducal title.

One of the few public houses in Nottingham licensed for Music Hall activities, the *'Albany'* for many years has been well-known for this form of entertainment. Such names as George Formby and Vesta Tilley have appeared on its programmes, and in 1936 the BBC broadcast a Variety Show from here.

CLOCK - *Craven Road*

Until December 1986 this was styled as the *'Avenue'* (Commercial Hotel), but because of the large public clock mounted on its outside wall it had always been known locally as *'The Clock'* - and on this date its present name was made official by the brewery.

The pub in times past has been variously described in journalistic terms as 'an oasis of Victorian architecture' and 'a classic Victorian gin palace' - so it is evidently worth visiting, if only to listen to the accordionist who plays here on Sunday evenings.

Clock, Hyson Green

CRICKET PLAYERS - *Radford Road*

It has often been quoted that the 'cradle' of our national summer game was the Broad-Halfpenny Down of the Hampshire village of Hambledon, enshrined as it is in the prose of several well-known writers. None of these is better-known than Neville Cardus who, in his book *'English Cricket'*, assures his readers that the Hambledon Club was 'not much heard of' by 1744, in the June of which year the county side of Kent played 'All England' on the Artillery ground in London. This was a full forty years before the Kent side itself accepted a challenge from the Hambledon side, who then proceeded to win the match.

The Hambledon men, by the way, bowled 'underhand' in those days. They wore dark green breeches and snowy vests (waistcoats), with best silk stockings for the Gentlemen! 'Moreover,' writes Cardus, 'it was not regarded as prejudicial to a cricketer of Hambledon's technical skill on the field if he could play the violin and sing in a sweet tenor voice away from it.' One of their players even hung a sign outside his house which announced, not too modestly:

> 'Here lives John Small
> Makes Bat and Ball,
> Pitch a Wicket, Play at Cricket
> With any man in England.'

Old Cricket Players, Nottingham

The sign here at Hyson Green looks astonishingly like the one which hangs outside the celebrated 'Bat and Ball Inn' at Hambledon. It, too, shows the wickets having only one bail and two stumps apiece. The striking batsman wields a bat with a slightly-curved blade, and the fielders all have jockey-style caps worn back to front - the height of fashion, it seems, in the latter half of the 18th century.

At some time in its history, this pub (recorded in the 1832 Directory as the *'Cricket Players and Tea Gardens'*) had the word 'old' inserted at the beginning of its title but this has since been dropped. There is still another *'Old Cricket Players'* in Barker Gate, Nottingham, which was first mentioned in the Town Directory of 1799, and which was subsequently rebuilt in 1884.

OLD GENERAL - *Radford Road*

Two other pubs of the same name (and presumably the same derivative) were closed down on Christmas Day in 1908, one in Cross Street and the other in Wellington Street. The name comes, strangely enough, not from any nationally-known soldier, but from a former inmate of St Peter's Workhouse at Broadmarsh whose proper name was Benjamin Mayo. His military title was acquired through being the ringleader and self-constituted marshal of the raggle-taggle schoolboy troops of Nottingham in the early part of the 19th century, Micklethorn (i.e. Middleton) Monday always being one of his special review days in the Old Market Square. The Middleton Jury would assemble in the open twice a year, in March and September, for the due performance of 'beating the bounds' ceremonies. It was their duty to see that the sons of burgesses, while yet schoolboys, were made thoroughly acquainted with the various boundaries of the Borough, pointing them out in succession and at the same time smartly tapping the lads in order to sink the knowledge in.

Mayo, born in 1779, was small in stature, being well under five feet in height, and this no doubt would accentuate the comical aspect of his posturing whilst drilling his obedient platoons in public - especially as one of his legs was shorter than the other, thus giving his body a peculiar up-and-down motion when he was in a hurry. An extract from a contemporary pen-picture has this to relate: 'Previous to the jury commencing their survey, away trots the General, with several hundred boys at his heels, to secure the sacred and inviolable rights of a holy day ...' and on another occasion: 'View the General at 11 o'clock, with his forces drawn up in front of the Castle Lodge, demanding admittance into the Castle yard - a summons always evaded by the distribution of a quantity of cakes and gingerbread. On the General's word of command, the precious sweets are thrown, one by one, over the gate - and the confusion of a universal scramble ensues ...'

No wonder that this short but formidable figure was recognised by all the citizens of Nottingham as:

> 'Commander of some forces there,
> And intimate with Mr Mayor!'

Ben was regarded by all as a harmless idiot but, during his frequently-permitted periods of liberty from the workhouse at Broadmarsh, he would exercise a surprising degree of business acumen in his roaming role as a 'flying stationer' - vending his penny-ballads around the town and successfully hawking his innumerable broadsheets on the topics of the day. Like many another military man, he was a great favourite with the ladies. One of his customary promises (following a premeditated assault-by-ogle from one of his admirers) was to marry the hussy in question 'next Sund'y mornin' - often adding with a beguiling leer that the wench had better not be later'n 7.30 for fear someone else should get him.

Old General

The Old General died in 1843 after a fall down the steps of the workhouse, and no doubt his passing was bemoaned by all his troops. Unlike the Iron Duke, who died nine years later, he was not accorded a State funeral, but all the same a statue was erected to him and a plaster-cast of this can be seen, enclosed in a glass case, above the entrance to this pub which bears his name. It is not known what happened to the original statue, which was carved out of a block of Caen stone in 1878 by a Mr Joseph Holmes, but this work was carried out in a field just off Hyson Green and a labourer named John Major was the model. Mr Holmes's brother, who was a stonemason, built this pub and became its first licensee.

Cedric Bonnell's own valedictory epigram to Benjamin Mayo sums up this remarkable man's life most fittingly:

> 'O, rare Ben! Sure, doth not thy name declare
> How MAYO fell but little short of MAYOR?'

RADFORD ARMS - *Radford Road*

Around 1887, a builder called Morrison bet £100 that he could erect a pub in less than a month. When the wager was taken up, his men worked every day and every night to build this house (then called the *'New Inn'*), completing it with time to spare, and winning for Morrison his bet.

In later days, this pub became a favourite meeting place for thespians performing at the old Grand Theatre which once stood nearby.

KELHAM

FOX INN - *Main Street*

This very popular inn was probably a farmhouse before it began selling beer in the early 1830s. The first landlord was Richard Fox, victualler, so why look further for a suitable name! Several decades ago the inn had a sign of some individuality - sadly the present sign is one of the John Smith Brewery silhouette interpretations which have become very stereotyped and devoid of character. It depicts a fox eyeing the weathercock on a church spire.

Fox Inn, Kelham

KEYWORTH

FAIRWAY - *Nottingham Road*

When it was opened on the 2nd August 1963 by Mr J.C. Green, the then joint managing director of Home Brewery, this was the first new pub to be built in the village for more than half a century and the 44th new house to be opened by this company since the Second World War. The site on which it stands was once a field used by cattle to graze.

Through its title, this pub is linked with the game of Golf - no doubt a reference to the nearby Stanton-on-the-Wolds Golf Club. In golfing terms, a 'fairway' is the cut stretch of grass leading towards the green from the tee, as opposed to the uncut area called the 'rough.'

The original sign that used to hang outside this house, displaying a golfer driving down the fairway, has been replaced by a most unusual double 'swinger' (a sign showing a different picture on each side) portraying scenic views of what appears to be the village in former days.

KEYWORTH TAVERN - *Wolds Drive*

Opened by Mr James Shipstone, former chairman of Shipstones Brewery on the 1st December 1966, this pub takes its name from the village in which it stands.

SALUTATION - *Main Street*

Mentioned in White's 1844 Directory, this is the oldest pub in the village.

The sign of the *'Salutation'* is a religious one - referring to the Annunciation, the greeting and proclamation of the Archangel Gabriel to the Virgin Mary. At one time this pub displayed the traditional interpretation of this - two hands clasping each other. Strangely, this has since been replaced with a picture of a sailing vessel - an explanation for which we have not been able to discover.

KIMBERLEY

GOLDEN GUINEA - *Maws Lane*

This pub takes its name from the George III Golden Guinea which was the registered trademark of Hanson's Brewery, established in 1847. This brewery once stood near the railway station in Kimberley, but was demolished in 1973. Its roof was topped by 4 large representations of golden guineas. Hanson's brewery merged with the adjacent Hardy's brewery in 1930.

The pub was opened by Colonel T.E. Forman Hardy, the then Chairman of Hardys & Hansons Brewery, on 19th April 1978.

The guinea (worth 21 old shillings) was a gold coin widely in use from 1663 until 1917. Gold then became too valuable a commodity to be made into coins.

NELSON AND RAILWAY - *Station Road*

The *'Nelson and Railway,'* or more properly the *'Lord Nelson, Railway Hotel,'* was formerly a farmhouse.

Recorded in the 1832 Directory as the *'Lord Nelson,'* this pub stands on the site of an earlier one dating back to the early 1600s when it was called the *'Pelican.'*

During the latter part of the last century, when the pub found itself strategically placed between the lines of two railway companies, the Midland and the Great Northern, both competing for the lucrative coal trade around Nottingham and Derby, it underwent a change of name to its present sign - one which records both its association with the railway and acknowledges the feats of Lord Nelson.

STAG - *Nottingham Road*

The origins of this old pub can be traced back to 1817. The sign of the *'Stag,'* a male deer in its prime, is most likely a reference to stag hunting - a royal sport in times past.

KINOULTON

NEVILE ARMS - *Owthorpe Lane*

This former farmhouse became an inn in 1835, and was known as *'Nevile's Hunting Lodge'*. It took over the license of an inn on the Fosse Way, closed because of "infestation by highwaymen". Kinoulton was once part of the Gainsborough estate. The daughter of the 4th Earl of Gainsborough married Christopher Nevile of Wellingore in Lincolnshire, and the inn sign incorporates the arms of both the Nevile and Noel (Earls of Gainsborough) families.

The estate was sold to Sir Jesse Hind (a Nottingham Solicitor) at the turn of the century. His son 'Monty' was killed at the battle of Vimy Ridge during the first World War and, as a memorial, Sir Jesse planted an avenue of 188 poplar trees (one for each of the officers who died there) just outside the village.

Nevile Arms, Kinoulton

The pub was bought by Sir Jesse in 1928 and became the *'Hind Arms'* very much against the wishes of the locals who successfully petitioned for the name to be changed back to the *'Nevile Arms'*, which it did in the early 1940s.

The Belvoir Hunt, with which Prince Charles rides, meets at the *'Nevile Arms'* each year.

KIRKBY-IN-ASHFIELD

Cricketers Arms, Kirkby-in-Ashfield

CRICKETERS ARMS - *Nuncargate Road*

Built in 1668 as a farmhouse (several of the old farm buildings still remain), this pub stands next to what was once a famous cricket pitch - the hallowed turf on which locally-born Harold Larwood first turned his arm and on which Joe Hardstaff and Bill Voce also played.

In 1977, both Voce and Larwood visited the pub and a picture recording this event, together with other cricket memorabilia, is proudly displayed within. (See also the *'Badger Box'* and *'Larwood'* inns).

The Larwood, Annesley Woodhouse

53

DUKE OF WELLINGTON - *Church Street*

An inn since the 17th century, it is thought that this pub was once a chapel or church hall. Centuries ago it was known as the 'Silent Lady,' and in 1717, about the time the rectory was built opposite, an underground tunnel was constructed from the cellar of the pub to link the two buildings together. Long since bricked up, great amusement can be derived at the thought of the then rector of St. Wilfrid's having his own private access to the inn's supply of ale. It is the oldest pub in Kirkby-in-Ashfield, and was acquired by Mansfield Brewery in 1895.

The name here honours Arthur Wellesley (1769-1852), the 1st Duke of Wellington who, after Lord Nelson, is the most popular military figure to appear on signboards.

Born in Ireland, the son of the Earl of Mornington, he sat for a time in the Irish parliament. Upon entering the army he was soon knighted for his distinguished military service in both India and Spain. After his defeat of Napoleon Bonaparte at Waterloo in 1815, he became a British national hero.

Known as the 'Iron Duke,' Wellington entered politics as a Tory, serving as Prime Minister from 1828-30. Whilst holding this office he modified the Corn Laws, but became unpopular due to his opposition to parliamentary reform and for conceding Roman Catholic emancipation in 1829. From 1834-5, he served as Foreign Secretary, and was a member of the Cabinet from 1841-46.

He is buried in the crypt of St Paul's Cathedral in London.

LEG OF MUTTON - *Ashfield Precinct*

This pub, opened on the 7th February 1969, perpetuates the name of an old house of the same sign which once stood nearby and which closed in 1958.

At one time, like the 'Shoulder of Mutton,' this sign was fairly common. Served in many an inn, the dish itself was central to many a celebration - such as that which marked the completion of an apprenticeship.

WILD ORCHID - *Southwell Lane*

Opened on the 3rd December 1991 by Hardys and Hansons, this pub occupies the site of the former Blue Orchid Club which was destroyed by fire.

The name here appears to be a derivative of its former title when it was a club - a place that to all accounts, had something of a 'wild' reputation.

KIRTON

FOX AND HOUNDS - *Main Street*

Kirton is an attractive village between Ollerton and Tuxford, with some fine farm buildings. The 'Fox and Hounds', a large inn on Main Street, has been serving ale since the early 1800s. The name is a very popular one, not just in hunting country. The inn sign is somewhat puzzling - the hounds are half out of the picture, and where is the fox?

Other pubs with this name can be found at Blidworth Bottoms and Walkeringham.

Fox and Hounds, Kirton

LAMBLEY

NAG'S HEAD - *Main Street*

Originally a farmhouse, this pub was built in 1732, demolished in 1833 and then rebuilt shortly afterwards. Though listed as the 'Nags Head' in the 1832 Directory, it began life as the 'Chequers' - the landlord at the time specializing in brewing his own mild, the dregs of which were given to the pigs.

An explanation for the origin of the name the 'Nag's Head' as an inn-sign can be found by referring to the pub of the same name at East Leake.

ROBIN HOOD - *Main Street*

Though still recorded in the telephone directory (and the 1844 Directory) as the 'Robin Hood And Little John,' the sign that hangs outside this pub refers to it as merely as the 'Robin Hood' - Little John, his trusty lieutenant, having being lost somewhere along the way.

Over one hundred pubs in Britain are named after this legendary outlaw - an explanation for which can be found by referring to the house of the same name at Sherwood.

Woodlark, Lambley (c.1910)

WOODLARK - *Church Street*

This pub, recorded in Wright's 1900 Directory, has an ornithological connotation - its name derives from the bird that years ago frequented this rural area. The bird itself is now quite rare - the preferred haunts of the woodlark in this country, namely open countryside scattered with trees and some shrub, are becoming overgrown with birch. Formerly, rabbits kept the young birch under control, but with the advent of myxomatosis many trees grew to a size too big for the rabbits before their recovery.

LANEHAM

BUTCHERS ARMS - *Main Street*

The *'Butcher's Arms'*, parts of which are 400 years old, acquired its name because it did indeed have a slaughterhouse for many years. Its suitably appropriate signboard shows the heraldic arms granted in 1540 to the Butcher's Company.

Bernard Minnitt, the nonogenarian local writer of the highly readable book of reminiscences *"A Trentside Narrative"* tells how one of the early innkeepers John Rodgers, and his wife, had to give up the pub because they couldn't make it pay. He also remembers the 'Black Minorca', the energetic landlady who took over from John Rodgers and certainly did make a living from it, quite willing, for example, to accommodate gangs of boisterous Irish navvies employed carting building supplies from Laneham to Rampton.

Today, the *'Butcher's Arms'* is a pub with much character, with its low beamed lounge bar and inglenook fireplace contrasting with the new conservatory extension. The pub even has a gym and health studio!

Butchers Arms, Laneham

FERRY BOAT - *Trent Lane*

The ferry at Church Laneham existed in the 13th century and remained until Victorian times. One of the Archbishop of York's manor houses was sited here and he would travel all the way by river to visit it. The *'Ferry Boat Inn'* has existed for over 150 years and, considering its somewhat remote location, has had its fair share of activity over the years. Bernard Minnitt, in *"A Trentside Narrative"* recalls some of the trials and tribulations the pub has seen, from constant flooding to invading crowds of daytrippers arriving in the their hundreds aboard the *"Shilling Shockers"*, (fishing trips for Sheffield anglers organised by the Great Central Railway). The *'Ferry Boat'* is a popular pub with visitors from far and near who come to enjoy its riverside setting.

Ferry Boat, Laneham

LANGAR

Unicorn's Head, Langar

UNICORN'S HEAD - *Main Street*

The tarmac car park of this inn was formerly the village green and once contained the village pond. Built in 1717 (the date, in dark brick, can be seen on the side of the rear gable), probably as both a farmhouse and an alehouse, the *'Unicorns Head'* had its own brewhouse which is identified by its unusual three tier, 19th century chimney.

One of the earliest innkeepers was Robert Simon who died in 1732 when the inn was known as *'The Feathers'* - part of the arms of the Howe family being a plume of five ostrich feathers. The Howes lived at Langar Hall and were Lords of the Manor. The Howe descendants included the celebrated Admiral, Richard 1st Earl Howe, Commander of the Channel Fleet when war broke out with France in 1793. (See also the *'Earl Howe'* pub in Nottingham). The inn acquired its present name around 1825 when John Wright, the new Lord of the Manor, was able to use his family's newly granted coat of arms - a unicorn's head.

The *'Unicorn's Head'* was a coaching inn in the 19th century and there are stables at the rear of the building. In 1848 the innkeeper was Pilate Scothern, "victualler and farmer occupying 100 acres and employing two men and one boy."

Langar was the birthplace of author Samuel Butler, whose autobiographical novel *'The Way of All Flesh'* is well known. He occasionally drank at the *'Unicorns Head'*.

LAXTON

Court Leet at the Dovecote Inn, Laxton

DOVECOTE - *Laxton Village*

Built as a farmhouse during the early part of the 19th century, it is first shown as a pub in the 1832 Directory. Although it used to form part of the Thoresby estate now, like most of the village, the *'Dovecote'* is owned by the Ministry of Agriculture.

The pub is the annual setting for the 'Court Leet,' a medieval form of justice, exercising its duties of administering the ancient 'open field' system of cultivation by farmers. Laxton is the only place in England where this medieval tradition still survives and the three-field rotation system of winter wheat, spring crops and fallow (or forage crops) is still followed to this day.

LENTON

BOAT INN - *Priory Street*

The name here derives from the fact that in times past canal boats and barges could be seen daily on the adjacent River Leen. The sign itself, however, is more adventurous - it shows a Viking longboat with a striped red and yellow sail. The building is listed in the 1832 Directory as an alehouse, brewing its own beer.

Local legend has it that a former landlord's wife was burned to death, many years ago, in an attic room above the pub, despite her husband's frantic attempts to save her. The poor soul had evidently suffered from fits of dementia for more than thirty years.

GROVE - *Castle Boulevard*

Like a number of Home Brewery owned houses, this particular hostelry displays a plaque on an outer wall which gives an insight into its history. It reads:

"At the turn of the 19th century, the Grove was known as 'The Struggler' public house and it stood adjacent to the canal. 1830 saw the passing of the Beer House Act by Parliament. This allowed any householder to sell beer provided that they bought an excise permit, resulting in the number of beer retailers in Lenton doubling that year. A man by the name of John Ward was the licensee at the time, and he became worried that the pub really was struggling and that the name was no longer a good one for the house. It was for this reason that the house was renamed The Grove. There exists an advertisement placed in the Nottingham Journal in 1882 from The Grove, which offers excellent Bottle and Draught, Porter, Cider, Ale, Spirituous Liquors, a room for dancing, public baths and tea gardens. 1844 saw Castle Boulevard built, and the area between it and the canal was quickly acquired for housing. As a result of this, the Grove Tavern was demolished and in 1886 it was rebuilt on its existing site. The Grove Tavern was bought by Home Brewery in 1890 for the sum of £6,385. Over the last hundred years or so, the pub has gone from strength to strength and today, it continues to be one of the finest ale houses in Lenton."

HAPPY RETURN - *Church Street*

When redevelopment took place in this area during the 1960s, three pubs of Shipstone's in Willoughby Street were reduced to rubble - the *'Town Arms,'* the *'Smiths Arms'* and the *'Nag's Head.'* However, as from July 1966 their patrons were able to join forces in a new pub just around the corner. Its car park occupies the site of the old Methodist Church and the pub itself stands almost opposite the present Baptist Church. The latter is unique in being named after Thomas Helwys, a former squire of Broxtowe Hall who became the founder of the very first Baptist church in England in 1612.

The main reason for this pub's name is therefore implicit, but the complementary reason is quite subtle - the *'Happy Return'* happens to be the title of an exciting adventure in the Captain Hornblower series, and as such was a favourite volume of the then brewery chairman's favourite author, C.S. Forester. The signboard interpretation is that of a jolly-looking angler. He has his dog alongside him, his equipment slung over his shoulder, and he proudly holds at arm's length an enormous pike. Unusually, this sign was designed and painted by a woman artist, Mrs Mary Austin of Sileby, Leicestershire.

JOHNSON ARMS - *Abbey Street*

Originally known as the *'Abbey Tavern'* it was frequented by bargees who travelled along the canal between Nottingham and Langley Mill (the river Leen now flows there).

In 1904 the building was purchased by local grazier, auctioneer and valuer, Frank William Johnson who, in 1912, completely demolished it. That same year, he rebuilt the pub and renamed it the *'Johnson Arms'* - after his family name. He died in 1952, and the pub was sold to the Star Brewery (Shipstones) a year later.

RED COW - *Gregory Street*

Red Cows are by no means as popular as Red Lions on signboards (or Cows as common as Bulls either, for that matter) - but this particular sign is displayed in a most unusual fashion. The realistic model of the animal's head is shown projecting from the building as though it is looking-out at passers-by from within a cowshed - in fact, any stranger would have a distinct shock!

Interestingly, it was thought, at one time, that milk produced by a red cow was of a higher quality than that produced by any other coloured bovine - perhaps leading to the popularity of this inn-sign.

17th/21st LANCERS - *Sherwin Road*

Opened on the 9th February 1973, this pub stands on the site of the former *'Albion'* which was demolished in January 1972. Its name was chosen in honour of his old regiment by Colonel W.G. Hanson, who at that time was chairman of the Kimberley Brewery.

At the colourful opening ceremony the original Balaclava bugle, which sounded for the Charge of the Light Brigade in 1854, was blown by Corporal Chris Benson of the 17th/21st Lancers. Afterwards the first pints of ale were pulled by Major-General R.E. Coaker, former Colonel of the Regiment, who presented them to two Chelsea Pensioners. Standing sentry outside during the ceremony, two Saracen armoured cars flew the flag of the regiment whose motto is *'Death or Glory.'*

Mounted on the front wall near to the entrance of the pub is a plaque bearing this motto surmounted by a skull and crossbones - and inside is a display of military regalia..

In June 1933 this regiment was restyled The Queen's Royal Lancers.

THREE WHEATSHEAVES - *Radmarsh Road*

The first reference to this old tavern was in an advertisement placed in a local newspaper in 1810 - it later appeared in Pigot's Directory of 1822. Originally a farm, it was acquired by Shipstones, in 1938, from the Gregory family, who had been lords of the manor of Lenton since 1630.

The name here is unique, coming from a motif on the Gregory coat of arms which shows three stooks of corn.

In April 1986, during decoration of one of the pub's bedrooms, strange markings were uncovered. These markings, in the form of 4" tall Roman numerals, were drawn on three of the room's four walls. Despite investigation by the local history society, it is still unclear as to how long the figures had been there or what purpose they may have served.

WHITE HART - *Gregory Street*

This old inn was originally a farmhouse dating from the reign of Charles II (1660-1685). Subsequently it became a popular coffee-house, renowned locally for its gardens and bowling-greens and as a favourite haunt of Nottingham folk. It gained a quite different reputation between 1790 and 1848, during which period part of its premises were used as a prison! The latter was a small brick building, two storeys high with three windows to each storey, which looked out into a small courtyard surrounded by a high wall. This yard was later roofed in and used as a skittle alley.

White Hart, Lenton

This prison, known as Peveril Prison, was abolished in 1849, when the 'Court of Peveril' ceased to function. This court supposedly goes back to the time of William the Conqueror - and, at the height of its power, had jurisdiction over 127 towns and villages in Nottinghamshire and 120 more in Derbyshire. Most of the later cases to be tried were for debts and the adjoining prison was used for the confinement of those unable to meet their liabilities. However, conditions don't appear to have been too rigorous, as prisoners were allowed to act as waiters, serving refreshments to the inn's customers on the bowling greens. This court was removed to the 'Lenton Coffee House' (as the inn was then called) in 1790. Its name was changed to the 'White Hart' in 1804 and it was the centre for all local activities. The Lenton and Radford Society for the Prosecution of Felons met there, as did the Amicable Society in 1797, one of the earliest of the 'Friendly Societies.'

There is a framed notice-board in the pub forecourt which contains an Ordnance Survey map of 1881 - together with a map of Old Lenton of the same date, a picture of the White Hart in 1889, and a detailed sketch of Peveril Prison. In addition, further details of the inn's history are given:

"*In May 1786 George Wombwell opened his gardens for the summer season, and in 1804 he built the present frontage on to the farmhouse behind it. The old jail still exists at the rear of the premises. It is worthy of note that the Innkeeper was responsible simply for the custody of the prisoners; their food and clothing - and heating during the winter - had to be provided by friends and/ or relatives. In 1927 the outbuildings and surroundings were removed during the construction of the Abbey Bridge.*"

A pair of old mounting-blocks from the days of horsemanship can still be seen outside the main entrance. On the wall above them could be seen, and admired, until recent times the largest and most attractive signboard to be seen anywhere in the county - portraying a truly noble white hart resting in the parkland once adjoining Nottingham Castle (the medieval castle itself being shown as part of the background to this panoramic picture). A smaller version of this pictorial sign can still be seen outside the pub.

The earliest instances of this still-common sign coincide with the beginning of Richard II's reign in 1377, as it was that monarch's heraldic symbol. He ensured that all members of his household wore the device, and it would have been a sound move on the part of tavern-keepers to show their allegiance by displaying it. Curiously, this tradition has continued down the centuries, as similarly with the ubiquitous *Red Lion!*

LINBY

HORSE AND GROOM - *Main Street*

These premises are over 300 years old and until 1921 ale was still being brewed here.

Signs depicting horses are a popular emblem for pubs, especially those to be found in more rural areas. In former days the animal was used for a variety of work such as hauling carts laden with produce, pulling ploughs or as a means of transport for travellers. The name of this pub no doubt identifies the ancillary services it once provided to both locals and travellers alike.

Horse and Groom, Linby

LOWDHAM

MAGNA CHARTA - *Southwell Road*

The colourful sign outside this pub depicts King John appending his seal to the famous document at the instigation of his barons and the Archbishop of Canterbury (Stephen Langton), who had extracted it from him in order to obtain certain privileges and a constitution. Later, when the King repudiated the *charta* on the grounds that he had been forced to sign it, civil war resulted. King John succeeded his brother Richard the Lionheart to the throne of

England in 1199 AD and was an extremely unpopular monarch. On the 15th June 1215 (the year before his death from dysentery at Newark Castle), in a Thamesside meadow at Runnymede, John put his royal seal on a lump of wax to show that he had signed and accepted the 48 articles embodied in the *Magna Carta*. Twelve copies of the Latin script were sealed and sent to the Lords of the Manors throughout England. Of these, only four remain - the most legible of which can be found at Lincoln Cathedral.

The 'charta' did not ignore drink. It decreed: *'Let there be one measure of wine throughout our realm and one measure of ale.'*

In former days, with its prominent

Magna Charta, Lowdham

position at the intersection of roads to Nottingham, Southwell and Newark, this former coaching inn was a stopping-place for a four-horse stagecoach called the 'Magna Carta' which commenced service on the 26th August 1823 and ran between Nottingham and Scarborough, calling at Southwell, Newark, Lincoln and Hull on the way. It ceased running in the mid-1840s. A deed dated the 2nd October 1835, records the sale of the inn by John Foster and Henry Brett, both of Nottingham, and Elizabeth Deverill to Thomas Abbott, a farmer of Marlock in the Parish of Lowdham, for the price of £1,040. The name should correctly be spelt 'Magna Carta' in the Latin, or 'Magna Charter' in an anglicized form. The local story is that the pub's name was a deliberate mistake to attract people to drink there!

OLD SHIP - *Main Street*

Mentioned in the 1844 Directory, this pub dates back to the early part of the 18th century.

Given its rural setting, the name here may appear to be an unusual choice, unless of course, it was first opened by an old 'salty dog,' home from the sea. Most likely though, is that the sign has a religious connotation and is a reference to 'Noah's Ark.'

WORLD'S END - *Plough Lane*

Believed to have been built around the mid-18th century as a blacksmith's, this pub used to be called the *'Plough.'* During the 1970s its owners, the Grice family, renamed it the *'World's End'* after an old coaching inn that used to stand in nearby Red Lane.

The sign here has been in use since the 17th century and was often given to inns that stood on the very outskirts of a town or village. In former days, the remoteness of the sites on which these premises stood often led to them being frequented by shady characters.

LOWER BAGTHORPE

DIXIES ARMS - *Main Street*

A pub of this name has stood here since at least 1750. It takes its name from Willoughby Dixie, a former landowner in the area and Lord of the Manor of Selston, whose family later moved to Market Bosworth in Leicestershire.

This family can recount many notable events. Sir Wolstan Dixie was elected Lord Mayor of London in 1585, and in the Leicestershire village where they took up residence (and where a pub of the same name can also be found), they endowed a grammar school and welcomed the then unknown Samuel Johnson to its academic staff, when he took up his first teaching post in 1741.

In 1993 Lady Dixie, on her way to Selston Church to research her family tree, made a twenty minute stop at this pub at Lower Bagthorpe - it is thought she may be the last surviving member of this illustrious family.

In 1850, the first recorded owner of this pub was a blacksmith called Edward Holmes. Later, it was run by a Thomas Wilson and his son until 1892, when it was purchased by Hutchinson's Brewery of Basford. During the 1920s it was again sold, this time to its present owners, Home Brewery of Daybrook.

The splendid sign that hangs outside the pub was the subject of much research by the present landlord's wife, and wasn't erected until 1993 after she had scoured the archives in London for the correct coat of arms with which to adorn it. Home Brewery then agreed to have the new sign painted. Outside, the landlord has erected a set of 'stocks' - no doubt a warning to any would be miscreants who might dare to disturb the peace and tranquillity to be found at this pub. Inside you will find the smallest bar in any county pub. It measures just 6' long, and replaced a small serving hatch.

Morris Dancers at the Shepherd's Rest, Lower Bagthorpe

SHEPHERD'S REST - *Main Street*

Set in a truly rural area, this pub used to form part of a farm and takes its name from the employment of Shepherding.

Many years ago (or so the story goes), a smallholder kept several ducks in a pen situated on a bank close by one of the two bridges over the brook. One night there was a cloud-burst which caused violent flooding in the village and the ducks were swept under the bridge, becoming trapped in a gully. Without respite, a flood of water cascaded over them with such force that they eventually drowned. Close to this hallowed spot, known as Millington Springs, is a trough to which the local women used to bring their buckets in order to obtain drinking water. The stream that flows through Bagthorpe has its source in Stafford Wood and still contains pure spring water.

MANSFIELD

BOOTLICKER - *Market Street*

Occupying premises once owned by the National Westminster Bank, this pub was opened by Tom Cobleigh, the independent pub operators, on the 1st April 1993. During the conversion the company took into account the former bank's special architectural features, like the elaborate moulded ceiling above its banking hall, retaining them in their design.

Prior to naming their new houses, Tom Cobleigh allocate them a code-name - in this instance the *Bootlicker*. This code-name became so popular with the employees of the company that they decided to adopt it as the title for this house.

At its opening, the story was told of how the bootlicker was a person who held his master's boots whilst he put them on. When his master changed his footwear from boots to riding shoes, the bootlicker would introduce the leather tongue behind the shoelaces to keep the weather out. It was also announced that as the pub was being opened on April Fools' Day, its title might possibly have an alternative meaning - perhaps a reference to what it might have taken to obtain a loan from its former owners!

BOWL IN HAND - *Leeming Street*

This old hostelry, originally called the *'Bowling-Green Inn,'* is recorded in the 1832 Directory under its present sign.

At the rear of the pub (acquired by Mansfield Brewery in 1898) there is, a bowling-green dating from 1720, which is said to be the second oldest in England. The oldest, dating from around 1299, belongs to the *'Bowling Green'* pub in Southampton. Quite obviously, the name here is a reference to the existence of this green and to 'Bowls,' a game of which Sir Francis Drake is said to have finished before setting sail in the *Revenge* to help defeat the Spanish Armada in 1588.

In 1800 the premises were kept by John Wright, and as well as sporting the splendid bowling-green, it had a billiards room. In an assembly room at the rear of the house, facing out onto the green, the local justices used to meet once a fortnight, and for many years the members of the 'green' also held their annual dinner dances here.

BRIDGE TAVERN - *Bridge Street*

Acquired by Mansfield Brewery in 1896, this pub takes its name from the position it occupies on a bridge across the River Maun.

At one time, most likely, this pub would have been occupied by jovial anglers, all with clinking pewter tankards, recounting tales of the big fish they had caught, or the ones that had got away. Trout from the River Maun (hard to believe now) would have graced their table, along with game obtained from the estates in the area.

Brown Cow, Mansfield

BROWN COW - *Ratcliffe Gate*

Prior to becoming an inn, this building was the home of Robert Dodsley (1703-64), a poet, publisher and bookseller.

After leaving school, Dodsley became a stocking-weaver's apprentice. Dissatisfied with this line of work, he ran away to London and took up a post as a footman in the service of the Honourable Mrs Lowther. Whilst in her employ (in 1729) he wrote a poem called 'Servitude' and completed a book of poetry, before leaving to pursue a literary career.

Dodsley started a bookshop and publishing business, making his mark with a successful play *"The King & Miller of Mansfield"* based on the old legend (see also entry for *Sir John Cockle*). He went on to write several plays, including one, a musical (in 1741), entitled *'The Blind Beggar of Bethnal Green.'*

He is chiefly remembered, though, as the publisher of works by Alexander Pope, Laurence Sterne, Edward Young, Oliver Goldsmith, Thomas Gray, Mark Akenside and Dr. Samuel Johnson - which included such literary masterpieces as *'Tristram Shandy'* (1759), and the didactic and reflective poem with some 10,000 lines of blank verse, *'Night Thoughts on Life, Death and Immortality'* (1742).

In 1758, in conjunction with Edmund Burke, Dodsley founded the *'Annual Register'* (an annual review of events of the past year) which still survives. A close friend of Dr. Johnson, it was Dodsley who first suggested to him that he should compile a dictionary of the English language - this was published in 1755.

By 1747, the birthplace of Mansfield's famous poet had become one of the town's largest inns, the *'Brown Cow'*. With its cellars cut into the rock, it boasted a large brewhouse and stabling for 60 horses. At one time a social advantage of being the licensee here was in having his own special large pew in the parish church. In 1892 the pub was acquired by its current owners, Mansfield Brewery.

Cows feature on many a pub's signboard - the colour brown is most likely a variation of the more common *'Red Cow'* (see pub of this name at Lenton).

COOPERS - *Leeming Lane North*

At the official opening of this pub in February 1980, the only remaining 'Cooper' employed by Mansfield Brewery, Mr. Brian Oldham, was handed the first pint by the brewery chairman.

The pub takes its name from Coopering - the trade of wooden barrel and cask making - which, since the modern practice is to manufacture them out of metal (called canisters), is becoming a dying art.

A trade included in the medieval guilds, Coopers used to attend an initiation ceremony upon their transition from apprentice to craftsman. When the young apprentice finally emerged from his six years' qualifying period, he was subjected by his work-mates to a loss of dignity which, although temporary, is most peculiar, and varied from place to place.

At a Blackburn brewery they used to follow the tradition whereby an apprentice would have to make a barrel, into which he was then trussed and covered in muck, before being rolled around the yard. After climbing out of the barrel, he had to knock on the yard door twice and ask for re-entry into the craft, after which, when the door opened, he was re-engaged as a fully-qualified Cooper and downed a celebratory pint with the head brewer.

At one time in Cheltenham, after the barrel-rolling had taken place, a speech which mentioned *'the mysteries of the craft into which the journeyman had entered'* was read, and the successful apprentice was tossed aloft in a blanket.

CUCKOO BIRCH - *Jubilee Way South*

Opened on the 27th November 1980 by former Councillor John White, Chairman of Mansfield District Council - the first pint being handed to local man, Ivan Wigley, the winner of a 'Name-A-Pub' competition organised by the brewers, Joshua Tetley & Son Ltd, in order to find a suitable title for their new house.

This name commemorates a remarkable piece of local phenomena and was first coined by former schoolmaster, Mr. Stan Bennett of Warsop, after he had discovered a silver birch tree growing out of the trunk of a dead oak tree in Sherwood Forest.

After forest fires devastated the tops of a number of oak trees between 1937 and 1939, it left them as 20 foot high stumps. It was out of one of these stumps that the silver birch tree grew, reaching a height of about 30 feet.

Within the pub a photograph of the actual tree can be seen on display, and the signboard outside also records the event.

DIAL - *Market Place*

This old pub is shown in the 1832 Directory as the *'Old Dial'* but appears under its current title in the 1848 Directory.

Acquired by Mansfield Brewery in 1887, the name is probably a reference to a nearby clock.

GREEN DRAGON - *Broomhill Lane*

The original pub of this name (built in 1800) stood in Leeming Street, Mansfield, until it closed on the 2nd October 1962. Its licence was transferred to this new house which was opened the following day.

An explanation for the origin of the name *'Green Dragon'* as an inn-sign can be found by referring to the pub of the same name at Hucknall.

King's Head, Mansfield

KING'S HEAD - *Stockwell Gate*

Opened in September 1975 by the then Chairman of Mansfield Brewery, Mr Robin Chadburn, this pub replaced a house of the same name that had stood on this site for centuries.

Though recorded in the 1832 Directory, the former house (a coaching inn) was much older than this. Years ago one of its 18-inch thick walls collapsed, revealing old wooden beams shaped like trees, suggesting that the pub was then more than 300 years old. In its stone-built arched cellar was one of the thirteen wells from which Stockwell Gate takes its name.

Once, a mounting-stone stood near to its door to assist passengers boarding and alighting from the coaches that used to pull in here - a relief team of four horses being stabled nearby. Travellers would often take a room for the night at a lodging house belonging to the landlord. This used to stand at the rear of the pub before being demolished in 1941. Rates for lodgers taking a bed for a night were 9d, and for those who slept seated with their heads leaning against a rope, 6d. It is said that in the morning, to wake up the sleeping guests, a regular would undo the knot and let the rope go.

It is believed that the old pub was once called the *'Maiden's Head,'* and in 1733 the Earl and Countess of Oxford let the house to Benjamin Maymott, a tradesman, on a 21-year lease at a cost of £7 a year.

The sign on the wall has a fine portrait of Charles I. Royalty often features on inn-signs - Henry VIII's distinctive figure appearing on most signs representing the *'King's Head,'* and Elizabeth I's the *'Queen's Head.'*

LADYBROOK - *Ladybrook Lane*

Built by Mansfield Brewery in 1958, this pub takes its name from a brook (now covered over) which flows nearby.

LING FOREST - *Eakring Road*

This pub was built in 1954 by Mansfield Brewery in an area once occupied by woodland called the 'Ling Forest,' part of which can still be seen. Ling is another word for heather.

LOCAL - *Armstrong Road*

Opened in December 1960, this pub, like the *'Village Inn'* at West Runton, Norfolk, does not have a proper name - but it manages to describe itself nevertheless.

LORD BYRON - *Quarry Lane*

Built during the early 1950s as a replacement for a former house of the same name that once stood nearby, this pub commemorates Nottinghamshire's celebrated poet George Gordon Byron (1788-1824).

Born in London, the son of an eccentric Captain, 'Mad Jack' Byron, and his wife Catherine Gordon of Gight, Aberdeen, a Scottish heiress, he was lame from birth, but grew to be a handsome man who was adored by women. In 1798 upon the death of his great-uncle, the 'Wicked Lord,' he succeeded to the title of Lord Byron and inherited Newstead Abbey.

In 1823 he joined the Greek insurgents who had risen against the Turks in a war of independence and died of marsh fever at Missolonghi in April 1824. His body was returned to England and buried in the family vault at St.Mary Magdalen Church in Hucknall. A white marble memorial was placed in the floor of Westminster Abbey, London in the South Transept, now known as 'Poets Corner,' by the Poetry Society on the 8th May 1969.

Hucknall also has a *'Lord Byron'* - and the poet's name is represented obliquely in Nottingham's North Church Street by *'Byron's.'*

OLD EIGHT BELLS - *Church Street*

Mentioned in the 1832 Directory, this pub briefly lost its licence in the 1870s when a former licensee was found guilty of supplying ale after hours. It was formerly the home of Samuel Brunts whose charity founded by his will (proved in 1711), is one of the wealthiest in the country. The inn was acquired by Mansfield Brewery in 1895 and rebuilt in 1925. In 1986 it was sold to Camerons who, after closing it for refurbishment, re-opened it as *'Russells'* but it soon reverted back to the old name.

Since eight are the normal number of bells in a peal, this sign is a fairly common one - especially for pubs situated near to churches, as this one is. The name also commemorates a later 18th century inhabitant of the house, Robert Watson who, by paying for one bell himself and sharing in the cost of another, was instrumental in completing the peal in the church.

PORTLAND ARMS - *Albert Street*

The name of this pub (acquired by Mansfield Brewery in 1895) is a reference to the Dukes of Portland, descended from William III's favourite, Hans Bentinck. The dukes owned a great many estates in different parts of the country as well as property in London.

William Henry Cavendish Bentinck, 3rd Duke of Portland was Prime Minister in 1783 and again between 1807 and 1809.

Old Eight Bells, Mansfield

RAILWAY INN - *Station Street*

Mentioned in the 1853 Directory, this pub's name derives from its close proximity to the former Mansfield Railway Station, which was closed under Beeching in 1963.

During the 1970s the pub became a veritable railway museum, being decorated with all sorts of memorabilia including a ganger's horn and a season ticket belonging to a former Chief Constable of Nottinghamshire, Mr W. Plackett. The ticket covered the period of January to March, 1893 and took him from Nottingham to Draycott at a cost of £2 16s. 8d. Other items amongst the collection include railway plates, rail timetables, water gauges and photographs of famous locomotives.

RAM - *Littleworth*

Opened in 1960 (though not acquired by Mansfield Brewery until 1983), this pub replaced a 200-year-old house of the same name which had once stood on a site opposite the brewery.

The sign of the 'Ram' has been in use since the 14th century. An heraldic symbol, it appears in the arms of the Worshipful Company of Clothworkers and other companies having connections with the wool trade.

REINDEER - *Southwell Road West*

Recorded in the 1832 Directory as the *'Little Reindeer,'* this pub was acquired by Mansfield Brewery in 1879.

Closed for refurbishment in June 1966, it reopened under its present sign. An explanation for the origin of the name *'Reindeer'* as an inn-sign can be found by referring to the pub of the same name at East Bridgford.

RUSHLEY - *Nottingham Road*

This pub was built in 1964 by Mansfield Brewery on an area of land once occupied by Rushley Farm - hence the name.

SIR JOHN COCKLE - *Sutton Road*

Opened in April 1937, the sign here recounts the story of a man, who as far back as the 12th century, at a time when Sherwood Forest was easy to get lost in and even Robin Hood had not yet appeared on the scene, became nationally famous as the Miller of Mansfield.

An old ballad (containing 21 stanzas in 'Part the First' and a further 19 in 'Part the Second') is kept in the Dodsley Collection at Mansfield Public Library. It tells how King Henry II was hunting in Sherwood Forest when he lost his way. As night fell he became separated from his escort of faithful retainers and nobles. After a fearful journey, he arrived, footsore and weary, outside a rude cottage on the edge of the forest. Even his palfrey had rebelled against his feeble navigation and he'd had to drag the poor beast unwillingly behind him for the last few leagues.

Salvation, however, was now at hand, for the hospitable cottager, the miller John Cockle, gave Henry comfort as a traveller in need - not knowing this ragged loon to be his king. The miller dined him expansively off His Majesty's own succulent venison, with which, it seemed, he always kept his larder plentifully-stocked from his son's daily foraging and marksmanship. Morning came, after a restful night's sleep 'neath the smoky thatch, and with it the search-party still frantically combing the forest for their missing monarch. Incognito inevitably became cognito, and the jolly miller realising how he had unwittingly flouted the royal prerogative in flogging the king's own deer, stood before Henry afraid and trembling.

It seems though that the king's sense of magnanimity was equal to the occasion, and if we may now quote from the final stanzas of the ballad:

Sir John Cockle sign, Mansfield

*"The King perceiving him fearfully trembling
Drew forth his sword, but nothing he said.
The miller downe did fall, crying before them all,
Doubting the King would have cut off his head:
But he his kind courtesye for to requite,
Gave him great living, and dubb'd him a Knight.*

*Then Sir John Cockle the King call'd unto him,
And of merry Sherwood made him o'er-seer;
And gave him out of hand three hundred
pound yearlye;
'Now take heed you steale no more of my deer:
And once a quarter let's here have your view;
And now, Sir John Cockle, I bid you adieu.'"*

The story of the Miller of Mansfield is also remembered by the sign of the *'King and Miller'* at Retford. Another pub of this name once stood in Mansfield's Stockwell Gate until it was pulled down in 1957.

SWAN - *Church Street*

This old coaching inn, one of Mansfield's premier houses, has stood here since 1584.

Over the years many changes have occurred at the *'Swan.'* During the 18th century the building became the headquarters for the many coaches that provided the town with its links to the rest of the country. The 1832 Directory records that the following coaches, with such splendid names as the 'The Royal Hope' (to Derby), 'The Volunteer' (to Liverpool), 'The Champion' (from Manchester to Lincoln), 'The Royal Union' (to York), 'The Hope' (from London to Sheffield, Huddersfield & Halifax), and 'The Express' (London to Leeds), all departed from the office of Samuel Stirrup in the Swan's yard, as well as five daily services to both Nottingham and Gainsborough.

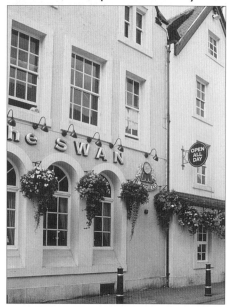

Swan, Mansfield

The inn once had large stabling accommodation where relays of post-horses were kept in readiness. These fine animals were nearly always hunters or carriage horses that were past their prime, and it was reckoned that, including time for changing, eight miles an hour was a good speed for a coach - the journey from here to York taking nine hours!

The inn's yard was accessed through a narrow archway leading off from the street and set at a lower level. This tested a driver's ability to the full, as he had to guide his coach down a steep drop whilst avoiding collision with the archway walls. Until the archway was pulled down to make way for alterations it still bore the marks of numerous collisions, the stones on either side of it being worn quite smooth by the constant friction of the traces.

In 1814 a coach entered the yard, bringing with it the news of Napoleon's defeat at the Battle of Toulouse on April 10th (the Emperor having abdicated the following day). Amidst the tumultuous excitement the horses were removed from the harness and a number of men grabbed the coach, pushing it out of the yard. As they did so, one of them slipped and was killed. In the Parish Church registers for June 18th, the entry of this man's death is recorded: *'Wm. Coop, aged 21 years. N.B. - This poor worthy young man lost his life by the mail-coach running over him when drawn out of the Swan Inn yard by men to testify their exultation at receiving news of the recovery of Europe from the tyranny of Bonaparte which took place in ye year 1814 - a glorious one for Great Britain. Give God to ye glory!'*

This sadly was not the only tragedy that occurred here. In 1816, a Mrs Millart was killed by the Leeds bound mail-coach as it entered the yard, crushing her against the wall.

By the end of the 18th century, the fast-expanding rail network reached Mansfield, and one by one the coaches ceased to run, until only a skeleton service to Nottingham remained. In order to move with the times, the *'Swan'* provided customers with a 'Town Omnibus' service, transporting them to and from the railway station.

At the forefront of the town's history and a popular place for public meetings, this house has witnessed many notable events. On the 14th July 1823, the Mansfield Improvement Commissioners met here for the first time. They drew up a petition, asking that Parliament pass an Act to improve Mansfield (which then had a population of 8,000) and provide it with gas lighting, new roads and scavenging (cleaning) of its streets.

Many famous people have passed through the 'Swan's' doors. In 1822 the Duke of Sussex stayed here on his way to Newstead and people thronged Church Street in an attempt to catch a glimpse of him. The third son of George III and therefore a royal personage, this visit of his is said to be the reason for the name of the pub (the 'Duke of Sussex') at nearby Fulwood. Before its residential and catering facilities were removed during the mid-1970s the inn had been host to a number of celebrities - The Beatles, Jayne Mansfield and many of the original cast of Coronation Street all having stayed here at one time or another.

Acquired in 1929 by Mansfield Brewery, the pub underwent major refurbishment in 1989, when major efforts were made to return it to something like its former glory. Interestingly, it is reputed to be haunted by five ghosts, one of which is said to be a cat!

The sign of the 'Swan' is extremely popular and has been in use since the 14th century, either as a direct allusion to the bird itself or to the coat of arms of Henry VIII or Edward III.

TOWN MILL - *Bridge Street*

The building in which this pub is housed was once a thriving 18th century cotton-mill - hence the name.

The mill itself (built in 1776), ceased production in 1907 when it was severely damaged by fire. In later years it was used as a television repair shop before being converted and opened as a pub in November 1984. Prior to its official opening by the then managing director of William Stones, Mr Douglas Townsend, a tour of the town was conducted by the brewery's shire-horses, pulling a dray.

Incorporated in this hostelry's design is a working water-wheel which can be viewed from a spiral staircase connecting the upstairs lounge to a smaller bar downstairs.

WIDECOMBE FAIR - *Oak Tree Lane*

Opened on the 24th August 1993 by Tom Cobleigh the independent pub operators, it stands on a site adjacent to this company's registered office.

The name here is a clever adaptation of the title of a late 18th century popular folk-song in which Tom Pearce lends his grey mare to Bill Brewer, Jan Stewer, Peter Gurney, Peter Davy, Dan'l Whiddon, Harry Hawk and old Uncle 'Tom Cobleigh' to carry them to 'Widecombe Fair' for a feast of fine ale and food. Sadly, during the journey, the horse takes sick and dies and is still seen to be haunting the moor at night.

Widecombe Fair, Mansfield

Ye Old Ramme, Mansfield

YE OLD RAMME - *Church Street*

Though a plaque above the door of this old inn bears a date of 1777, it is thought that parts of the building are much older, dating back to the 1600s. Acquired by Mansfield Brewery in 1877, it is reputedly haunted by monks.

Over the years, this pub has revealed some of its secrets. In 1976 a late-17th century clothes press was discovered in its attic, and in August 1987 old newspaper cuttings were found by workmen who had removed wooden panelling to reveal the inn's original wattle and daub walls. A number of these cuttings, dating from 1860, once formed part of the *Bells London Life* newspaper and several other smaller pieces, dating from 1859, were from either the *Nottingham Evening Post* or the *Express*.

During alterations (in 1987) a stone slab was raised in the area of the bar, uncovering a makeshift tunnel filled with rubble and bricked up at one end. It is said that this tunnel was once used by monks, who used it to travel to and from the inn from nearby St Peter's Church - more likely, though, is that it once offered a facility to the house in the form of a vaulted cellar.

Like the sign of the 'Ram' at Littleworth, this pub's name has connections with the wool trade.

MANSFIELD WOODHOUSE

ANGEL - *High Street*

The sign of this old pub (recorded in the 1832 Directory) derived from that of the 'Salutation' and is often found near to religious establishments. At one time pilgrims seeking shelter and refreshment would stay at hostelries such as this.

ANVIL - *Portland Street*

This former grocer's shop was opened as a pub in 1884. It is only 29 years younger than Mansfield Brewery itself (established in 1855).

The name here reflects the important position once held by the village blacksmith - which saw him making tools and weapons for members of the community, as well as shoeing their horses.

FOURWAYS - *Leeming Lane South*

This late Victorian building originally served as the Mansfield Cottage Hospital, before its closure just prior to World War II.

After the war the premises were registered as the Elm Club, named after a weeping elm tree which can still be seen in the grounds of the current house. During the 1960s the premises were purchased by Stones Brewery and reopened as the 'Fourways.'

The name here is a reference to the pub's prominent position at a crossroads with roads leading off in four directions towards Pleasley, Warsop, Forest Town and Mansfield.

Angel, Mansfield Woodhouse

Fourways sign, Mansfield Woodhouse

PARLIAMENT OAK - *Church Street*

The sign of this pub (recorded in the 1832 Directory) originates from a tree of the same name which still stands in Sherwood Forest on Peafield Lane, Mansfield Woodhouse.

It is said that whilst travelling to Scotland in 1290, King Edward I summoned Parliament to meet on St Michael's Day (1st October) under the branches of this massive oak. There is no written record of what passed between the gathered assembly, though it is suggested that they discussed the recent revolt of the Welsh under Llewellyn, and resolved to march against him. It is quite likely such a meeting did occur, particularly as the King was known to enjoy hunting in the forest.

STAR - *Warsop Road*

Recorded in the 1832 Directory, this former coaching inn is believed to be more than 300 years old.

In 1975, amongst numerous items of bric-a-brac discovered in its loft was a small book bound in animal skin. This book documents the financial dealings of the landlord of the inn between 1798 and 1803, though his name itself is not recorded. Made in faded brown ink, the entries detail the delivery and payment of hops, 'molt,' 'tobacker,' ale and bread. Most interesting though, is a record of the debts accumulated by a number of the landlord's former patrons - a certain Mr George Unwin, for example, who owed various amounts at one time or another - his most serious bout of drinking being one ten-pint session for which he owed the princely sum of 2s 6d.

The origin of this pub's name can be found by referring to the entry for the house of the same name at Basford.

SUNNYDALE - *Brown Avenue*

Built by Mansfield Brewery in 1956, this pub takes its name from Sunnydale Farm and Cottages which are situated nearby on Cox's Lane.

Animals

Lion Revived, Bulwell

Black's Head, Carlton

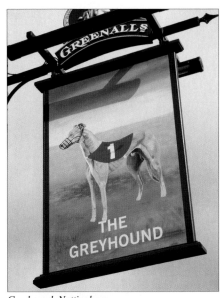

Greyhound, Nottingham

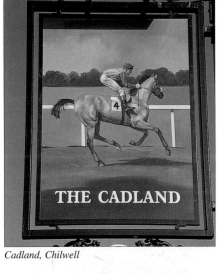

Cadland, Chilwell

Fox, Sneinton

Roebuck, Wollaton

Badger Box, Annesley Woodhouse

Greyhound Inn, Arnold

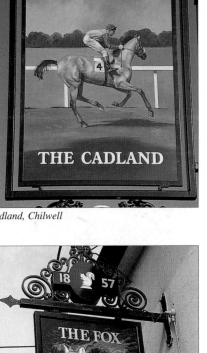

Unicorn Hotel, Gunthorpe

Red Cow, Lenton

Plate III

Birds

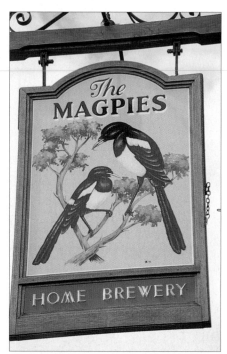

Lark's Nest, Nuthall

Pelican, Bilborough

White Swan, Basford

Magpies, Sneinton

Flamingo, Worksop

Peacock, Clifton

Eagle, Arnold

Bird in Hand, Blidworth

Tree Tops, Mapperley

Plate IV

MAPLEBECK

BEEHIVE - *Maplebeck Village*

Maplebeck boasts the smallest pub in the county, and one of the prettiest, - the '*Beehive*', built in 1803. Before 1844 it was called the '*Gate Inn'*, but since then has always been known under its present name. Originally, the pub had just one small room, but has now expanded to two, even so, 30 people cause it to bulge at the seams! 'Regulars' come from elsewhere in the county to drink at this delightful little local, - one American in 1950 even offered to buy the pub, take it down brick by brick and ship it back to the States! For over seventy years, the '*Beehive*' was run by the Whitworth family, one of whom, 23 stone Percy Whitworth was actually born in the pub.

The Beehive has long been a symbol of industry, but in many cases, it must have appealed as a sign because of its distinctive shape. And, oh yes - there is a beehive among the flowers in the garden!

Beehive, Maplebeck

MAPPERLEY

PLAINSMAN - *Woodthorpe Drive*

The naming of this pub (opened in December 1969) is a pleasant attempt to integrate local topography with American history, and touches of the Wild West are visible inside - where the eye-catching murals are the work of Ernest Bottomley, former senior art lecturer at the Manchester Polytechnic. His silver bison herd on a golden range is featured on a straight wood carving (there are also samples of wood-relief figures of varying sizes) and as preliminary research he studied these animals closely beforehand at a zoo. A hunter's buffalo gun, a life-size Colt .45 and other reminders of tough frontier living are incorporated in a composition of wood and leather.

As to the inn-sign itself, this is an impressive interpretation of the Western theme. We tried to persuade ourselves, in gazing up at it, that the rugged features of the foreground character did in fact remind us of the late, great Gary Cooper (who took the part of Wild Bill Hickok in that memorable film '*The Plainsman)*' but we don't reckon the easy-going Cooper ever looked as stern and forbidding as the feller on the signboard. No foolin', pardner, he sure is a 'plain' case of the Big, the Bad and the Ugly!

TRAVELLERS REST - *Mapperley Plains*

This inn, once known as the '*Half-Way House'*, originates from 1872 and was rebuilt in 1925. Its first owner was a farrier, who attended to the re-shoeing of horses after they were watered here. In those days carriers' carts made their twice-weekly trips to Southwell from the '*Black Boy,*' the '*Crown*' and the '*Maypole*' on Long Row, Nottingham. This pub, with its strategic position, would certainly have occasion to be 'restful' to these travellers.

Travellers Rest, Mapperley

Tree Tops, Mapperley

TREE TOPS - *Plains Road*

This pub (opened 9th October 1963) was formerly a commercial and residential guest house. Situated at one of the highest points in the district (a factor from which it takes its name), it affords scenic views over the neighbouring countryside.

MEADOWS

CREMORNE - *Queens Drive*

This Victorian pub was named after the Derby winner of 1872, a portrait of which appears on the signboard. Captain Henry Savile of Rufford owned the horse, which is buried in an animal cemetery at Rufford Country Park. The original skittles alley, dating back to 1880, is still used in the beer garden.

The pub is said to be haunted by a 'poltergeist' named Wally - a former countryboy-turned-cellarman who stayed on here after his death. According to the licensee, his apparition knocks bottles off the wall and mischievously removes other objects.

In May 1941, during the Second World War, the Meadows area was visited by the *Luftwaffe*, who reaped far greater havoc than the aforesaid Wally. Their screaming bomb-loads laid waste to vast tracts of land, smashing the nearby caravans of Proctor's Fair (which had settled behind the pub) and killing the owner's wife.

PLUMPTRE ARMS - *Bunbury Street*

The name here honours two local and related benefactors. The first John Plumptre was Mayor of Nottingham in 1385, 1394/5 and 1408. He endowed a hospital in 1390 which in 1823/4 was demolished and rebuilt. It is the city's oldest Charity, and has its location in Plumptre Square.

The second John Plumptre was a promoter of education among the poor. In the Deed founding the Bluecoat Charity School in Weekday Cross in 1720, his name stands first of all the Trustees.

The pub itself (opened in December 1938) and Bunbury Street in particular were filmed in September 1968 by a BBC-TV camera crew during scenes for a screen play entitled *'Sling Your Hook'* by ex-Bestwood Colliery miner Roy Minton, the pub being re-named the *'Mustard Pot'* for the occasion. The play was about a group of Nottinghamshire miners who take a bus ride to Blackpool for a riotous weekend - essentially a comedy about the social and home life of miners which contained an element of fantasy. Its director was reported as saying, "We chose Bunbury Street for the location because we wanted to depict Nottingham as outsiders see it - back-to-back streets and terraced houses . . ."

POETS CORNER - *Kirkewhite Walk*

In common with too many other pub-names, the requisite apostrophe here is conspicuous by its absence - so it is not clear whether the original pub in Kirkewhite Street (closed in 1975, whereas its successor opened in 1977) was once the haunt of poet or poets. Even though 'plural' may be implied, however, there is no doubt that the principal poet commemorated in this way was indeed a 'singular' one.

Henry Kirke White's modest place in Literature would almost certainly have been enhanced but for a tragically early death in 1806, following a brilliantly-successful studentship at Cambridge. His birthplace in the old 'Shambles' of our city was swallowed-up in the building of the Council House, opened on 22nd May 1929 by the then Prince of Wales. On a wall just inside its shopping arcade is a bronze plaque depicting the little butcher's shop owned by Kirke White's father. Arthur Mee's volume *Nottinghamshire - the Midland Stronghold,* reveals that his father showed a fine disregard for the lad's literary gifts by taking him early from school and setting him to deliver meat before apprenticing him to the stocking-loom. But eventually his mother, who had been a schoolmistress, managed to get him transferred to a lawyer's office where the working hours were merely from 8am to 8pm - after which he was free to devote himself to the study of Latin and Greek by the light of the midnight candle!

Through the influence of friends he gained entrance to St John's College, Cambridge, and whilst preparing for the University he came with his books to stay in the village of Wilford and lodged in a cottage with a garden reaching down to the river, finding both here and at Clifton the inspiration for much of his best work. As Arthur Mee wrote, 'there he would dream as he looked out on a scene which was Wilford's great joy, a never-to-be-forgotten landscape of swift-flowing river, meadowland carpeted with crocuses in Spring, and Nottingham with its castle silhouetted against the sky . . .'

From an early age young Kirke White had been writing verse, and his poem *'Clifton Grove,'* which helped to raise his university fees, was perpetuated in the pub of this name in Waterway Street which closed in 1975. His natural abilities at Cambridge placed him first in every examination and promised a dazzling career, but too much exertion in the pursuit of knowledge exhausted his feeble frame, and his burial took place soon after his 21st birthday.

His work was much admired by Lord Byron, whilst Robert Southey (then Poet Laureate) championed him royally, wrote his biography and published his writings. The hymn *'Oft in danger, oft in woe'* is one of several by which older congregations can still remember him. An attempt to commemorate his birthplace by an inn-sign was made in the early 1860s by a circle of admirers, who obtained the consent of the licensing authorities to change the sign of an inn in Exchange Alley to the *'Kirke White Tavern'* - but this of course has been lost to view long since.

SPINNING JENNY - *Meadows Way West*

The name of this pub (opened in November 1979) is echoed by one in Belper, Derbyshire. They both refer to an early form of spinning machine in which several spindles were set in motion by a band from one wheel. This labour-saving device predated Richard Arkwright's spinning-frame and was the invention of James Hargreaves about 1764, though not patented until 1770. The latter was a Lancashire-born mechanic (as distinct from Arkwright, who was originally a barber from the same county) who came to Nottingham to set up a cotton-mill of his own and died here in 1778.

Sadly, his revolutionary invention met with much opposition and he died a poor man (unlike Arkwright, who gained fame, fortune and a knighthood - plus having a pub uniquely named after him, this being in Arkwright Street, of course, and closing down in 1974).

The immediate area of the *'Spinning Jenny'* runs across that part of Nottingham where the local cotton industry developed. When The Meadows was still in fact meadow-land, the machines of both Hargreaves and Arkwright were still in full operation, and their workers would spread out the cloth on the grass to dry.

THREE BRIDGES - *Gritley Mews*

Opened on the 21st December 1983 by Mansfield Brewery's then chairman, Robin Chadburn, who travelled there in a Victorian horse-drawn coach. This was their first purpose-built pub in the Nottingham area.

The name here was suggested by housewife Rita McMinn who won a Name-a-Pub competition - it signifies that there are three bridges across the River Trent in this locality, the Lady Bay, Trent and Clifton Bridges. A fourth one is at present under consideration.

MEDEN VALE

THREE LIONS - *Netherfield Lane*

The three lions rampant used as the sign for this pub (opened in December 1967), are taken from the coat of arms of the Fitzherbert family, principal landowners in the area.

MISTERTON

PACKET INN - *Station Road*

Misterton village has never had many licensed premises because the Temperance movement was very strong here. This pub, parts of which are over 250 years old, takes its name from the packet boats which transported grain along the Chesterfield Canal, which today has been taken over by leisure craft and privately owned, colourful narrowboats. In the early 1800s, a packet boat passenger service ran between Retford and West Stockwith, calling at Misteron Wharf and passing the *'Packet Inn'*. The horse drawn boats took five hours to complete the 15 miles between the two places. Later, steam packets became increasingly common.

MOORGREEN

HORSE AND GROOM

Originally a farmhouse, built some 300 years ago, on the Greasley Castle Estate, this pub was extended 100 years ago to its present form and is very popular with visitors to D. H. Lawrence countryside.

MORTON

FULL MOON - *Main Street*

The sign of the moon, a romantic symbol, is not as popular in Nottinghamshire as that of the *'Sun.'* Whilst a *'Full Moon'* welcomes us here, a *'Half Moon'* is visible at Hucknall and the *'Moon and Stars'* adorn Eastwood. The sign of the *'Sun'* can be found in other parts of the county, including Gotham, Retford and Eastwood.

Heraldry accepts the moon as a charge, but the crescent is favoured more often than the full moon. With the horns of the moon turned upwards it represents the sign of the second son, and when they point downwards to the sinister (or left) the device is known as decrescent.

A genial man-in-the-moon extends the following welcome on the sign of this pub:

'Step in my friends, and take a cup,
It is not dark, for the moon is up.
Sit down, refresh, and pay your way,
Then you will call another day.'

This pub is thought to have been built in the early 1840s.

NETHER LANGWITH

JUG AND GLASS - *Queens Walk*

A traditional coaching inn, built in the 1690s, which has a most attractive riverside frontage overlooking the River Poulter, complete with waterfowl. Visitors in summer will often find a variety of events, such as Morris Dancing, taking place outside the pub.

The name is a reference to the times when beer was brought up from the cellars in jugs, from which it was poured into drinking glasses. Another pub with this name at Edwinstowe has a humorous sign.

NETHERFIELD

FOX AND HOUNDS - *Station Road*

A large pub, also a hotel, built in 1876 to serve the needs of the very rapidly expanding community. The pub's name is a common one nationally and not just in hunting country.

RAILWAY HOTEL - *Victoria Road*

The birth of the railway as a mode of transport in the 19th century had a major impact on life in Britain - a fact reflected in many public house signs such as this.

This Victorian pub, known locally as *'Jackie Bell's'* after its original landlord, has stood here for around 140 years and has significant links with the LMS railway. A room above it (now used for functions), once served as a dormitory for engine drivers and their stokers who often used to visit the large locomotive sheds at Netherfield, a site now occupied by the Victoria Retail Park.

Railway Hotel, Netherfield

NEWARK-ON-TRENT

BLUE MAN - *North Gate*

Recorded in the 1832 Directory as a beerhouse, the sign of this old pub has a colour common to many former hostelries that once stood in Newark. A glance at this same Directory reveals that an inn called the *'Blue Lion'* (closed in 1884) once stood in Middle Gate, and that besides the presence of the *'Blue Man'* in Newark, there were a further two beerhouses sporting this colour as part of their sign, namely the *'Blue Goat'* and the *'Blue Sergeant.'* Directories also record the existence of the *'Blue Swan'* (1861-1911) which once stood in North Gate.

Though the sign outside this house depicts a 'blue' diver fishing underwater with a rod, this is merely the artist's own interpretation of the name. The true meaning behind the popular use of this colour as a prefix for so many of Newark's inns is its association with the Manners family, the Dukes of Rutland, whose ancestral home is Belvoir Castle. The Manners gave their political support to the Whigs, whose party colour was then blue, and for a number of years it was customary for many pubs owned by, or connected with, this family to include the colour as a prefix to their signs.

BRIDGE INN - *Lincoln Road*

Opened in 1936, this pub stands near to a bridge on Lincoln Road which carries vehicular traffic over the main East Coast railway line. A section of this bridge occupies the site of the former *'Walnut Tree'* public house which closed in 1936, having stood there since 1853. The colourful signboard outside depicts the engine Lord Farringdon (named after a director of the LNER). Another *'Bridge'* inn can be found at Dunham on Trent.

BROADWAY - *Bowbridge Road*

Depicting scenes from Broadway shows, the attractive signboard that hangs outside this pub (opened in 1939), suggests that it takes its name from the famous street in New York which is renowned for its theatres in the section nicknamed 'the Great White Way.'

CARDINAL'S HAT - *Jersey Street*

Although inns named after monarchs, politicians and military figures are common enough, those named in honour of ecclesiastical dignitaries are rather rare - certainly as far as the Roman Catholic Church is concerned. Even then they seem to focus on one man, the great Cardinal Wolsey (1471-1530). In his time, signboards were used to honour a leader of the (Catholic) hierarchy in the same way as showing the crest of a nobleman. Before the Reformation began in 1534 (when Henry VIII took control of the English Church), hats were the outward sign of a cardinal's rank and dignity - recognisable by two golden cords and innumerable tassels.

The signboard of this house (opened in October 1958) does in fact portray such a hat and is an excellent example of the craftsman's art in its design and colouring.

The original house of this name stood from 1494 in Newark's Market Place until, under its new sign as the *'Clinton Arms,'* it closed in 1990. The former pub's title was a tribute to William Booth of Southwell, who became a cardinal at the end of the 15th century - although by tradition it also pays compliment to Wolsey, who, almost forty years after the pub was first christened the *'Cardinal's Hat,'* stayed at Southwell (in 1530) and visited Newark several times before being arrested for high treason by King Henry VIII. At some time in the 17th century it became known as the *'Talbot,'* after the heraldic dog which features on the coat of arms of the Earls of Shrewsbury (Talbot being their family name), gaining notoriety as the headquarters of 'Quick Nick' Nevinson, the notorious highwayman whose execution took place at York in 1684.

From 1828 to 1831 it was known as the *'Kingston Arms,'* the Earl of Kingston being a local landowner and a popular military figure, but was then again renamed, this time in honour of the Duke of Newcastle (who put up Gladstone as Newark's MP in 1832), using his family name of Clinton.

CASTLE AND FALCON - *Beaumond Street*

Rodney Cousins, in his excellent booklet *'Newark Inns and Public Houses',* published by Nottinghamshire County Council indicates that the history of this former coaching inn can be traced back to 1788 when the then licensee William Clark offered a reward for the arrest of the thieves who had broken into the hostelry.

The 1832 Directory records that such stagecoaches as the *Regulator,* the *Magna Charta* and the *Rockingham Union* all called here daily to transport travellers to London, Southwell, Gainsborough, Lincoln, Hull and Nottingham.

The name is a reference to Newark Castle which was built in the 12th century by Alexander, Bishop of Lincoln. During the Civil War the fortress was held by the Royalists for King Charles I from 1642 until May 1646, when His Majesty ordered the Royalist Governor of Newark, Lord Belasyse, to surrender the town to the opposing Parliamentarian forces. Soon afterwards Cromwell's soldiers laid ruin to much of the castle, leaving only the gatehouse and the north and west walls standing. The Castle and Falcon was also the badge of Catherine Parr, the sixth wife of King Henry VIII.

CASTLE BARGE - *Town Wharf*

With a length of 94ft and a beam of 17½ft, the *'Castle Barge'* must be one of the most unusual pubs in the county. Opened in December 1979 by North Country Brewery Ltd of Hull, this floating hostelry was once a 45-ton steel sailing barge called the *Ril Elsie.* Built in 1923, she once used to regularly navigate the Trent in her role as a grain carrier.

To re-model the *Ril Elsie* for her new employment she underwent extensive strengthening and modification at Hull dockyards, before being floated upriver to Fiskerton for final conversion into a pub - a bar being built in her hold.

Owned by Mansfield Brewery since 1985, the *'Castle Barge'* (as she was re-christened) has a number of onboard features designed to enhance the feeling of being afloat, including a ship's wheel and a telegraph. The name is a reference to the siting of the barge close to the ruins of Newark Castle.

CAVALIER - *Middle Gate*

The site on which this pub stands was once occupied by an old tavern called the *'Angel,'* whose origins are recorded in a deed of 1471. In 1965 the former house was completely rebuilt and restyled as the *'Cavalier'* - a sign which recalls the town's strong Royalist connections during the Civil War (1642-1646). It is said that King Charles I's wife, Henrietta Maria, lodged at a dwelling in nearby Kirk Gate (now a greengrocer's shop) for almost a month during June 1643, having arrived with over 4000 volunteers who were to take part in an offensive against Nottingham Castle later that year.

CROWN AND MITRE - *Castle Gate*

Prior to this pub assuming its current sign (in March 1989) it was known as the *'Exchange Hotel,'* and before that the *'Wagon And Horses.'*

Dating back to 1799, it once had stabling for a large number of horses as well as its own malt-house, features of many pubs at that time. During the early part of the 20th century it was the local resort of pianist and artist Elliot Etwell - a number of whose watercolour paintings can be viewed in Newark's Museum and Art Gallery.

The pub's current sign recounts Newark's religious and royal links with history - which include the building of Newark Castle by Bishop Alexander of Lincoln and, by tradition, King John's death there in 1216.

HORSE AND GEARS - *Portland Street*

The origins of this old inn can be traced back to 1801. Once owned by the Duke of Newcastle, it was sold as part of his estate in 1888.

The name here is a traditional reference (popular until the 19th century) to the harness worn by a draught horse.

MAIL COACH - *Beaumond Street*

Formerly known as the *'Cross Keys,'* the origins of this old hostelry can be traced back to 1788 when it was sold by the Mayor and Alderman under the authority of the Turnpike Act for the sum of £150. Its current sign, adopted after it underwent refurbishment in 1989, recalls a former inn of the same name which once stood nearby.

MALT SHOVEL - *North Gate*

The origins of this old inn are recorded in an 1861 census which documents that the patron of a beerhouse called the *'Malt Shovel'* was a Mr William Footitt. By the beginning of the 20th century the premises of number 23 North Gate were being used as a bakery and a grocer's shop, whilst number 25 was serving ale. In February 1973, the bakery long since gone, the pub was obliged to close due to commercial pressures.

The property did not stand idle. For a brief spell it was used as accommodation for students, later becoming the offices of Macarthy Hughes International. In December 1986 it was re-opened as a pub amid talk of ghostly happenings. Rumour has it that during the early hours of the morning the eerie sound of voices could be heard echoing throughout the building - perhaps the spirits of former bakery workers 'rising' to commence their early shift!

At one time Newark was an important centre for the malting and brewing trade with companies such as James Hole's 'Castle Brewery' (established in 1885 and taken over by Courage of London in 1967) conducting their business from the town.

Refer also to the pub of the same name at Hucknall.

MAPLE LEAF - *Winthorpe Road*

Opened in August 1968 by former owners James Hole and Company, the sign chosen for this pub followed the brewery's trend at the time of naming their new houses after particular themes - which had previously included the *Wild Life* at Lincoln, *the Sea Around Us* at Loughborough and the *Burmese Cat* at Melton Mowbray.

Inside, in line with the chosen Canadian motif (the maple leaf being the national emblem of that country), the pub displays maps of the Wild West and photographs of the territories along with totem poles carved by local resident and nationally renowned sculptor, Robert Kiddey (1900-1984).

OLD KINGS ARMS - *Kirk Gate*

Mentioned in the 1832 Directory as the *'Kings Arms,'* the name of this old inn honours King George IV (1762-1830). Shortly after the king's death, when the less popular William IV acceded to the throne, the pub changed its name to the *'Old Kings Arms,'* in remembrance of the former monarch.

According to Rodney Cousins, the house was offered for auction in 1759, when it was described as a *'very good accustomed inn, with stabling for 30 horses, a large yard, with the London - York coach dining here on the upward journey.'*

On an outer wall above the entrance to this pub is the Royal Coat Of Arms which was in use between 1816 and 1837. This brilliantly-coloured cast-iron

Old King's Arms sign, Newark

plaque was created by William Midworth, a skilled Newark foundryman who showed his work at the Great Exhibition in 1851, over forty years before the Newark Cycling Club held an early meeting at this hostelry in 1897.

In 1885 the pub was sold to the Trent Brewery of Richardson, Earp and Slater (later part of Warwick and Richardsons of Newark). At this time the premises consisted of a bar, bar/parlour, bagatelle room, tap room, kitchen, pantry, larder, club room, four bedrooms, lumbar room and an adjacent brewhouse.

Due to economic reasons, the pub closed in 1971. The building then served as offices until 1977 when it was again re-opened as a public house.

PACKHORSE - *Albert Street*

This house was opened in July 1829 as a replacement for an earlier *'Pack-horse'* inn which used to stand on the corner of Stodman Street and Middle Gate.

The name is a reference to the animals that, prior to the days of canals and railways, were used to transport goods. These horses would carry items, such as wool and corn, to and from market, often in caravans of up to forty at a time. Their human companions would no doubt have used an inn such as this to quench their thirsts (and of course that of their animals).

The sign depicts a packhorse passing a milestone on its way to Hawton, 1½ miles away.

QUEEN'S HEAD - *Market Place*

In existence since 1560, this is one of the oldest inns in Newark.

The name commemorates Elizabeth I (1533-1603) who was Queen of England from 1558, and who had been on the throne for only two years when this house started to serve ale. Because of the esteem in which Elizabeth was traditionally held, most pubs under the sign of the *'Queen's Head'* depict her portrait on their signboards.

Interestingly, during her reign, signboard artists had to exercise extreme care as to how they portrayed their queen. It was Sir Walter Raleigh in the introduction to his literary work, *The History of the World* (1614), who passed comment that under the Queen's own proclamation of 1563, portraits of her made by 'unskilful and common' painters were to be knocked to pieces and cast into the fire.

Queen's Head, Newark (1929)

ROBIN HOOD - *Lombard Street*

Recorded in the 1832 Directory, this former coaching inn once had stabling for 30 horses and provided a daily service for market carriers. (See also the *'Robin Hood'* at Sherwood for a more detailed explanation of the name).

ROYAL OAK - *Castle Gate*

Once owned by the Duke of Newcastle, this old inn (dating back to 1775) is, like many of Newark's old pubs, a listed building. It is named after the tree in which Charles II concealed himself to hide from the Roundheads, following his defeat at the Battle of Worcester in 1651.

The pub is supposedly haunted by a friendly ghost in the guise of an elderly woman, who often appears in an upstairs passageway and kitchen.

RUTLAND ARMS - *Barnby Gate*

The history of this old pub can be traced back to an indenture dated the 31st May 1657 which records it under its current sign. In 1991 the premises were refurbished and it was restyled as the *'Newark Royalist'* - recalling Newark's royal allegiance during the English Civil War (1642-1646).

On the 28th December, 1994 the house reverted to its original sign as the *'Rutland Arms'* - a reference to the family owners of Belvoir Castle (see also the *Blue Man* at Newark).

SAWMILL - *Beacon Hill Road*

This pub, opened in October 1981, is built on the site of an old woodyard and steam sawmill once owned by Thomas Smith and Sons (Newark) Ltd. The mill itself had stood on Beacon Hill from the early part of the 1860s until it closed around 1970.

Officially opened by former Mayor of Newark, Mrs Maureen Dobson, she would have noted Mansfield Brewery's attempts to recapture the history of the sawmill in this pub's design. Amongst various woodworking tools on display inside are framed copies of bills issued to customers by the former mill owners, including one found in a cupboard in a Millgate house. Dated 1867, this bill belonged to a Mr Isaac Lawson, whose orders included *'six clothes poasts'* at a cost of 18 shillings.

SPRING HOUSE - *Farndon Road*

The name of this old inn (mentioned in the 1832 Directory) is derived from the legend surrounding nearby St Catherine's Well (situated in Devon Park), which is filled with pure water from a freshwater spring.

The story goes, that a knight called Sir Everard Bevercotes was besotted with a fair damsel called Isabel, the daughter of Alan de Caldwell. But Sir Bevercotes had a rival for the lady's affection, a certain Sir Guy Saucimer. When it appeared to Sir Guy that the lady Isabel was more attracted to his competitor, he cowardly slew Sir Everard and fled abroad. At the scene of the murder, a stream of pure water issued forth from the ground. But this was of no comfort to Isabel, who later died of a broken heart. Nor did Sir Guy himself escape without punishment, for terrible sores began to manifest themselves about his body, and he vowed to return to England to seek a cure. Pained from his journey, he had just set himself down to rest in the Forest of Avold, when suddenly, a vision of the holy St Catherine appeared. She proceeded to give council to Sir Guy, advising him that the only cure for his ulcerated body was to be found in the waters of the stream, now gushing from the spot at which he had foully slain Sir Everard.

And so, it came to pass, that heeding the words of St Catherine, the wayward knight became a hermit and returned to the place where he had slain his rival. There he built himself a small humble abode, and using the clear waters taken from the stream, cured himself of his ailment. By the time he died at the ripe old age of 87 he was much revered by the local community for his kindness and grace.

The modern sign ignores the legend and illustrates the Spring House as a bird's nest!

WATERMILL - *Mill Gate*

Built around 1782, this old hostelry was acquired by Mansfield Brewery in March 1992.

The name originates from the pub's close proximity to a former watermill which used to stand nearby. Initially owned by the firm of J.T. Thorpe, this mill was originally used to spin cotton. In later years it underwent a change of ownership and became known as Parnham's Mill, being used to produce flour. Sadly, during the early 1960s it was burned to the ground and only its footings remain.

WHEATSHEAF - *Slaughterhouse Lane*

A lease of 1801, revealing that this house was once known as the *'Crispin Arms,'* reads, *'All that messuage dwelling house or tenement situate standing and being in Newark Upon Trent aforesaid, of the East side of a certain street or place there called Saint Leonard's Court now for some time past used as public house and formerly called or known by the name of the Crispin Arms but now commonly called or known by the name of the Wheatsheaf.'*

An explanation for the origin of this sign can be found by referring to the pub of the same name at Burton Joyce.

WING TAVERN - *Bridge Street*

When the *'Green Dragon'* was demolished in Newark's Market Place in 1773 to make way for a new south wing to Newark Town Hall, the innkeeper opened a new house nearby and called it the *'Wing Tavern'* in honour of this extension.

The latter stood in the Market Place from 1775 until 1871, when it was replaced by the present house which perpetuates this name.

WOOLPACK - *Stodman Street*

Built in 1452, the name of this old house reflects Newark's connections with the wool trade. The age of the building was established in 1993 by tree ring dating techniques used by Nottingham University's Dendrochronology Unit. At one time, the wool would have been transported by river to Boston, from where it was shipped to Calais and traded for cloth and wine. The inn was once the home of a well-to-do merchant (possibly a wool merchant), and is the only example in the East Midlands, of a 'Wealden House', a style of building with an open, central hall and projecting first floor bedrooms.

Ram Hotel and Royal Oak, Newark, (1929)

The wool-pack is a package in which wool was prepared for carriage, or sale, and is said to have had a definite weight of 240 pounds. The word is similar in origin to that of the woolsack, which has now taken on a more specific meaning, referring to the large square sack of wool covered with scarlet on which the Lord Chancellor sits in the House of Lords - a reminder of how much the nation's wealth at one time relied upon the wool trade.

YE OLDE MARKET - *Castle Gate*

The earliest record of this pub's existence was when it appeared in the Duke of Newcastle's deed of settlement in 1775 under its former name, the *'Ram Hotel.'*

In 1868 the novelist Mary Ann Evans (1819-80) boarded here - describing the hostelry as *'an old inn, opposite the ruins of the castle.'* Under the pen-name of George Eliot, she wrote such literary works as *'The Mill on the Floss'* and *'Middlemarch.'*

In 1939 the house was purchased by Home Brewery (now owned by Scottish and Newcastle) who retained its former name until September 1994 when, following refurbishment, it was re-opened under its current sign - a reference to Newark's fame as a medieval market town. A plaque outside the pub attempts to recall the origins of this market, in prose which will make traditionalists recoil in horror!

ZOO - Carter Gate

Until the early part of 1994 this old pub (mentioned in the 1832 Directory) was called the 'White Hind', a derivative of the more popular 'White Hart' (see pub of this name at Lenton).

The new name here appears to be in keeping with the modern craze of turning hostelries into so-called fun-pubs, where they are re-christened with a trendy name that befits their proposed new image! In order to enhance the modern-day theme of this pub, a number of prints depicting various wild animals have been incorporated in its design.

NEWTHORPE

LORD RAGLAN - Newthorpe Common

Depicted here astride his favourite charger, this gallant soldier was Lord Fitzroy James Henry Somerset, youngest son of the fifth Duke of Beaufort, who was born in 1788 and had a most distinguished military career. As a young man he served in Spain as Wellesley's aide-de-camp during the Peninsular campaign, and was later wounded at Waterloo - losing his sword arm as a result. Thereafter, he sat in Parliament as MP for Truro but, following the death of Wellington in 1852, he succeeded his old chief as commander of the British Forces, being created the first Baron Raglan. Subsequently, at the outbreak of the Crimean War, he was promoted to field-marshal and sent, in charge of the troops in an alliance with France, to oppose the Russians.

His first battle of the campaign was crowned with victory, but only a month later, in October of 1854, came the terrible blunder of tactics by which the heroic charge of the Light Brigade became a doomed venture from the very start. This bloody fiasco at Balaclava brought down the wrath of Raglan on the head of the Earl of Lucan, whom he held responsible, and the latter was summarily recalled to England.

After showing sound judgement and almost rash bravery at the Battle of Inkerman a month later (Queen Victoria sent him her personal congratulations on this success) Raglan was made the unfortunate scapegoat for Army mismanagement during the shockingly severe winter that followed, and died ten days after the failure of the mistimed attack on the Redan in June 1855, 'the victim of England's unreadiness for war.' It had been a grossly ill-equipped force from the very beginning. Swift pursuit of the Russians after his victory at the River Alma might have ended the whole campaign by Sebastopol's imminent capture, but the French dragged their feet, as they continued to do, unreproached by the British Government through the ensuing weary months of siege warfare. In effect, Raglan's intended conduct of operations was sacrificed to the preservation of an uneasy alliance, with himself as Commander-in-Chief, the scapegoat for the dithering and indecision of the Cabinet at home. Sir John Fortescue, the military historian, wrote of this valiant and patriotic soldier, 'Never was there a nobler or more self-denying public servant.'

It is conceivable that the original pub of this name was named by its first licensee in honour of his old general, under whose command he served.

NORMANTON-ON-SOAR

PLOUGH - Main Street

This 'Plough', one of nearly a dozen pubs with this name in the rural south of Nottinghamshire, started life as a farm in the 16th century. It later acquired a coal wharf, the coal being transported by barge along the River Soar, which flows behind the pub. The half timbered, Tudor-style frontage, makes this one of the most impressive looking village inns in the county.

During the 1930s, one room was used as a mortuary after a group of very drunken anglers from Sheffield slept on the river bank, but some did not live to tell the tale!

Plough, Normanton on Soar

NORMANTON-ON-THE-WOLDS

PLOUGH - *Melton Road*

An extremely pretty pub which was converted from several farmhouses. The original oak beams give this popular inn, great character. Emerging from the mass of creeper which covers the walls, is an old plough recalling the age of simple, pre-industrial farming.

NORMANTON-ON-TRENT

Square and Compass, Normanton-on-Trent

SQUARE AND COMPASS - *Eastgate*

This quiet, and little known, village has one of the very oldest pubs in the county. Its history can be traced back to around 1550 when, as a beerhouse, it stood adjacent to two cottages. These have now become part of the pub. In the 18th century, a man was hanged at Nottingham Gaol for failing to pay his bill in the pub. It appears that he hasn't forgotten the place as his presence remains and has led to strange things happening over the years!

Around 1860 the pub acquired its present name - an indenture of 1865 records that it was "latterly known by the sign of the *Freemans Arms*". Square and Compass is a reference to the basic tools used by carpenters, joiners and stonemasons.

During its history the pub has had many landlords, sometimes being run by a Brewery but mostly being in private ownership. A document at the pub indicates that it was sold in 1837 for £400. Between 1971 and 1975, the *'Square and Compass'* had the tallest landlord in the county. 6' 8" John Claridge, affectionately known as 'Long John', now lives in Australia.

The sign is different each side - one shows a builder's square and compass on a cushion, whilst the other depicts a mariner's square and compass on a map.

NORTH MUSKHAM

MUSKHAM FERRY - *Ferry Lane*

The villages of North Muskham and Holme once stood side by side but, during Elizabethan times, a flood caused the River Trent to change course and it now flows between them. A ferry used to link both places but today, only the inn marks this river crossing point. The ferry ceased operating in the mid 1940s, although boat moorings remain, with pleasure craft tying up here during the summer months.

The pub itself is now 303 years old, built in 1692 to serve the needs of the village, but later extended as a coaching inn. It was known as the *'Newcastle Arms'* (cf pub of the same name at Southwell) until 1980 when it acquired its unique, and much more appropriate, name.

Muskham Ferry, North Muskham

NORTH WHEATLEY

SUN INN - *Low Street*

The delightful red-brick village of North Wheatley, had three inns in the early 1800s - the *'Red Lion'*, the *'Sherwood Ranger'* and the *'Sun'* (the innkeeper in 1832 was William Bosley). There was also a *'Plough'* by 1848 but today only the *'Sun'* survives - a very popular family pub. The unusual old sign of the *'Sun'* is set into the frontage of the pub and is presumably contemporary with its building (see pub of the same name at Eastwood, for further details).

Other *'Sun'* inns to be found in North Nottinghamshire include those at Darlton, Everton and Tuxford.

Sun Inn, North Wheatley

NOTTINGHAM

ADMIRAL DUNCAN - *Lower Parliament Street*

Opened in October 1935, this pub was sold by Home Brewery to Ansells in March 1979. It is named after Adam Duncan (1731-1804), an English admiral who achieved a notable victory over the Dutch near Camperdown (North Holland) in 1797 and later became Viscount Duncan of Camperdown.

ALMA - *Alfreton Road*

The name of this pub, opened in February 1936, relates to a river in the Crimea (Ukraine). It recalls the first battle of the Crimean War, when in September 1854 General Sir Colin Campbell (later Lord Clyde) led the Highland Brigade up the Heights of Alma to defeat a Russian army of 40,000 troops. National jubilation over this Allied victory was such that the name *'Alma'* became widely used for pubs, streets, and the daughters of soldiers who had fought in this battle. It was in fairly popular usage until the 1920s in all English-speaking countries.

ARBORETUM MANOR - *Arboretum Street*

The word 'arboretum' has a Latin derivative, meaning 'a botanic garden of trees,' and since this former hotel overlooks the Arboretum park, the name here is implicit.

Originally built as an inn in 1852, it became a hotel named the *'Spread Eagle'* in 1864 before being demolished in 1952 due to redevelopment of the area. It was rebuilt, but came to grief when destroyed by fire in 1969. Again re-built, it re-opened in 1972 as the *'Arboretum'* but in 1992 it again changed its name to its current title.

AVIARY - *Trent Bridge*

This building is one of the few remaining on view, which is shown on the "Location of Licensed Premises" map prepared by S.V. Cherry in 1947. Cherry was the Architectural Assistant to the Nottingham City Engineer at that time and his map shows the location of pubs which existed within the Nottingham Borough boundary between 1758 and 1764. Cherry's map is based on Badder and Peates' 1744 map of Nottingham. In those times *'The Aviary'* was known as the *'Town Arms'* - a name it held until December 1985. It then took its present (and unique) name, changing its decor to one based on caged birds. These have now been 'released' due to further refurbishment. However, the four flying ducks still used as a sign have managed to maintain their composure on an outer wall.

Town Arms, Trent Bridge (c. 1900)

BEHANS - *St James's Street*

November 1994 saw the opening of 'Behans', the recreation of a traditional Dublin pub in the heart of Nottingham, providing a venue for live Irish folk music, and the traditional pint of Guinness.

Dublin has produced many 'literary greats' including Beckett, Joyce, Shaw, O'Casey and Yeats. Another famous name to add to this list is that of Brendan Behan, one of Ireland's best-loved and flamboyant characters. His plays 'The Quare Fellow' and 'The Hostage' are well known.

The pub was opened by Brian Behan, who described the bar as a "fitting tribute" to his brother.

BELL INN - *Angel Row*

It is not certain when the original inn was founded on the present site at 18 Angel Row, but around 1976 the curator of the Castle Museum dated this building with a "crown post roof" as being between 1400 and 1450. In those days the inn was known by the sign of the *'Angel'* (from the Latin word *Angelus* meaning 'the noon-day bell') and served as the refectory of the Carmelite monastery then sited on Beastmarket Hill, just below the present premises. Naturally enough, the cellars form the oldest part of the building - the majority of these, which stretch the whole length of the inn, being Norman. Their age is revealed by the marks of the implements wielded by the monks who enlarged the cellars whilst in charge of the premises. These same cellars, carved out of the sandstone rock, are on the Civic Society's list of places to visit, with tours being conducted down to view them.

First mention of this ancient hostelry in the city's archives dates back to 1638, when Alderman Robert Sherwin bequeathed the profits of his half of *'a messuage known as the Bell Inn'* as an endowment for his Charity in favour of the poor of St Peter's parish. It must be said however, that this detail differs somewhat from the account in the *Bell's* own information booklet published in 1958 - the latter cites the date of the will as 1623, and the legacy *'to be equally divided between the poor of the two parishes of St Nicholas' and St James'* (the *Bell Inn* standing on the old boundary line) *each Michaelmas and Lady Day.'*

After the dissolution of the smaller monasteries by Henry VIII in 1536, the premises became a secular alehouse, taking its name from the Angelus bell which formerly tolled outside the monks' refectory. Its modern counterpart is clearly visible high on the (1810-1820) Regency facade of the present *'Bell'*, now a Listed Building. The original

Bell Inn, Nottingham

flagstones still exist in the main passageway, down which the horsemen and coachmen of a later era led their passengers first to the stables and then to the buttery.

At one time the *'Bell'* became a billet for soldiers of the Horse Guards regiment, perhaps attracted by the fearsome reputation of the local brew. The last of these to be registered were four Dragoons whose overnight stay in 1746 cost them three shillings. The story goes that this same Nottingham ale accounted for a Derby coachman seventy years on, in the year after Waterloo. Drunk in charge of his carriage, he overturned it and the horses, causing the death of one of his passengers.

It is of interest to note that in White's Directory of 1832 the ancient inn is shown as the *'Blue Bell,'* whether by accident or design, with that redoubtable cricketing character William Clarke as 'Mine Host' - having recently wooed and wed the widow of the licensee of the *'Trent Bridge Inn'* (qv).

An interesting gastronomic feature provided by the *Bell* during the Edwardian era was its 'Market Dinners' - with luncheons according to the hour of the day but definitely 'dinner' in quantity. These were prepared in the basement kitchen, carried up a flight of stairs into what is now the Elizabethan Bar, and up two further flights into what is now the kitchens but was then known as the 'Clubroom.' This 'Market Dinner' was a two-course meal including a real man-sized cut of the joint, the very best cheeses and a pint of old Nottingham Ale, all for the princely sum of one shilling - those were the days! Another feature at the *'Bell'* has always been its 'Critics Corner,' a bastion for men only - one of the last to survive in city pubs - until, in 1969, this Bar 'went mixed.'

In 1928, the year that building work started on the

Council House, Robert Jackson was the first to introduce snack-bar meals, and in 1974 permission was granted to place outside tables and seating in front of the pub. Pioneering continued here in the early 1960s when the 'Bell' became the first pub to launch tank beer in the City before joining the keg revolution.

In 1957 a tradition commenced at this pub which is still followed today. On the first Wednesday in November each year, two suckling pigs are roasted, carved and served to customers, and the president of the students' union at Nottingham University is honoured by having his or her name inscribed on a silver tankard after they have served a year in office.

But without doubt the one factor in the 'Bell's' long history that sets it apart from its peers today is the sturdy independence deriving from the 'Jackson Tradition,' which has continued unbroken here since 1898. In fact, when Hardys and Hansons took control of the 'Trip to Jerusalem' this left the 'Bell' as the only truly independent pub in Nottingham, in so far as the Jackson family doesn't rely on brewery money.

BLUE BELL INN - *Upper Parliament Street*

This old hostelry dates back to 1761, being rebuilt in 1904 - but prior to 1928 it was called the 'Bell.' The reason for the renaming was perhaps in memory of the bluebells which once covered the fields known as Burton Leys (cp. nearby Burton Street). This same sign was formerly found on Bluebell Hill, the uplands of which were massed with such flowers when Spencer Hall wrote these lines in Victorian times:

> *'Glad as a poet's thought, as wild and free,*
> *The lark from Bluebell Hill this morning springs!*
> *By St Ann's Well the thrush as sweetly sings*
> *While light the linnet's lay floats o'er the lea ...'*

The sign here, however - unlike that of the 'Blue Bell' at Attenborough (qv) - is represented by a single blue translucent hanging bell. This inn also has another frontage, and entrance on Forman Street.

BRITANNIA - *Beck Street*

The *Britannia* originally opened in 1934 and in 1964 became a 'Berni Inn', operating as such until 1974.

'Britannia' was the Roman name for Britain, its first mention of the symbolic female figure occurring in the diaries of Samuel Pepys and referring to a medal struck in 1665. The model for this figure was Frances Stewart, a mistress of Charles II and later Duchess of Richmond. 'Britannia,' resting on her familiar shield, had earlier appeared on Roman coins.

Some pub signs, like the one here, make use of the traditional coin representation - others refer in some way to a ship which bears the name of *Britannia,* the first of which was commissioned by the Royal Navy in 1682.

CASTLE INN - *Lower Parliament Street*

A familiar name, this, of course, but the pub here has only had it since November 1985, when its title was changed from the 'Nottingham Castle' because too many telephone enquiries were being received by the licensee from folk believing his house to be the real Castle!

In fact the present pub replaced the former 'Nottingham Castle' in November 1968, the latter having stood on an adjacent site for more than 150 years before being demolished to meet the march of progress. Mercifully, the break with tradition was quite brief, and there was a mere month's hiatus in drinking time for the regulars.

Inside the pub can be seen a series of old prints framed along the walls, showing views of Nottingham Castle from various vantage-points - the original engravings of these are to be found in the Art Gallery of the castle itself. Perhaps the most fascinating of all is a replica of the picture on the signboard outside which, unlike the sign of the 'Nottingham Castle' public house at Kirk Hallam near Ilkeston which shows the present building, portrays the castle in the 16th century. Those were the days when it really looked like a castle - with its medieval turrets, moat, drawbridge and all ...

The original castle, made of timber and earthworks, was built by order of William I in 1068. It was rebuilt in stone by Henry II in the late 12th century, enlarged by both King John and Henry III, and underwent its main construction by first Edward IV and then Richard III between 1468 and 1485. After this, it slowly fell into ruin and was mostly demolished in 1651 after the Civil War, following its defence against the Royalists by the garrison under Colonel Hutchinson (see entry in *Soldiers On Parade*). Two years earlier, Cromwell's Parliament had given the garrison the sum of £1,000 as a reward for holding Nottingham Town against these troops of Charles I.

Subsequently, William Cavendish (1592-1676) the Duke of Newcastle, cleared away the ruins, and began the transformation of the former castle into a ducal mansion. On Newcastle's death his son Henry completed the work. The work started in 1674, and took five years to complete at a total cost of £14,002! The 'castle' later passed to the Pelham Clinton Dukes of Newcastle. It was the 4th Duke's opposition to the Reform Bill which led, in 1831, to a mob burning down the great mansion. It remained a blackened and roofless shell for more than forty years. Its long place in the political history of England was over, and its new life was begun in the year 1876, opening as an Art Museum two years later in 1878.

CATTLE MARKET TAVERN - *London Road*

This important tavern (now a Free House) is leased by the City Corporation, and dates from 1928. Until 1993 it served the purpose indicated by its name, and its drinking facilities were distinctly irregular - bar open only twice a week (Mondays and Saturdays) from 10am to 3.30pm, plus Goose Fair Thursday at the beginning of October. A quick running commentary of the time would be on these lines:- "The bell goes at 10.30, when all present troop out for the Cattle Auction; half an hour later, it's possible to nip back for a 'quick one' before the Sheep Auction starts. Then it's the Pigs!"

The notice-board then at the entrance to the Cattle Market warned of the dangers of 'Sheep Scab' and 'Warbles' - the latter referring to the painful swellings on the hides of cattle, caused by the larvae of warble-flies - but this of course accompanied the general exodus to the modern premises at Newark, although the handsome casts of bulls' heads affixed to the gates are still there.

The tavern now plays host to the personnel of the Wholesale Market formerly held at Sneinton, and its opening hours remain, naturally, irregular - that is to say, at lunchtime and on Friday, Saturday and Sunday evenings.

CITY GATE TAVERN - *Long Row*

Until May 1994 this former inn had been known as the *'Dragon'* since March 1982, when to general surprise it achieved the dubious distinction of being the sign of the only *'George and Dragon'* (its previous name) in the whole of England whereby Saint George was vanquished by the dragon instead of vice-versa!

Previously our patron saint had been on view here for at least 200 years, having been shown as the *'George'* (although then possibly in honour of the reigning monarch, George II) on Cherry's map (see *'The Aviary'*, Trent Bridge for details). The inn itself was rebuilt in 1879, and now at last the Dragon is no more .

COACH AND HORSES - *Upper Parliament Street*

The original building is shown on Cherry's map (see *'The Aviary'*, Trent Bridge, for details) as the *'Waggon and Horses'* and is thought to have dated from about 1650. It later changed its name to the *'Bell and Holland,'* but in 1854 magistrates closed the house due to the bawdy behaviour of its patrons.

The inn was completely rebuilt in the early years of the 20th century in a similar style to the old building, but with only one Dutch gable instead of the previous two. The new building possessed one of the earliest slate roofs seen in Nottingham. These slates came from a quarry near Swithland in Leicestershire and were pegged-on with oak.

At one time the inn housed a boisterous *Copper Kettle Club*, mentioned in one of J.M. Barrie's tales entitled *'When A Man Is Single.'* Its date of founding is not recorded, but it was still going strong in 1883. A correspondent to the local Press, writing in this same year, describes the activities of the Club as follows:

Coach and Horses, Nottingham (c. 1903)

"*On the gas brackets of the cosy smoke-room are hung dainty little tin kettles, about two inches in diameter, and if any Member should relate any picturesque experience of his own - the truth of which his fellow-members hold in serious doubt - he has to wear one of these symbols in his coat buttonhole for the rest of the evening. There is an elected 'Chaplain' whose duty it is to fix the kettles to the coats of prevaricating members. He is a genial old cock, with a cluster of dark curly hair, and always referred to as 'Phineas' because he bears such a remarkable resemblance to the famous American showman Phineas T. Barnum. The initiation ceremony at the Club takes this form:- Upon the applicant for Membership being introduced by two sponsors, a copper kettle holding about a pint is filled with ale. The applicant then has to place the spout in his mouth and absorb the contents of the kettle without pausing for breath. It seems that very few candidates have so far failed to accomplish this modest feat, and there remains a formidable waiting-list for others who wish to aspire to the test. Among the assets of this remarkable Club is included a wooden box, to which those betrayed into using 'unparliamentary language' are required to contribute, in order to purge their offence. The elected Chaplain by common consent acts as adjudicator as to the size of the contribution ...*"

COOPERS ARMS - *Porchester Road*

During the 1914-18 War there was only one house anywhere in the vicinity of this pub. This stood right opposite, and was occupied by an old gentleman named Cooper, who was said to own a fair amount of property locally. It is possible that in negotiation with the brewery it was agreed that his family should appear in the pub's naming, but this is only conjecture.

It is more likely that this is one of the many Victorian pubs named after a particular trade that was flourishing at the time somewhere in the neighbourhood. There is another *'Coopers Arms'* in Bulwell (qv), too - as associations of tradesmen were in the habit of meeting on licensed premises. There have been in Nottingham a sizeable sample of these *Arms* - from a national collection of some 260 different names - of which the following remain:

'Foresters Arms' - St Anns Street
'Masons Arms' - Church Street, Basford
'Framesmiths Arms' - Main Street, Bulwell
'Mechanics Arms' - Alfred Street North
'Smiths Arms' - Radford Road, Hyson Green

Other examples can be added from areas within the county (see 'Blacksmiths Arms' at Everton).

City area pubs in this category, now no more, were as follows:-

'Bleachers Arms' - Lincoln Street
'Bricklayers Arms' - Lewis Street
'Butchers Arms' - Lincoln Street
'Coachmakers Arms' - St Anns Well Road
'Goldsmiths Arms' - Shakespeare Street
'Masons Arms' - Commercial Road, Bulwell
'Millers Arms' - St Agnes Street
'Moulders Arms' - Bovill Street, Radford
'Sawyers Arms' - Greyfriar Gate
'Smiths Arms' - Willoughby Street, Lenton

The reason why there should be a proliferation of these trades can be traced back, in the majority, to the Industrial Revolution. By the 1820s coaching and innkeeping had soared to the heights of prosperity, but the wind of change was already preparing to blow across the face of England, and after Stephenson's 'Rocket' had made its historic trial run in 1825 it was clear to all that the locomotive had come to stay. Pubs with such names as the 'Live And Let Live' marked the change of the era, proving to the disquieted world that the roads and inns were in danger of being neglected.

Intensive industry was now entering its domain - and in consequence, publicans were not slow to encourage Artisan customers, putting up signs in recognition of Colliers in mining communities, alongside foundries to salute Fettlers and Puddlers, in proximity to timber yards to tempt Joiners, Carpenters and Sawyers, and so on ...

It is indeed apparent that, at all stages throughout their history, our inn signs have faithfully recorded the coming and goings of the times. Many of these trades, of course, are either in the process of redundancy or have died out long since, but several of those included in the medieval guilds still cling to the initiation from apprentice to craftsmen. Sadly, the ancient craft of Cooperage is no longer one of the latter, since the barrels themselves (known as kegs or canisters) are nowadays manufactured out of metal.

COURT - *St. Peters Gate*

This pub, which occupies the former County Court building, is Grade II Listed. Furbished in a Victorian style, it opened on the 13th July, 1993.

CROSS KEYS - *Byard Lane*

There are very few hostelries which can claim that at one time they advertised *Ale sold here by the yard'* - but such indeed was the case when a notice to this effect was painted on the wall of this busy city pub in 1896 - thus making a pun on its location.

Whenever this claim was challenged, answer would be made by supplying the suspicious patron with a yard of glass or copper piping - on the same principle that a churchwarden pipe was called a yard of clay! Unsuspecting country cousins found that they were required to quaff the contents of this measure within a certain time, but if the urgency of their thirst was equal to the occasion, they were not prevailed upon to pay for the privilege! No doubt the old term 'ale-drapers' for publicans came about due to such hilarities which were a standing joke at many a tavern - as witness the 'Copper Kettle Club' at the *'Coach And Horses,'* Nottingham (qv).

Court, Nottingham

As to the origin of the name, the sign of the 'Crossed Keys' is of particular Christian significance. It is commonly found in Christian heraldry, referring to the Apostle (later St Peter) to whom Jesus said, "I will give unto thee the keys of the kingdom of heaven" (St Matthew chapter 16, verse 19). This same emblem became the personal badge of the Popes and a vital part in the make-up of the Arms of the Vatican City.

Early inns and ale-houses depended upon the Church and Crown for recognition, patronage and legal acceptance.

Not only did a favourite emblem encourage trade via those all-powerful authorities, but it also carried a 'certificate of approval' from them - in much the same way as the 'royal appointment' on a product today. In an age when ale was the staple family drink and most households brewed their own, it was necessary - if you wished to sell your product - to advertise your own expertise. Almost anyone could brew ale, but only ale tested and approved could be sold to the public. Thus, the sign of the 'Crossed Keys' showed approval by the (Catholic) Church and would therefore gain the trade of travelling dignitaries, pilgrims and the Christian populace at large. The same sign occurs in the Arms of various bishops whose cathedral is dedicated to St. Peter.

Mention of this hostelry first appeared in Pigot's Directory of 1822, and rebuilding took place in 1900. The news-magazine of the Nottingham branch of CAMRA reported in 1993 after its recent 'face-lift' that the 'Cross Keys' had undergone a tasteful refurbishment and redecoration which enhanced all the best features of its late Victorian pedigree. Concerning the latter, the December 1994 issue of the local magazine 'Bygone Nottingham' featured the following story which no doubt explained why this same pedigree had been tarnished prior to the rebuilding programme which followed soon afterwards ...

"At the end of the nineteenth century the owners of Cross Keys' pub in the Lace market area of Byard
Lane were mystified as to why their beer was disappearing so quickly. Then they noticed that there was a gang of navvies just down the road working on the Great Central Railway tunnel. Using their initiative, they had put their skills to good use during their free time and managed to tunnel into the cellars of the pub, helping themselves to some of the stock on the way!

In their defence, they claimed that railway building was "very thirsty work."

DUKE OF DEVONSHIRE - *Carlton Road*

Like a number of Home Brewery owned houses, this pub has a plaque outside which recalls part of its history. It reads:

"This Public House has for many years been known locally as 'THE MADHOUSE.' This nickname originated at the time when patients from the General Lunatic Asylum, originally sited on Dakeyne Street opposite, were allowed out to visit families and friends and also to visit the original public house built on this site. The Lunatic Asylum was opened on 12th February 1812, the total cost being £21,000. Accommodation in 1816 was provided for a total of 84 men and women. Part of the Asylum wall is still to be seen at the top end of Dakeyne Street."

EARL HOWE - *Carlton Road*

This gallant naval officer (shown in uniform on the signboard here but minus his tricorn hat) is Admiral Richard Howe (1726-1799), a member of an old Langar family who gave famous sons to serve their country. The admiral's two brothers both became generals and, like him, distinguished themselves in battle against the enemy. He himself was created Earl in 1788, the same year in which he was promoted to First Lord of the Admiralty. He has a monument in St Paul's, but is buried in the village church at Langar which overlooks the Vale of Belvoir.

He was recalled to sea-going command in 1793 as Commander-in-Chief of the Channel Fleet, and in the following year he achieved a spectacular victory over the French in the naval battle off Ushant. Second only in importance to Trafalgar, it became known as 'The Glorious First of June' when seven French ships of the line were taken, and six were towed triumphantly into Spithead. The battle destroyed the morale of the French Navy and paved the way for Nelson's later victories.

Earl Howe, Nottingham

Fellows, Morton and Clayton, Nottingham

FELLOWS, MORTON AND CLAYTON -
Canal Street

This sounds like a firm of family solicitors - but in fact the pub takes its name from an old, well-known canal haulage company which previously occupied this site. Situated alongside the Nottingham Canal Museum, there is no connection between the two, other than the fact that they are both full of narrow-boat artifacts and paraphernalia. As can be seen from the stone inset high on the outer wall, the building dates from 1895 - but did not become a pub until December 1981, having previously served as a warehouse and also, at one time, a shop.

This is nowadays the only pub in Nottingham where beer is brewed on the premises, and the brewhouse itself can be viewed at the back through an extra-large window. Below, and extending towards the canal is the beer-garden where the hanging flower baskets in summer have twice earned the 'Fellows' first prize in the *Nottingham in Bloom* competition in recent years.

FILLY AND FIRKIN - *Mansfield Road*

On the 12th July 1993 one of the best-known of the city's pubs, which had for years rejoiced in the patriotic name the *'Rose of England'*, the cricketing name of the *'Yorker,'* and briefly the mundane *'City Alehouse'*, suddenly changed to the much more intriguing combination of the *'Filly and Firkin'* - the first name having either two or four legs, whichever you fancy, and the second representing a barrel of only 9-gallons capacity.

The building itself (standing on the corner of York Street and Mansfield Road) dates from 1898, and is a superb example of the architectural imagination of the much-respected Watson Fothergill whose father-in-law Samuel Hage was a founder member of Mansfield Brewery. The pub's history is well worth detailing, as follows:-

The original name of the very first pub on this site was, amazingly enough, in Portuguese - the *'Filho da Puta,'* meaning 'Son of a Whore.' Its first landlord was the stud groom of Sir William Maxwell, the owner of this horse which won the St. Leger in the year of Waterloo, 1815. The pub became the *'Rose of England'* in 1876 but it was pulled down in 1896 to make way for the new Victoria Railway Station. In 1898 it was rebuilt for

Filly and Firkin, Nottingham

the Nottingham Brewery Company, and existed under this splendid name until October 1967, when it was restyled by Whitbread as the *'Yorker'* - with a handsome 'pairing' sign featuring on one side the bushy-bearded W.G. Grace and on the other, the hatchet-faced features of his Test Match opponent the Australian 'Demon Bowler' Frederick Spofforth. He invented the infamous 'Yorker' delivery which led to the legend of *'The Ashes'* in 1882. When Ansell's took over, they replaced the signboard with another 'double-sider,' this time depicting two cartoon-type cricketers of a batsman and a bowler. The original, beautifully carved wooden 'Rose of England' can still be seen over the porch.

The present sign, as may be expected, is also of a humorous nature, and follows the almost inevitable trend these days of being - well, at least a little bizarre even if pertinently alliterative ...

FIVE WAYS HOTEL - *Edwards Lane*

Opened in April 1936, this mock Tudor-style house takes its name from its position at a point where five roads converge.

FLETCHER AND FIRKIN - *Castle Road*

Known since 1980 as the *'Old Castle'*, this pub stands almost opposite the gatehouse entrance to Nottingham Castle. The new name, in use since August 1995, combines the medieval word 'fletcher', an arrow maker, with 'firkin', a beer barrel with only 9 gallons capacity. The amusing new signboard illustrates this accordingly.

The building is another of those idiosyncratic concepts of local architect Watson Fothergill (see also the *'Filly and Firkin'*).

FOUNTAIN - *Bridlesmithgate*

This pub was rebuilt and reopened under its present name in February 1966, before that it was the *'Gate Inn,'* dating from October 1937. The name *'Fountain'* is a reminder of the well-known 'Walter Fountain' put up in Lister Gate in 1866 at a cost of £1,000 by the son of John Walter following the latter's death in 1847. It was removed for road widening in 1950.

John Walter himself had been not only the town's MP, but the proprietor of that world-famous daily newspaper 'The Times.' The tower which had stood for so long in his honour was 50 feet high and had at its base four drinking fountains, each containing a chained metal cup topped by a medallion portrait of the great man. The former signboard reminded us of the old drinking fountain, which once stood in Lister Gate.

FOX - *Valley Road*

Opened in November 1938, this is built on a reclaimed river-bed and its foundations go down 25 feet. It was reopened after refurbishment in 1987 by John Barnwell, then the manager of Notts County Football Club.

An explanation for the origin of the name here can be found by referring to the *'Fox'* at Sneinton.

Gatsbys, Nottingham

GATSBYS - *King Edward Street*

Formerly the *'Central Tavern'* until June 1983, when this distinctly unpretentious name (suitable for its rather seedy surroundings, some said) changed to the pretentious title it now has - presumably meant to hint at the high-living style of the 1920s by the American upper classes, and referring in particular to the fictitious playboy created by the American novelist Scott Fitzgerald in his book *'The Great Gatsby.'*

GENEROUS BRITON - *Alfreton Road*

In the 1880s, this Victorian pub was run by a fellow named Bill Hulse who in his former butchering days had chopped-off several digits belonging to the notorious criminal Charlie Peace.

This unpremeditated act occurred in self-defence when Hulse was driving home in his trap from selling a beast at market. It seems that Peace held up his horse on some pretext or other and grabbed the side of the trap whilst loudly demanding money. He was armed with a revolver, and seeing the desperate nature of this unexpected customer, Hulse picked up a cleaver lying handy beside him and made a professional slash at the menacing hand, parting several fingers from their rueful owner. He then drove off and, on reaching Nottingham, reported the matter to the police, who found the severed remains in the bottom of the trap.

Perhaps this sharp lesson put the brakes on Charlie's infamous activities. It was soon after this digital mishap that he was arrested, tried, and finally hanged for his crimes at Armley Gaol, Leeds, in 1879.

The political reason for the unusual title of this pub can be found under the similar naming of the village pub at Costock. Perhaps in the former case it should have been called instead the *'Butcher And Cleaver'*!

GOLDEN FLEECE - *Mansfield Road*

Though this Victorian pub, whose colourful signboard depicts the fleece of a ram hanging from a tree, appears to take its name from the Greek legend concerning Jason and the Argonauts - it is more likely that it is styled after the Knights of the Golden Fleece, a chivalric Order founded in 1429 for the protection of the church.

The pub itself has a number of storeys, three of which are above ground level, with three to be found beneath the surface in caves. At the lowest point, some 30 feet below the surface, the cave contains what appear to be ancient pick marks. It is thought that at one time these caves may have been used as a cattle pen - a theory borne out by a number of holes in the walls of the caves, suggesting that at one time, wooden beams may have been fitted to them to form a fence. On occasions, the current landlord runs pre-booked guided tours of these caves - a trip well worth exploring!

There is also a *'Golden Fleece'* at Upper Broughton.

Golden Fleece, Nottingham

GOLDSMITH PITCHER -
Goldsmith Street

This imposing, early 20th century pub was known, for many years, as the *'Spread Eagle'* until June 1984 when, with a radicalism matched only by the students attending the nearby Trent Polytechnic, it became *'Fagins'*. They felt that the change of name would create the right image to encourage these very students to drink there. It still attracts them today, with its 'Student Nights' and convenient location, but since November 1994 it has been renamed the *'Goldsmith Pitcher'* — imaginative and unique!

GOOSEBERRY BUSH - *Peel Street*

This pub, opened in December 1984, takes its name from the fact that it was built on the site of the former Women's Maternity Hospital.

GROSVENOR - *Mansfield Road*

Above the main entrance to this Home Brewery owned house is a large plaque detailing its history and the likely origin of its name. It reads:

"The property and surrounding land was purchased by John Robinson (who in 1875 started the Home Brewery Company Ltd.) on July 4th, 1873. The premises were described, at that time, as a 'retail beer house' known for many years as the Black's Head. The name Grosvenor Inn probably derives from the fact that The Grosvenor was also the name of the last horse to win at Forest Racecourse (on the site of the public house) before its demise and relocation to Colwick Park - Nottingham's then new racecourse. It should be noted that there is a restrictive covenant in the deeds preventing the erection of a steam engine in or upon any part of the premises."

Grosvenor, Nottingham

Since the early 1900s, the large white horse which stood on an archway by the entrance to the pub, was a very well known local landmark. This horse has now been vandalised beyond repair. However, high up at the front of the inn, another white horse can be seen emerging from a barrel - unusual and amusing!

HAND AND HEART - *Derby Road*

Named after a local Friendly Society in the 1860s, this pub's back room is hewn out of solid sandstone.

Hearty Good Fellow, Nottingham

HEARTY GOOD FELLOW - *Mount Street*

A pub of this name has stood on Mount Street since at least 1799. The present pub was built in the 1960s when its predecessor was demolished, along with many other buildings, to make way for the development of Maid Marian Way. The large and jovial figure to be seen on the outside wall suggests the popular ballad sung in the music-halls of a previous era:

'I am a hearty good fellow, I live at my ease
I work when I'm ready, I play when I please.
With my bottle and glass many hours I do pass.
Sometimes with a friend, sometimes with a lass.'

Another pub with this convivial name can be found in Southwell.

HOLE IN THE WALL - *North Sherwood Street*

Verses from the book of Ezekiel (chapter VIII, verses 7-10) are thought to have been responsible for earlier examples of this curious name (*'... and when I looked, behold, a hole in the wall'*) although the following verses are by no means inviting! Another belief is that the sign referred to the hole in the wall of a debtors' prison (see mention of the latter in the entry for the *'White Hart'* at Lenton) through which the inmates received money, broken meat, or other donations from the charitably-inclined. Two other reasons for the name were (1) a hole in the wall of a cell in which a condemned man was confined, through which he was allowed to speak before his execution: (2) a hole in a leper's den through which certain brave spirits of the Church would thrust their hands to bless the dying men and women inside. Yet another derivation could be from a snug and narrow entrance to a pub from a comparatively wide street (as formerly at Ashby-de-la-Zouch).

A remarkable feature of this area (like others in and around the city) is that it was originally built on catacombs, and at one time there were underground passages linking the neighbouring

Hole in the Wall, Nottingham

pubs. Building work being carried out adjacent to the *'Hole In The Wall'* during 1980 uncovered a large hidden cellar carved out of solid sandstone, thought to be the only remains of another pub long since gone - possibly the one of the same name which was built in 1860. As it was unable to accommodate more than 12 at a time, it was pulled down and rebuilt in the 1930s. Whitbread's records show that in August 1935 it was leased by the City Corporation to Nottingham Brewery (closed in May 1952) for a period of 99 years. The aforesaid cellar, by the way, was about 40 feet long and 14 feet wide, had a brick arch ceiling, and contained a number of earthenware pots and glass bottles, a large mirror and a bottle rack. After major refurbishment in December 1984 the present pub (styled by its predecessor as *'Ye Hole In Ye Wall'*) became a Mansfield Brewery house in March 1994.

IMPERIAL - *St James's Street*

The shell of the present house was erected just after the turn of the century, but the facade itself, being older, counts as a Listed building. Further extensions took place in July 1964. In 1900, the end of sixty years of Imperial rule was imminent and the death of Queen Victoria close at hand. For that reason one would expect to see on the signboard some portrayal of a Raj concept - the Taj Mahal, perhaps - but disappointingly, the passer-by has to be content with a crown perched on top of what appears to be a lamp-post . . .

Today it is difficult to realise that, in more alcoholic times, there used to be at least half-a-dozen pubs in St James's Street. One of these was formerly a Music Hall, as is evident when one steps inside the present 'Potter's House.'

JACEYS - *Heathcote Street*

This progressively-minded and music-orientated pub was established in November 1982 by two young gentlemen named Jim and Charlie - Messrs. J. and C., naturally. They have now moved on, but their notion of updating the pub as a venue for 'Alternative Trendies' is continued by their successors, and successfully so. It is not exactly one of the new breed of Fun Pubs (or whatever), but neither is it anything like the rather unsavoury place it once was when tied to a local brewery.

In fact 'Jaceys', or rather, its predecessor has had a long and honourable history. It was formerly known as the 'Old Plough', and there is also reference to it as the 'Plow' in Borough Records dated August 1705.

JUBILEE - *Marmion Road*

This pub opened on the 14th July, 1977, a month after the Queen's Silver Jubilee Thanksgiving celebrations had commenced on the 7th June in London with a State pageantry.

LANGTRY'S - *South Sherwood Street*

This house has existed under its present name since April 1981. Before that it had been known as the 'Peach Tree' (a pub name thought to be unique) since 1761, and its large illuminated sign after dark was once a sight to behold.

Lillie Langtry (1853-1929) was a famous actress and noted beauty, known as 'The Jersey Lily' (and commemorated by a pub of this name at Bristol). She was born in St Helier, Jersey, as Emilie Charlotte Le Breton. Edward VII was one of her most ardent admirers, as was Oscar Wilde, who wrote the celebrated play *Lady Windermere's Fan* as a vehicle for her talent. She made one film, in 1913, *His Neighbour's Wife,* and had her portrait painted by both Sir John Millais and Edward Burne-Jones.

The pub itself has a photograph of the actress on display in the bar, together with posters that remind us of her appearance at the Theatre Royal in 1885. Sadly, the old signboard portraying the lovely Lillie has been removed after a recent refurbishment.

Other pubs named after her, also called *Langtry's,* can be found in Lillie Road, Fulham, in Norwich and in Southsea where, in 1989, a trunk full of her costumes and other possessions was discovered in a secret alcove during extensions.

Limelight, Nottingham

LIMELIGHT - *Wellington Circus*

A most appropriate name, as this pub adjoins the Nottingham Playhouse which, over the past thirty years, has been the venue for contemporary and traditional theatrical and musical works. It has given Nottingham theatregoers the opportunity of seeing many of the great stars of the stage. It is not uncommon to see familiar faces of the entertainment world relaxing in the 'Limelight' whilst in Nottingham for a performance.

'Limelight' was invented by Captain T. Drummond and was produced by a blowtorch flame directed against a block of quicklime. To be 'in the limelight' means to be the centre of attention, as are the actors on a stage.

LINCOLNSHIRE POACHER - *Mansfield Road*

This building started life as unnamed beerhouse in the 1830s, but became the 'Old Grey Nag's Head' at a later date, perhaps in rivalry to the 'Nag's Head' (qv) almost opposite. It first opened its doors under its present name in June 1989 - the name of a folk-song once familiar to generations of schoolchildren and which could be described as carrying the banner for Bateman's Brewery at Wainfleet near Skegness, whose ale was introduced into Nottingham in this manner.

Inside the pub - whose walls are a mass of memorabilia - can be seen a brass plaque which proclaims that the *Poacher* is twinned with the 'In der Wildeman' bar in central Amsterdam, owned and run by Henk Eggens. The twinning of pubs may seem an eccentric idea, but when it is realised that it came from the jovial Henk, joint winner, with popular local licensee Tony Green, of the Eccentric Landlord competition at the Nottingham Beer Festival of 1991, then it seems perfectly natural.

LION - *Clumber Street*

Rather surprisingly, although there are hundreds of pubs (and hotels) entitled the 'Red Lion' - and some named after lions of other colours - it is unusual to find one simply called the 'Lion' (as witness this particular example and others in Basford and Worksop), especially as the lion was probably the first beast to appear in Heraldry.

The premises at 11, Clumber Street were leased by the Town Corporation to its occupier in 1646, its address then being Number 2, Long Row (it joined with Number 1 in 1694). Restyled as the 'Whyte Lion' in 1684, it was rebuilt at some time before 1848, in which year it was renamed as simply the 'Lion.' In 1675 it had been mentioned as an inn by a celebrated traveller who had publicly praised the excellence of its beds, its food and its ale. A century later it housed the Duke of Cumberland, brother of George III, when he came to Nottingham in order to receive the freedom of the town.

According to the Nottingham Date Book this same inn was, from its foundation, the headquarters of the local Tory

Lincolnshire Poacher, Nottingham

Party - whereas the Whigs centred themselves at the 'Moot Hall Inn' and removed from there to the 'Blackamoor's Head.' The 'Whyte Lion' itself, apart from its political affiliations, (including the Cavalier Party, followers of Charles II, which also met here regularly), upheld its prominent position locally for many years as 'the best place to go to and be seen at.' It fronted on to the Market Place, and its yard was at the rear, opening on to Cow Lane. The western side of this was the rear wing, which became part of the present 'Lion.'

Cow Lane, by the way, was widened and renamed Clumber Street in 1812, in honour of the Duke of Newcastle, the area's principal landowner. It has always been a narrow thoroughfare, and at one time a great beam traversed it on which was the swinging sign of the 'Whyte Lion.' This beam crossed Cow Lane at the end of Long Row, and (again, according to the Nottingham Date Book) when criminals were conveyed from the gaols to the gallows *'the beam was made much use of by a string of vulgar people, who indulged their morbid taste with the sight of the malefactors passing underneath them on their way to execution.'*

During the coaching era, this inn was one of several in Nottingham providing an overnight stay for passengers. In fact Borough Records of 1761 reveal that in that year alone it had stabling for as many as 200 horses, with coaches continually arriving 'from all points of the compass' and 'departing for anywhere and everywhere.' The local historian William Stevenson, in his book 'Bygone Notts,' recollects the fame of the 'White Lion' as a coaching-house during the early part of the 19th century. *'I well remember the open yard, the busy coach office in the rear of the late Mr. Skinner's (wine & spirits) shop, and the many coaches with their red-coated guards, the sound of whose clarions were so familiar to the ear . . .'* By 1814, when Wellington's armies were assembling for a final onslaught against Napoleon, the inn was serving three lines of daily coaches to Leicester, Leeds and London. In 1815, the year in which victory at Waterloo caused church bells to ring throughout England, the *Nottingham Review* carried an advertisement for a coach journey starting from the 'White Lion' at 5am which was scheduled to arrive, some 200 miles later, at Holyhead in no more than 32 hours. The fares to be £4 (inside) and 42 shillings (outside).

By 1830 the 'White Lion' had eleven lines of daily coaches - to London, Scotland, Leeds, Manchester, Liverpool, Birmingham, Lincoln, Hull, Derby, Newark and Leicester - also two other lines to London and Doncaster every two days. Shortly after this, however, and with the advent of the railway, the inn's coaching services gradually disappeared. It did have the distinction of being the last house in Nottingham to be associated with the old mode of travelling - namely the Mansfield and Sheffield mail service, which was continued long after the opening of the Midland Railway in 1839.

Apart from its fame as a coaching inn, history remembers it for its sporting associations, and as a regular rendezvous for the local gentry and nobility. At one notable meeting here, in 1776, it was decided to erect a grandstand by the side of the racecourse on The Forest (4 miles long and reaching to Radford), and the considerable sum of £2,460 was subscribed forthwith. This grandstand was built the following year, but in 1891 the Town Corporation decided not to appoint a Race Committee, and in consequence racing on The Forest was discontinued. The promoters then purchased Colwick Park, on which was built the now nationally-recognised racecourse (see the entry for the 'Starting Gate' at Colwick).

Cockfighting remained the most attractive 'sport' during most of the inn's long history, and it catered quite extensively for its patrons - mostly wealthy businessmen and aristocratic landowners, who wagered huge sums of

Lion, Nottingham

money on the results of such gruesome combats. During the August race meetings in 1695, the best blood of England (mostly blue in those days, of course) gathered here. The early part of each day was spent in the great cockpit, which had been installed in 1668 and was the scene of many of the country's most important contests. This pit was still in existence until 1890 and then used as a chandlery, its entrance being via Pawlett's Yard in Long Row. A pub called the *'Old Iron Pot'* once stood here until it closed down in 1916, but in those days of course it was literally connected to the inn.

The year 1763 witnessed a great contest between the gamecocks of the Gentlemen of London and those of the aristocracy of Nottingham. The London fowls were stowed away in the cellar of the inn, where access was later obtained to them by some daring townsman. To influence the betting in his favour, he poisoned the birds' water with arsenic and rendered them incapable of emitting even a squawk. The Nottingham Date Book reported as follows: *"This malfeasance led to an association for the defence of game fowls being formed in the three counties of Notts, Leics. and Derby, its HQ being fixed at the 'Red Lion' in Pelham Street, and a reward of £50 being offered for the apprehension of the dastardly delinquent."*

In July 1772 a great battle was fought in the cockpit between the Gentlemen of London and Derbyshire. The conditions were 'to weigh 51 cocks in the main, and to fight for 10 guineas a battle and 200 guineas for the champion' - a match which Derbyshire won by 16 bouts to 11. It was not until 1849 that this cruel 'sport' was made illegal.

One of the patriotic scenes affecting Old Nottingham in times of war took place in September 1794, when Admiral Sir John Warren (qv) returned home (after sharing with Admiral Earl Howe (qv) in the separate defeats of the French fleet) and, after the populace had paraded him around the Market Place, he alighted at the *'White Lion'* and partook of refreshment. The Date Book for that year reports, *'The people continuing to crowd around the inn, the gallant hero addressed them from a window, thanking them in the warmest terms for the honour they were conferring, and assuring them that it would henceforth be the pride of his life to deserve well of his King and Country.'*

LOGGERHEADS INN - *Cliff Road*

Mentioned for the first time in Borough Records in 1743, this old inn was at one time the headquarters of those notorious highwaymen Nick Nevison and Dick Turpin. Their agent, a man known as Coney, was a close friend of Lanky Dobbs, the landlord of the *'Loggerheads'*, his wife was recognised as 'Bounding Bella' and followed the profession of chimney-sweep! According to Paul Herring who, in 1926, wrote a graphic series of articles in the local Press on our city's inns and street names, *"this lovely trio were the leaders of as petty a gang of thieves and cut-throats as ever lived in Nottingham. When the Marsh grew too hot to hold them they migrated to the 'Salutation' until things cooled down, then returned to their headquarters."*

This former hot spot of Narrow Marsh once had a quaint sign which depicted two comical-looking yokels in full grin above the motto *'We Be Loggerheads Three'* - the beholder being (by sardonic inference) the remaining member of this trio. Some authorities believe that Shakespeare referred to a similar sign when he asked, through one of his characters in *'Twelfth Night'*, "Did you never see the picture of *'We Three?'* (Loggerheads be).

The present writer once saw another example of this curious sign at the tavern which has given its name to the village of Loggerheads, found on the A53 near Market Drayton in Shropshire. There also used to be a pub named *'We Three Loggerheads'* in Tonbridge, Kent. However, having for some years being connected with maritime matters himself, he prefers to believe that the *'Loggerheads Inn'* owes the derivation of its name to the term applied to the stout wooden post built into the stern of a boat, to which a rope is attached. This pub became popular with boatmen from the nearby canal.

The present pub is now the only one left out of a total of 17 in what was formerly the Marsh area.

Loggerheads, Nottingham

An unusual feature is the War Memorial board on the outside wall. The present board has been placed there by the Royal British Legion, in memory of the men killed in the two Great Wars. The original board was subscribed to by the people of the district, and on it was a list of names of those who died in the 1914-18 War (this board was replaced by a metal one in August 1977). The list was painted on paper, in a glass frame. As the paper became faded it was replaced, and a vase of flowers stood in front. Poppy wreaths were placed there each November 11th. However the people who cherished the memory of their menfolk moved from the district when old properties were cleared in the old Narrow Marsh area.

Another feature is a mammoth fig tree which soars high above the remarkable warren of cave-cellars and appears to be growing out of the cliff rock itself. In times past it has borne fruit in abundance, but not just lately - much to the present landlord's disappointment!

It is worthy of note that between 1930 and 1974 the pub was in the hands of only one family - the Rileys.

LORD NELSON - *Carlton Street*

This is the oldest of the pubs in the county which honours the name of our most famous admiral. Parts of it date back to 1668, and beneath the building is a well said to have a depth of 64 feet.

MARCH HARE - *Carlton Road*

The idea for this most unusual sign came from Major D. Warwick, one of the brewery directors at Warwick & Richardsons of Newark, now taken over by John Smiths of Tadcaster. The inn formerly standing on these premises was named the *'Carlton'* and something quite different in title was felt to be necessary, perhaps with a twin allusion - something truly rural yet with a literary connotation! At any rate, the *'March Hare'* emerged out of all this, and when built in 1958, was thought to be the only pub in Britain having such a name.

A youthful Englebert Humperdinck was just one of the acts which, on Friday nights, drew the customers in large numbers.

MECHANICS ARMS - *Alfred Street North*

This is not far from the prestigious 'Nottingham Mechanics,' a unique institution formed in 1837 firstly in St James's Street with a founder-membership of 400, at a time when Mechanic's Institutes were being set up in every major city in England to instruct and educate artisans and mechanics. They all originated from the work undertaken by Dr. George Birkbeck, who saw the need to educate under-privileged young people.

Education became so popular in Nottingham through 'The Mechanics' that it was found necessary to set up other educational establishments within the city area. This led to the formation of a University College in Nottingham which opened in 1881. Later, through the influence of Sir Jesse Boot (later Lord Trent), it became the University College of Nottingham in July 1928, attaining full university status in 1948.

MILL - *Woolpack Lane*

This pub is built on the site of Arkwright's original mill, and was opened in December 1981. A pity, indeed, that it wasn't named either the 'Hockley Mill' or, better still, as the successor to the *'Sir Richard Arkwright'* (in Arkwright Street until December 1974). However, it does have some memorabilia.

Sir Richard Arkwright (1732-1792) was a native of Preston, and in early life traded as a barber and travelling hair-dealer based in Bridlesmithgate. Becoming interested in mechanical problems, he set himself the task of inventing an improved cotton-spinning machine, and took out his first patent when his own horse-powered Hockley Mill was built in 1769. At this time the leading machine was that invented by James Hargreaves (see entry for the *'Spinning Jenny'*), but the yarn it produced could only be used for weft, it was not compact enough for warp threads.

Arkwright therefore experimented until, by adopting an arrangement of rollers that moved with different velocities, he succeeded in perfecting his 'spinning frame' - which successfully produced a yarn that could be used for warp as well as weft. After this he entered into partnership with Mr Jehediah Strutt, a former mayor of Derby, and became a manufacturer on a large scale. In 1771 Arkwright established the first spinning-mill worked by water-power at Cromford in Derbyshire. This revolutionised the cotton industry and gained him a knighthood.

NAG'S HEAD - *Mansfield Road*

Mention of this old pub is found in Pigot's Directory of 1822. Its present address dates from 1834, before that it was in Mansfield Terrace.

In olden days, the gallows of Nottingham was situated on the Forest side of Mansfield Road, near to where the present cemetery gates stand. Convicted criminals had to wend their way (or be taken by cart, if they were important enough) from the county and town prisons on High Pavement to meet their fate upon what was then called Gallows Hill.

Gradually the custom arose that the landlord of the *'Nag's*

Nag's Head, Nottingham

Head' - which stood just at the point where the gallows came into view - should provide a last jug of Nottingham Ale to any condemned man before he was 'turned off' at Gallows Hill. The last hanging here was of a certain William Wells on the 2nd April 1827 for highway robbery - the first here being in 1701 for the same reason.

According to legend, ghostly occurrences took place at this former coaching-house as recently as 1985. The gambling machine suddenly started spinning on its own with nobody near it, and a chair started to rock back and forth on its own. Perhaps one of the former prisoners came back for another free drink?

An explanation for the origin of this pub's name can be found by referring to the *'Nag's Head'* at Lambley.

NARROW BOAT - *Canal Street*

This old pub is shown on S.V. Cherry's map (see *'The Aviary'*, Trent Bridge, for details) as the *'Bowling Green'* by Leen Side. In November 1980 it changed its name to the *'Narrow Boat,'* and the signboard shows a handsome picture of a canal barge, a belated tribute to the fact that, in 1792, work on the Nottingham Canal had begun. A year later, the first stretch of the canal, from the town to Trent Bridge, was opened - with a Canal Wharf and Canal Street itself coming later.

Navigation Inn, Nottingham

NAVIGATION INN - *Wilford Street*

According to the Stretton Manuscripts kept in the County Library, this old pub was built in 1787. It was taken over by Banks's as their first City central-area house in 1985 and sits on a raised area affording an excellent view of the adjacent canal locks.

The name here is a reference to the canals or 'navigations' as they were once popularly called.

NEWMARKET INN - *Lower Parliament Street*

This old place, established about the turn of the century, was blessed with the rural name of the *'Plough and Sickle'* until 1926 when it changed to its current title to mark the opening of the new Central Market in Nottingham, located just across the road from the pub. There used to be a slaughterhouse at the rear, and then a home for donkeys. It is thought that there may be caves leading from under the pub to Greens Windmill in Sneinton.

The pub closed for refurbishment in 1995, emerging in the August as a splendid 'Victorian Gin Palace'.

NEWS HOUSE - *Canal Street and St. James's Street*

Both these pubs having the same name possess a venerable vintage, the former having been mentioned in the 1848 County Directory and the other in the first Town Directory of 1799. Like others of this name, these pubs employed professional newsreaders in times past to inform the illiterate masses and patrons-at-large of news in general (and sometimes in detail, too) concerning elections at home and naval or military victories overseas.

In the days before mass-circulation and mass-communication, it was deemed necessary for the *Nottingham Journal* and the *Nottingham Evening News* to print special 'Stop Press' editions by which professional readers at these two hostelries in particular could keep the townspeople up-to-date about important topical affairs. Newsboys would run around the streets shouting "Read all about it" - and the details of the Headlines would find plenty of literate buyers at all times of the day (or night).

NUMBER TEN - *Upper Parliament Street*

This pub was originally recorded as the *'Fox and Owl'* in an 1834 Directory, and changed to the *'Fox'* (still shown as a stone figure high on the facade) in 1928. Although its street number remains as 97, it changed to a more modern 'image' as from January 1989, its present 'name' suggesting the prestigious address in London's Downing Street. Initially there was a large picture of Winston Churchill gracing the interior, but this has now gone!

Incidentally, the sign of the *'Fox'* has been used since the late 15th century. It has been disappearing from urban areas in recent years, but is still common in the country, especially where fox hunting occurs.

OLD ANGEL - *Stoney Street*

Dating from 1676 in the reign of Charles II, this old hostelry can trace its varied history through Borough Records - even such sordid details as that mentioned on the 7th February 1736, *"The Constable Jury present Joseph Roe for keeping his cart in the street near the 'Old Angel.'"*

In Victorian times people used to come here before going to work in the Lace Market - but not for a pint! They went to offer prayers in the Chapel above the pub. The Chapel was built by a lace manufacturer who was obviously concerned with the salvation of his employees. The Chapel is still there - a long, draughty room with a lofty ceiling and umpteen pictures of the Royal Family framed around the walls. It was once used as a meeting-place by the Royal and Ancient Order of Buffaloes (Friendly Society).

An old haunt of the infamous outlaw Dick Turpin, the pub also used to house a soup kitchen. It is reputedly haunted by ghostly footsteps which are accompanied by the rattling of keys - supposedly those of a police sergeant who died here when a chimney collapsed on him in 1801 whilst he was working in the kitchen.

The sign of the '*Angel*' has been in use since the Middle Ages, reflecting the early connection between religious establishments and travellers' hostels.

OLD DOG AND PARTRIDGE - *Lower Parliament Street*

Thought to date from 1916, this old pub used to stand opposite the so-called '*Original Dog and Partridge*' which had been built during the latter part of the 19th century (the railway line into Victoria Station ran directly beneath it) and was pulled down in January 1970. Originally it had been known as the '*Dog and Partridge Brewhouse*' before Shipstone's took it over in 1890. When this present pub was built during World War I, the former house naturally assumed the name by which it announced to the world its premier position, as having been the 'original,' and there already, before its 'rival' had the audacity to put in an appearance.

The current pub won first prize in Shipstone's immensely-popular 'Paint-a-Sign Competition' culminating in July 1982 with the winning entries being hung in the city's Art Gallery. Its mournful-looking bloodhound, flopping down in picturesque meadow-land with the elusive partridge perched triumphantly on its head, has since been remembered as a masterpiece of inn-sign artistry. The following year however, the pub was refurbished and decorated in that curiously unappealing shade of cobalt blue - and the present less-attractive sign shows a King Charles spaniel gazing at a partridge perched upon a tree-stump.

The name itself is an allusion to the hunting of game-birds which, after being shot, are then retrieved by the dog.

Old Vic, Nottingham

OLD VIC - *Fletcher Gate*

This pub started life as a factory in Nottingham's Lace Market, but had a new lease of life as a pub in 1981 when Jimmy Etherington bought it, and supervised its conversion. With his interest in Old Time Music Hall he included facilities for live entertainment, attracting big names from the Jazz world in particular. Many regulars were very disappointed when it closed in 1989.

However the pub reopened its doors in September 1992 after further refurbishment, and is now resplendent in its rich red, green and gold decor, with plenty of ornate brasswork around the bar and fancy light fittings everywhere. The atmosphere is very much like that of a grand Victorian public-house-cum-music-hall, although the live entertainment offered daily (except Sundays) is of a much more recent era. The genial Roy Hudd was among the first week's attractions.

The name not only honours Queen Victoria, a popular monarch, but also has theatrical overtones.

OWD BOOTS - *Glasshouse Street*

Renamed from the '*White Hart*' in December 1982, its original title, planned as '*Boots the Pub*', was objected to by Boots the Chemists, whose superstore is nearby, so much so that the latter took out an interim injunction in the High Court against the pub's owners. Fortunately, the matter was resolved before it got to court, and the present name of the house was allowed to proceed (incidentally, there is an '*Old Boots*' pub in Cromer Street, London).

To nobody's surprise, customers at the grand opening found the place based on a footwear theme, with a wide variety of boots hanging from the ceiling. Moreover, as promised, they were awarded a free pint in return for any old boots they brought in with them!

PEACOCK - *Mansfield Road*

The name of this Victorian pub refers (like that of its namesake at Clifton, and the '*Old Peacock*' in Ilkeston Road) to the heraldic crest of the Clifton and Manners families. The pub itself was modernised in 1884 and 1930, and in July 1989 was refurbished completely. It has retained its attractive etched windows, and is one of the last of Nottingham's pubs to have table service in the Lounge - just press the bell and wait for someone to take your order!

QUEEN ELIZABETH - *Bottle Lane*

Affectionately known as the '*Q.E.*', this pub takes its name from the popular Queen Elizabeth I whose features adorn its colourful signboard. A pub of this name has existed on this site since at least 1885 and, at one time, the Great Central Railway Line which terminated at the former Victoria Station used to pass beneath it - no doubt causing a few glasses to rattle in the process!

When the pub was rebuilt in 1928, the landlord of the time, Jim Tacey, distributed pink invitation cards, inviting folk to come and partake of the fine ales to be had at the new '*Queen Elizabeth.*'

ROYAL CHILDREN - *Castle Gate*

This building is listed under its present name in the very first Town Directory of 1799. Although the inns and pubs of England are often named after the monarchs (or their children) of the time, this is the only one referring to unnamed royal progeny - and even so, their lineage is distinctly suspect. Local tradition suggests that the children of Princess Anne (daughter of King James II) played with those of the innkeeper whilst staying at the nearby Castle. It is highly unlikely that this was possible, although the picture on the inn-sign has always represented the tradition in this way, showing a pair of royalist-robed children (a boy and a girl) cavorting with a smaller and poorer-clad lassie.

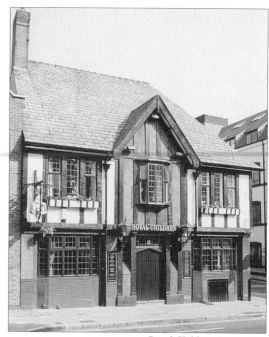

Royal Children, Nottingham

The historical facts are that the Catholic James II had six sons and nine daughters from two marriages. Anne herself married Prince George of Denmark in 1683 when she was only 18, and by him had five children from a total of seventeen confinements. Four of these children died before the age of two, and one (Duke William of Gloucester) died at the age of eleven, nine were still-born, and there were three miscarriages. The unfortunate Princess eventually became Queen and reigned from 1702 until her death (aged only 49) in 1714. She took refuge at Nottingham Castle in the year 1688 at the time when her father was deemed by legal fiction to have ended his reign by flight (the throne of England by then being too hot to hold him).

The hypothesis inherent in local tradition thus being overthrown (that Princess Anne's own children were involved), it therefore remains a possibility that these children were either those belonging to James II's other three daughters by his English wife Ann Hyde - or to his five other daughters by his unofficial Spanish wife Mary D'Este. The complexities of the situation would baffle many a historian!

At one time this pub used to sport a plaque which hung beside the shoulder blade of a whale. It read:

'This inn is probably one of the oldest licences in Nottingham. The present name was derived from the children of Princess Anne (daughter of James II) who when in residence at the castle were playmates of the innkeepers children – circa 1688 – The sign is the shoulder blade of a whale that was used to indicate whale oil was sold here. The inn was one of the first places to use lamps instead of candles and torches.'

At any rate, the pub's current signboards both show a cut-out trio of three children, two royals with differing blonde hairstyles and a brunette of presumably lower degree. Above the grouping is painted the title *'Royal Children'* and beneath it the logo entitled *T.J. Bernard* - this being the name of the Edinburgh brewery which the Scottish and Newcastle combine of today bought in 1900 and hastily disposed of, so it is said. All in all, quite a mystery . . . This pub as been completely refurbished, and not altogether to the liking of many who knew it of old!

Sir Charles Napier, Nottingham

SIR CHARLES NAPIER - *North Sherwood Street*

The date given by the brewery to this pub (adjacent to the Arboretum gates) is November, 1887. The person remembered was Sir Charles James Napier (1782-1853), a Victorian general who had a successful Army career, but is chiefly recalled to mind nowadays for a military joke expressed in classical fashion! In 1843, whilst campaigning in India, he announced the capture of the state of Sind (now in Pakistan) by sending a one-word telegram to the War Office: 'PECCAVI.' This translates from Latin as 'I have sinned' - and was enough to tell those at home that Sind had become an annexe of the Crown.

The victorious general is remembered in Nottingham as being the officer in charge of the troops who suppressed the local Chartist riots which took place on The Forest in August, 1839. It is unfortunate that the pub-sign is not of Sir Charles (James) Napier himself, but Sir Charles (John) Napier (1786-1860), who was in fact an admiral - and it is *he* whose portrait graces the board, wearing *naval* uniform, of course. One must point out that these distinguished cousins were often confused for each other - which must have been very tiresome for them both!

SIR JOHN BORLASE WARREN - *Canning Circus*

Discerning readers will already know that the above name is synonymous with the *'Happy Man'* at Stapleford, (qv) - and that the romantic aspect of his life is recounted elsewhere.

As a boy, his ruling passion was for the sea. He entered the Navy and was occupied with the troubles arising out of the French Revolution and the fight against Napoleon, for which he was later made a baronet and promoted to Admiral.

Two special reports from the second Nottingham Date Book are worthy of mention. The first of these is dated 19 September 1794, and refers to the action on the recent 'Glorious First of June' whereby the French fleet had been significantly defeated:

Sir John Borlase Warren, Nottingham

"*Sir John was met near the Trent Bridge by a great body of people, who saluted him with three loud cheers. The horses were then taken from his carriage, and the people laying hold of the shafts and pushing behind, the naval hero was drawn into the town amidst the acclamation of thousands, preceded by a company of the Light Horse, 12 sergeants and 5 drummers of the recruiting parties, a number of flags, and the 'Cock o'th' Blue' himself in his full-bottomed wig.*

After Sir John had partaken of refreshment at the 'White Lion,' the procession then reformed. Huzzas rent the air, the bells rang, blue streamers and cockades were displayed without number, flags of the same colour were mounted in the church towers. Thus accompanied by the utmost demonstrations of esteem, Sir John was conducted out of town en-route to his home at Stapleford Hall."

The second report is dated 29 October 1798, and relates to Sir John's victory off the coast of Ireland. An enemy French squadron of 9 ships of the line (destined for the supplying of troops and Irish rebels) was dispersed, and an important warship and 3 frigates were captured.

"*This glorious news,*" exclaimed The Journal, "*was received here in the most rapturous and loyal manner. The bells were immediately rung and continued without intermission during the day, and all ranks seemed to enjoy the event which saved the sister kingdom from the horrors of a second invasion - which in a few hours the enemy would have been able to accomplish, had it not been for the unwearied exertion of our gallant Representative.*" This enthusiastic report continues, "*A great number of sheep were roasted in the streets and distributed to the populace, who behaved in the most peaceable and loyal manner. At every village in the neighbourhood similar rejoicings took place.*"

As to the opening of this pub, Borough Records Vol. VIII gives it as 1814, the year before Waterloo. The Town Directory of 1799 records another *'Sir John Warren'* at New Buildings, Sion Hill - and the 1822 Directory lists another of this name in Old Street.

SMITHY'S - *Carlton Road*

Until April 1983 this pub (licensed in June 1939) was known as the *'Crown.'* It gets its present name from the fact that a blacksmith's shop and forge once occupied this site.

STAGE DOOR - *Upper Parliament Street*

Opened under its new and most appropriate name in October 1985, this old pub stands only a few yards away from the Theatre Royal. It was formerly the *'Hand Inn'*, listed in the 1822 Directory. This had its licence transferred from the *'Bird In Hand'*, demolished in 1865. The latter stood in Market Street, then known as Sheep Lane. Curiously enough, a sign showing a woman's hand in former times indicated a bawdy house, or brothel . . . whereas the sign of the Open Hand, formerly the trade symbol of the brewers Allsopp, was taken over by Ind Coope, who display it as their logo accompanied by the original date of its adoption in 1856.

TAP 'N' TUMBLER - *Wollaton Street*

This pub changed its name from the *'Rutland Arms'* in June 1985.

The signboard outside the pub gives this unusual combination name two different interpretations. One picture demonstrates the skills of the travelling acrobats and jesters who were popular showmen in medieval days, the other shows the tap on a beer barrel about to fill a glass. The pub is close to the Theatre Royal, and perhaps brings back memories of the former Empire music-hall nearby which was closed down in 1958 to make way for the Royal Concert Hall.

THURLAND HALL - *Thurland Street*

This stately specimen of the Bass empire was always renowned for the quality of its mahogany fittings, its accompanying brass rails and its unique Island Bar. It dates from 1900, and takes its name from the original Thurland Hall, part of which stood on this same site, and a 16th-century portrait of which can be seen above the fireplace.

The original Hall was built in 1458 by Thomas Thurland, an influential wool merchant who, at that time, controlled the entire European wool trade and was reputedly the richest man in Europe. Moreover, he represented the town of Nottingham in Parliament and was nine times Mayor. His splendid mansion in later years provided accommodation for several royal visitors, notably James I in 1612 and Charles I in 1634 and later in 1642 prior to the 'Raising of the Standard' which signalled the start of the Civil War. Before its demolition in 1831, the Hall was owned by the fourth Duke of Newcastle (whose ducal home was Clumber Park) and whose title still survives (as the 'Newcastle Arms') at pubs in Nottingham, Southwell and Sutton-in-Ashfield.

Writing in 1751, the local historian and map-maker Charles Deering described the social activities taking place at Thurland Hall as follows:

"The Monthly Assemblies of the genteel part of the town of both Sexes ... where the younger element divert themselves in the dancing, whilst the senior or graver part enjoy themselves over a game of quadrille or whist. One of these places of Meeting is on Low Pavement; the other, called the Tradesmen's Assembly, is held in a large room 70 feet long by 20 feet broad, where the town's wealthy Tradesmen, their wives and sons and daughters, meet for the same recreation. This is at Thurland Hall in Griddlesmith Gate."

According to another observer of the local Social scene ... *"For splendour and magnificence, Thurland Hall ranks second only to the Castle."* Reflecting on the national boom in pub rebuilding between 1898 and 1899, another writer declared that a quartet of town pubs stood out from all the rest. These, he said, were the *'Thurland Hall,'* the *'Rose of England'* in Mansfield Road, the *'Cross Keys'* in Byard Lane, and the *'Bodega'* in Pelham Street.

TURF TAVERN - *Upper Parliament Street*

This house is thought to have taken its title from the celebrated 'racing' house of the same name at Doncaster. After the Champagne Stakes there, it was customary for the winner to give six dozen bottles of 'Champers' to the guests who dined at that distinguished hostelry. When Lord George Bentinck won the aforesaid Stakes, he ordered an ample supply of magnums in pursuance of his victory before he left Doncaster to return home to Welbeck - and his first question after driving back to the racecourse on the following day was, "How did the dinner at the *Turf Tavern* go?" One marvels at his restraint in not honouring the occasion with his own lordly presence, but we are unaware what delights were awaiting him at his own ancestral home in the Dukeries.

It is not known in what year this building was erected, but the stone panel high on its facade clearly indicates 'Rebuilt in 1923.'

WINDMILL - *Alfreton Road*

Opened in December 1966, this pub's name evokes the fact that the last windmill in this area to survive was burned down in 1858. It had been built on The Forest in 1807, and was one of thirteen that once stood on Forest Road.

YATES'S WINE LODGE - *Long Row*

One of the chief inns of Tudor times in Nottingham was the *'Bull Head'* on Long Row - the site and sign of which there is some reason for thinking the present house has indeed succeeded. In 1566 a previous innkeeper named Robert Parke was 'presented' at the Brewing Sessions by the town constables for *'brewing and tippling without a licence.'* He was fined the goodly sum of eight pence - which kept him within the Law for the rest of his term of office.

Borough Records for the year 1590 show an item in the 'Chamberlain Account' for *'wyne and sugar bestowed upon Maister Henry Talbott at the Bull Head'* - from which the local historian many years later drew the ingenious conclusion that because of the association of the Talbot family with it, the *'Bull Head'* may have assumed at a subsequent date the family name of the Earls of Shrewsbury (who at that time had land and property in Nottinghamshire) - and changed its name to that of the large white hunting hound called the *'Talbot'* which still features in the noble Earl's armorial bearings.

In 1874 this inn was scheduled to be reconstructed in accordance with the campaign of improving Long Row promised by the then Town Clerk of Nottingham, a certain

Yates's Wine Lodge, Nottingham

Yates's Wine Lodge, Nottingham, interior (c. 1930)

Mr Samuel Johnson. Unfortunately for his plans, a local tycoon called Edward Cox, already notable for his connections with such Nottingham enterprises as dance halls, skating rinks and shooting galleries, decided instead to create on the site the most flamboyant 'Gin Palace' in the whole of the Midlands.

His carefully-veiled plans were passed by Authority in all innocence (it cost them no money to do so, anyway) and the old inn was pulled down. In 1876 there arose in its place the new plush drinking Emporium in all its splendour. *'With a huge tongue-shaped Bar down the middle of the main room, a handsome gallery, dazzling arrays of cut glass and chandeliers featuring lavish gas-lights, spirit fountains of the latest design, bronze statues, oil paintings, marble curios and other objets d'art . . .'* It was much more in keeping, actually, with the British Museum in London than a provincial public house! But whatever, it certainly drew customers like moths to a flame. Many of the paintings were by the chairman of the 'Palace of Varieties' on nearby Market Street - a place which opened at Christmas the same year. It was run in conjunction with the *'Talbot'* and eventually became the 'Scala Picture-House.'

This showpiece was of course a 'must' for all visitors to the town. During Goose Fair week in October they were charged at twopence a head to gaze in awe at its ornate decor. They passed through the building in their hundreds, in at Long Row and out at Market Street - consuming on their way one drink, which they were allowed inclusive with the entrance fee. Mr Cox, it must be said, quite nobly observed the religious scruples of those Victorian times by resisting all temptations to open his establishment's doors on the Sabbath.

However, the Town Clerk chose to stigmatise the *Talbot* by declaring it to be *'a resort of which there is no greater source of immorality and degradation'* - and this vitriolic attack naturally prompted a spirited retort from the proprietor . . . *'You can find no hole-in-corner snugs here!'* he thundered self-righteously, *'its frequenters have to guard their behaviour, because they are in the light of day or of a hundred chandeliers - and, at busy hours, under the observation of five hundred eyes - not to speak of the surveillance of the liveried servants of my establishment and alternate relays of prowling detectives. We venture to assert that in no Gin Palace in town is there less drinking per head of the frequenters. Multitudes use the Talbot as an attractive musical Lounge which is sufficiently crowded to save them from attracting awkward attention if they do not freely order refreshments!'* Correspondence on the subject was featured in local newspapers for several weeks.

On 1st May 1929 the *'Talbot,'* was sold at public auction for £34,500 to a gentleman named Yorke from Manchester, and since then has been known as his company's 'Yates Brothers' Wine Lodge.' Nowadays it is more spartan, of course. Its wrought-iron stairways, its balustraded gallery, its stained-glass windows and its huge grandfather-clock are still there, but its enormous oak-barrels racked on view behind the Long Bar - and that irresistible 'Palm Court Trio' playing at one end of the balcony upstairs - these are, sadly, no more. But the fact remains that, as Richard Tresidder remarks in his splendid booklet on Nottingham Pubs (published by the Nottingham Civic Society in 1980) *'the Talbot has always been unrivalled and exceptional, as a unique expression of Victorian opulence and enterprise.'* The pub underwent a complete refurbishment in October 1995.

YE OLDE SALUTATION - *Houndsgate*

The traditional sign of this and like-named hostelries (i.e. of the Archangel Gabriel 'saluting' the Virgin Mary) aroused the religious scruples of the Puritans when they came to political power (1649-1659) and formed the so-called *Commonwealth Government.* The innkeeper here was ordered by the new masters either to remove the offending sign or have it repainted and some approved sign substituted. Naturally, he wished neither to alter his sign out of all recognition nor to lose his licence, so he compromised - as did so many of his Royalist colleagues - by renaming his inn the 'Soldier And Citizen.' Most ingeniously, he further suggested that these worthies should be represented on the signboard as a pair of shaking hands. In this way - even in its Puritan guise - the original name would still be recognised. No doubt it went by the name of the 'Salutation' all along, despite official disapproval.

This old-time innkeeper was certainly an opportunist, because when the Restoration of the Monarchy was effected in 1660 he brought back the old name on an official basis, but he let his existing signboard of the 'Soldier And Citizen' remain until it was worn and weathered - making sure that when repainted, the 'salutation' (or greeting) was replaced by the sign of a hearty handshake. In fact, in recent times, a suspended wrought-metal symbolic hand was put up outside this ancient inn during extensions in 1966 - but this disappeared overnight, due to the action of a roving souvenir-hunter, and hasn't been seen since!

In former times there was no date painted on the outside walls here (only the name of the licensee's home-brewed ales), but for many years past the date of 1240 AD has been prominently displayed. This particular date, according to recent research, represents the first building on this site as being the homestead of an unnamed Master

Tanner, who made animal skins into leather. He, his apprentices and journeymen, would exercise their craft on the ground floor, and the upper floor would be the common domestic area for both family and workers.

However, beneath the foundations are several rock-hewn chambers and rock caverns. For many years these were accepted as having been rooms for the purpose of storing ale, but in 1937 the Thoroton Excavation Society made a thorough investigation and decided that these caves, apparently made in the 9th century, were intended for folk, who belonged to the local Saxon settlement, to live in.

The spectre of a small four or five-year old girl is still said to haunt these caves - supposedly a street urchin from Victorian times.

Richard Tresidder, emphasises that the medieval roof of the 'Salutation' is fully exposed, and that 'it is a challenge to the visitor to try to distinguish the ancient timbers from those put in recently by the brewery'. He says, further, that 'the earliest reference to the Salutation is in 1761.'

This brings us to the intriguing account, in the Recorder and Weekly Post dated 3rd September 1992, of a report from the tree-ring dating Laboratory attached to the University of Nottingham's Department of Archaeology - which had assessed the oldest timber of the inn as having an inner ring date of 1360. According to the then landlord, "Experts know that timber was not left to season as it is now, but was cut and used straightaway - so we can be certain that the original parts of the 'Salutation' were built in that year."

Ye Olde Salutation Inn, Nottingham

Borough Records do in fact mention a messuage (a term in law which signifies *'a dwelling and offices with the adjoining lands appropriated to the household'*) on the corner of 'Le Hundegate' (i.e. Houndsgate) in the year 1414. This building on the present site, however, was neither an Inn nor a Friary guesthouse, but a private dwelling-house *'belonging to a gentleman by the name of John Alastre.'*

All these facts seem to establish that the building under present discussion can surely be the oldest trading establishment in Nottingham still standing - but as Borough Records Vol. III mention under the date of 1460 specifying *'le Swan'* on High Pavement *'and Thurland gave to the Trinity Gild a messuage on the Hiepavement of this name,'* it may well be that the aforesaid 'Swan' (a sign recognised since the 14th century) represents the very first tavern-sign of Old Nottingham Town in historical perspective.

Finally, here is the text of the inscription framed and painted on the outside wall of the 'Salutation' which faces onto Maid Marian Way:

"The present house was built c.1240 on the site of the 13th century Ale House known as 'The Archangel Gabriel Salutes the Virgin Mary.' During the first Civil War 1642-1646 part of the house was used as Recruiting Rooms for both Factions. The original still existing Cave Systems was probably a Saxon Farm, later used for Servants Accommodation and brewing."

YE OLDE TRIP TO JERUSALEM - *Brewhouse Yard*

This was originally the brewhouse of the Castle, which towers above it. Hewn out of the rock on which the castle itself is built, it is honeycombed with caves and passages, and because of its unique features, is world-famous.

Tradition has it (largely due to the date of 1189AD painted on the outside wall) that this old inn is so named because as the Crusaders assembled from all parts, in order to fight the heathen Saracens in the Holy Land, they would halt here for rest and refreshment. 'Trip' (in its original spelling as 'Tryppe') is the old English word for 'stop' or 'halt'. The writer Palgrave used this term in 1530 - "He dyd but tryppe at ye yn" ("He did but stop at the inn"). Against the latter, one has to point out that the name 'Trip' cannot possibly date from the 12th century. The word was unrecorded in English in any sense that would be meaningful, until at least the 14th century. 'Trip,' incidentally, always seems to have meant a journey that was either short and sharp, or for amusement rather than a serious purpose - which is hardly fitting in a Crusading context.

The Third Crusade did in fact take place in 1189. Richard the Lionheart was one of the joint leaders but, sad to say, there is no documentary evidence to support the oft-held contention that the 'TRIP' fulfilled any such function of hospitality at that time (nobles and their retinue customarily staying under the Castle roof). However, the other part of the long tradition - i.e. that this inn began life in earnest being known as the 'Pilgrim' - is much sounder, although here too opinion has differed considerably as regards dates.

In County Archives (Manuscript 1768) there is a reference dated 1638 to 'Le Brewhouse' near Nottingham Castle - but whether this meant the 'Pilgrim' is a matter for conjecture. However, *Victorian Nottingham* (Volume Four p.74) says that the 'Pilgrim' makes its first appearance on Deering's plan of Nottingham Town dated 1751. Cherry's map (see 'The Aviary', Trent Bridge, for details) - does not include the 'Pilgrim' although Brewhouse Yard *is* clearly shown!

This is because the pub was *outside* the Borough boundary in the 18th century and Cherry's map only includes those premises *within* the boundary at that time. Whatever the true reason may be for this divergence of opinion, the William Stevenson Papers (dated 1909) in County Archives concerning the *'Pilgrim'* are certainly more helpful, and begin as follows:

'In 1760 Thomas Tenison of Sysonby in Leicestershire, Esquire, sold the property to William Marriott, Innkeeper. The purchase money was £52.10s. The property is spoken of as a messuage with garden and piece of ground adjoining, commonly known by the name or sign of THE PILGRIM. It is stated to be situate in Brewhouse Yard or within the precincts or territories thereof. It is sold subject to a yearly chief rent of 2s.8d to the Duke of Leeds.'

This is the earliest *documentary* evidence of the existence of the *'Pilgrim'* - which a generation later was followed by its further sale by auction as recorded in the Nottingham Journal of July 1785. It was then in the possession of 'the widow Footit' and bought from her by Mr Stanford, a bleacher in Castlegate. Soon afterwards, when Nottingham's very first Town Directory had been published by Willoughby in 1799, the name of the *'Pilgrim'* had somehow been transmuted into that of *'The Trip To Jerusalem.'* However, a possible reason, or at least an intriguing speculation regarding this, was offered by the local writer and historian J. Holland Walker in his book *'Links With Old Nottingham'* which was first published in 1928 and a salient part of which is reproduced below:

Ye Olde Trip to Jerusalem, Nottingham

'Brewhouse Yard itself was an extraordinary little area. It was legally outside the jurisdiction of the town, and consequently was much less carefully policed than was the rest of the district. It was apparently the resort of a curious semi-political, semi-religious body called the Philadelphians, whose particular shibboleth (by which they hoped to reach Heaven) was to refer to each other as 'Brother Pilgrim.'

By a series of curious legal chances, Brewhouse Yard later came under the jurisdiction of a court held at Cotgrave (which was under the headship of the Prior of Jerusalem) - and I think that some nickname concocted from 'The Pilgrim' and this Order of Jerusalem is the origin of the present name of the inn.'

It is perhaps worth mentioning that this 'present name' was confirmed in the deeds of the property in the year 1834, when the owner, George Langford, disposed of it. This celebrated inn last came up for auction in March 1954, when it was sold to the tenant (a member of the Ward family who ran it for so many years) for £17,500. As a tailpiece, it is no secret that *'Ye Olde Trip To Jerusalem'* was acquired by the Kimberley Brewery (Hardys & Hansons) in 1989 for a sum much more than that!

NUTHALL

LARK'S NEST - *Larkfield Road*

Opened in May 1957, this pub is situated in the middle of the Larkfields Estate which, before housing development took place, was the home of many wild birds - skylarks in particular.

THREE PONDS - *Nottingham Road*

In the 19th century the village had two inns - the *'Goat's Head'* (part of the heraldic crest of the Sedleys) and the *'Horse And Groom.'* The former hostelry closed down during the 1880s and the latter's licence was transferred to the *'Three Ponds.'*

Not far away from this pub is Temple Lake which was constructed out of a rock quarry in 1754 as part of one of the most remarkable stately homes in all England. Built to the order of Sir Charles Sedley, then MP for Nottingham, it was called Nuthall Temple and took a team of Italian craftsmen three years to complete. It was demolished in 1929. The lake itself was once complemented by three ponds, exceedingly ornamental in character, which it fed through a series of levels. Before the encroachment of the motorway, Temple

Three Ponds, Nuthall

Lake covered about 12 acres, and in high summer was ablaze with water-lilies of all colours. It is common belief that the *'Three Ponds'* was built over one of the ponds from which it takes its name, but this is not so. An inspection of the Basford RDC sewer plan of that time makes the point in dispute quite clear. A culvert was introduced to make a free outflow which eventually reached the river Leen, and the pub site is shown to be quite distinct from the pond site. Actually, with the ground being so low, and as several large trees had to be uprooted, concrete piles about 16ft long were driven into the drained ground on which the smallest of the ponds (known as the Dog-Kennel Pond, for some obscure reason) had once stood. This was covered with a concrete raft - upon which the rear portion only of the building was set.

OLLERTON

HOP POLE - *Church Street*

The 1832 Directory records that this former 18th-century coaching inn once contained a post office from which letters were despatched by mail gig to Newark at 7.15 every morning, with a return post at midday. Situated just off the Great North Road, it grew to serve some of the coaches which, when travelling northwards, left the main highway near Newark and took the more picturesque route through Ollerton to Worksop before rejoining it near Doncaster.

The 5th Viscount Torrington recorded his itineraries and travels between the years 1781-1784 in a diary which records:

'The Hop Pole at Ollerton is pleasantly situated upon a trout stream and fronting the forest woods, a house of good stop and station. Here we fared comfortably, and of the port wine, seemingly better than usual, we drank two bottles. The host was of a communicative turn; nor did we think our stay, of two hours, tedious, except the time thrown away looking at the new church as ugly, and ill-contriv'd, as ever was built.'

The hop industry, from which the house derived its name, was once a prosperous local trade which has long since disappeared. See also the *'Hop Pole'* at Chilwell.

OLLERTON HOUSE - *Wellow Road*

These premises, built in 1957 as a private residence of the same name, were once occupied by the chairman of Mansfield Brewery, Mr R. Chadburn, before being converted to a pub which opened on the 6th April 1962.

The licence for this hostelry was transferred from the former *'Royal Oak'* public house which used to stand some 50 yards away.

Snooty Fox, Ollerton

SNOOTY FOX - *Main Street*

This 17th-century building served as a post office and then a guest house before it was converted into the *'Forest House'* pub during the middle part of this century. In 1991 it was privately purchased, and the new owner decided to rename it the *'Snooty Fox.'* This pub name first appeared at Tetbury in Gloucestershire and has become more popular since the 1980s. It is possibly intended to portray the fox's ability to outwit and outrun the chasing hounds, and the disdainfully supercilious attitude he may feel entitled to adopt when he does so! The building itself is said to be haunted by the ghost of an elderly lady.

WHITE HART - *Market Place*

The present house was built during the 1770s on the site of the original *'White Hart'* which had been destroyed in a fire. Records dating back to 1873 show that the Collins family purchased the pub from the Rufford Estate and have owned it ever since.

A former coaching inn, the pub stood on the main Nottingham to Doncaster road until a by-pass was built to preserve Old Ollerton.

An explanation for the origin of the sign here can be found by referring to the pub of the same name at Lenton.

OXTON

GREEN DRAGON - *Blind Lane*

Mentioned in the 1832 Directory, this pub is at least two hundred years old. Until the 1920s it also incorporated a dairy farm which provided fresh food for the inn's customers and was a regular haunt for the Edwardian carriage and four. In those days it was not unknown for the hostelry to provide up to two hundred breakfasts for guests staying at a Lodge that once adjoined it.

Purchased by the Nottingham Co-operative Society in 1953, it underwent major refurbishment and the remaining farm buildings

Green Dragon, Oxton

were removed to provide a car park. At this time it sported a colourful sign of a green dragon on one of its front walls which, during the passage of time, has been removed. Surprisingly, having been acquired by Mansfield Brewery in 1968, this pub no longer displays a pictorial signboard - a rarity among pubs owned by this particular company who are noted for their famous circular signs.

An explanation for the origin of the name can be found by referring to the *'Green Dragon'* at Hucknall.

PAPPLEWICK

GRIFFIN'S HEAD - *Moor Road*

Recorded in the 1832 Directory, this old house underwent extensive alterations in 1992. During these modifications builders discovered in the dining area, a 30ft-deep well from which the villagers used to collect water using a hand-pump. In the late 1800s, this pub also served as the local mortuary!

The Griffin was a fabulous monster. Supposedly the offspring of a lion and an eagle it has appeared on the coat of arms of numerous families, including those of the Dukes of Marlborough (the Spencer Churchills).

A modern pub of this name can be found at Whatton.

PLEASLEY

NEW ENGLAND - *Chesterfield Road North*

Opened on the 20th December 1963, this pub stands in an area of Mansfield which was formerly called New England - hence the name.

Its colourful round signboard depicts the Pilgrims and Puritans who originally settled in the region of New England, USA (see entry for the *'Pilgrim Fathers'* at Scrooby).

WHITE SWAN - *Meden Square*

Built during the late 1800s, this inn was acquired by Mansfield Brewery in 1921.

Reputedly, the pub is haunted by the ghost of Florence Nightingale whose father was the first owner of nearby Pleasley Colliery.

An origin for the name can be found by referring to the *'White Swan'* at Basford.

PLUMTREE

GRIFFIN - *Main Road*

Many 19th century buildings in Plumtree owe their existence to the Burnside family, instigators of an extensive building and improvement programme for the village. This included the large inn which dates from 1843 as the datestone, with its carved griffin's head shows. In the 1920s, the inn belonged to Griffin Farm, the landlord being the farmer as well. The porch door is thought to be part of an old double coffin, made for two brothers, but not permitted by the church authorities to be used. See the *'Griffins Head'* at Papplewick for details about the name.

Griffin, Plumtree

RADCLIFFE-ON-TRENT

BLACK LION - *Main Road*

Mentioned in the 1832 Directory, the sign of this pub is less common than that of the *Red Lion*. An heraldic sign, it is mainly related to Queen Philippa of Hainault (1314-1369), wife of Edward III, but was also used as the royal ensign of Madoc ap Meredith, the last sovereign prince of Powys, who died at Winchester in 1160.

Manvers Arms, Radcliffe-on-Trent

MANVERS ARMS - *Main Road*

This former coaching inn stands on the site of the former *'White Hart'* whose cellars were included in the design of the present building which dates from around 1792. Long ago these cellars were utilised as a temporary mortuary, with beer barrels stored on one side and corpses on the other. Reputedly, the bodies were brought here from nearby St Mary's Church using two tunnels which ran from the cellars to the church, the entrances to which have long since been sealed.

It is said that the house is haunted by a poltergeist that occasionally breaks glasses and moves casks about the cellar.

The 1832 Directory records that like Cotgrave, Radcliffe-on-Trent was at one time owned by Earl Manvers, whose heraldic crest is displayed on the sign outside this pub. The pub was rebuilt around 1815, using a distinctive design by the Manvers Estate architect William Wilkins, who was also responsible for the estate workers' houses at Budby.

RADFORD

BOULEVARD - *Radford Boulevard*

This enormous hostelry was built in 1883, not long after boulevards as such were 'adopted' by Nottingham, the first English town to have them, in the 1870s, copying them from the Parisian boulevards which themselves were built only a decade earlier. The word itself is related to 'Bulwark' in its original sense of 'fortification'. A boulevard for the past century or so has come to signify simply 'a broad road, walk or promenade bordered with trees.'

No-one appears to know how many rooms are contained in this 4-storey building, but only the top floor is not used for any regular purpose. In the days when it was officially classed as a (Victorian/Edwardian) Hotel, it would usually be fully occupied (like, for example, the *'Grove Hotel'* on Castle Boulevard), by teams of canal navvies, railway labourers, or groups of artistes appearing in the local music-halls of that period.

CLINTON ARMS - *Radford Road*

The name of this Victorian pub possibly refers to the 4th Duke of Newcastle (1785-1851) - 'last of the feudal aristocrats' and one of the most important landowners in the county.

It is noteworthy for its fascinating *Terminus Bar* - a reminder that trams used to turn around nearby. This is decorated with old prints of public transport from days gone by, and also photographs of Nottingham's former trams and trolley-buses. The era of the trams began with a horse-drawn service in September 1878 which existed until 1897. After electrification had been completed, services resumed as from New Year's Day in 1901 until 5th September in 1936. (The London trams ran until 1952, and the service in Blackpool is still operating!) Trolley-buses in the Nottingham area ran from 1927 until 1966.

For an explanation as to why a tramcar is shown on the sign of the *'Forest'* pub in Bulwell, see the appropriate entry.

COLONEL BURNABY - *Hartley Road*

Acquired by Whitbread from the Nottingham Brewery Company in October 1887, this pub was named after one of the most unusual military adventurers of the entire Victorian era.

The legendary Burnaby (Frederick Gustavus, 1842-1885) was by profession a cavalry officer. He also found time to become a seasoned balloonist, diplomat, explorer, linguist, global campaigner and military correspondent of the Times - plus horseman most extraordinary. He became a national hero after his hazardous 300-mile trek across the frozen Steppes from Kazala to Khiva during the winter of 1875, and was made Colonel of his regiment (the Royal Horse Guards) in 1881.

Three years later he was sent out to the Sudan to join the Nile Expedition as second-in-command to General Wolseley and leader of the advance guard entrusted with the rescue of General Gordon at Khartoum. He was killed, as Gordon was, by a spear-thrust from one of the Mahdi's troops. This took place during a preliminary skirmish at Abu Klea, and provided a fitting and epic finale to a military career without parallel, even in the annals of the British Empire.

Not far away is Burnaby Street which is also named after him. With a curious twist of historical perspective, the pub itself was renamed in 1982 as the *'Penny-farthing'* (presumably as some indication of affinity with the local Raleigh cycle works which had their origin in 1888) - but it reverted to its former name in 1986.

JOLLY HIGGLERS - *Ilkeston Road*

The original pub (listed in the 1832 Directory) was closed in September 1970 and reopened almost three years later on an adjacent site.

There has always been speculation about the true meaning of the word 'Higgler' - often thought of as an itinerant pedlar on foot or a 'hawker' with a horse and cart, both with goods to sell and both with a willingness to higgle or haggle as to a fair price. However, when the present writer visited the pub in 1966 shortly before the retirement,

after thirty years, of the landlady, Mrs Nellie Allen, and asked for her explanation of the title, she told me with conviction that it came about long ago, before shafts were sunk, to denote those stalwarts (women among them) whose unenviable task it was to carry crates of coal up to the surface from the pit bottom. Whether these particular, and so-called 'higglers', were employed at Radford Colliery (closed in 1963) or Wollaton Colliery (closed in 1965) she could not say. Coal higglers were in fact waggoners who carried coal from the pits.

At any rate, Shipstones weren't fully committed to providing pictorial signboards until the success of their 'Paint-a-Pub-Sign Competition' in 1980 became apparent - and even then, due to some administrative oversight, the long-awaited

Jolly Higglers, Radford (c.1920)

'Swinger' wasn't actually affixed and unveiled for all to see until the 1st February, 1982! As many of us will know, the picture presented to Joe Public's admiring gaze shows a trio of amiable fellows engaged in friendly discussion - but about what, we cannot be sure.

MARQUIS OF LORNE - *Salisbury Street*

This Victorian pub was named after John George Edward Henry Douglas Sutherland Campbell (1845-1920), who succeeded his father as Duke of Argyll and Marquis of Lorne. Once MP for Argyllshire (now Strathclyde), he married the fourth daughter of Queen Victoria, Princess Louise, in 1871. From 1878-1883 he was the governor-general of Canada.

MARQUIS OF WATERFORD - *Ortzen Street*

This was the title accorded, on his further elevation in the peerage, to Field-Marshal Earl Roberts, VC (1832-1914), one of the most popular and successful of Queen Victoria's generals.

He served first in the campaign to quell the Indian Mutiny, where his bravery gained him his VC, and by 1885 he was Commander-in-Chief of the Army in India. After distinguished service both in Ireland and in South Africa, he became Commander-in-Chief of the British Army from 1900 until 1904, when this archaic office was finally abolished.

The pub named *'Lord Roberts'* in Broad Street, Nottingham refers to the same man.

NOTTINGHAM ARMS - *Dulwich Road*

Purchased by Mansfield Brewery in 1983, this pub's distinctive circular sign displays the coat of arms of Nottingham, whose motto is *Vivit post funera virtus* (Virtue lives beyond the grave).

There are pubs of this name in several places, including Westgate-on-Sea in Kent, where the first landlord named it as such in memory of his birthplace (perhaps he was once a 'regular' at the Radford pub). Incidentally, there are pubs named *'Nottingham House'* at Heanor and in Sheffield, the latter can be found near the university and shows Robin Hood on its sign. Even more interesting is the fact that at Mutley Plain, Plymouth, there was, until recently, a pub called the *'Nottingham'*, which displayed a signboard showing the castle and the coat of arms of the city of Nottingham. The original inn stood in Nottingham Place, Plymouth, this area having several streets named after English towns.

SIR GARNET WOLSELEY - *Denman Street*

This pub was closed for alterations in December 1970 and re-opened in March 1972. The soldier whose name it honours (1833-1913) was born in Dublin and rose to the rank of Field-Marshal. It was his skilful planning and organizational ability which gave rise to the expression used throughout the British Army during the late 19th century - 'Everything is all Sir Garnet' - meaning that all aspects of military preparedness in a particular situation were beyond reproach. The scope of the world-wide campaigns in which he successfully participated were such that he became one of the nation's favourite 'Sons of Empire'. At the end of his active career he was promoted by a grateful Queen Victoria to the post of Commander-in-Chief of the entire British Army (from 1889-1895), as well as being elevated to a Viscountcy.

Wolseley joined the Army in 1852, was wounded in the Burmese War of 1852/3 and served in the Crimean War, in which he lost an eye. He fought during the Indian Mutiny in 1857/8 and served in the Chinese War of 1860. Ten years later he put down the Red River Rebellion in Canada without losing a man, and in 1873/4 he was also in command of British troops during the Ashanti War in West Africa. In Natal and the Transvaal his flair for simplifying all aspects of operations gained him a reputation as a superb planner and organiser, and in 1882 he was appointed Commander-in-Chief of the expedition sent to Egypt to subdue Arabi Pasha. His sole set-back was that his Relief Expedition, authorised by Gladstone to bring General Gordon out of the Sudan, arrived just too late to prevent the latter being speared to death in Khartoum.

Wolseley's legacy, left to the Empire on his retirement in 1895, was a thoroughly professional British Army, with proper supply lines and an integrated command structure. However, there are two facts concerning him that are not generally known:

- He helped establish the famous Wolseley car company, started by his younger brother, by supporting him with money when cash flow proved problematic.
- It was he upon whom was based the idea of 'the very model of a modern major-general' introduced with such success by Gilbert and Sullivan in their comic opera 'The Pirates of Penzance,' first performed in London in 1880.

WHITE HORSE - *Ilkeston Road*

It is generally thought that a pub of some kind has stood on this site since 1660. In the 19th century it was a coaching inn, with its own brewhouse. The pub acquired its distinctive green tiled exterior when it was rebuilt in 1912.

The sign of the 'White Horse' has been in use since the fifteenth century and is popular because of its widespread use in heraldry.

This pub has now been immortalised in "Saturday Night and Sunday Morning", the literary classic of local author Alan Sillitoe. The novel is about Arthur Seaton a cycle factory worker who, when the day's work is done, is off to the pub, thirsting not only for the beer, but for adventure also. The opening paragraph tells how, with *"eleven pints of beer and seven small gins playing hide-and-seek inside his stomach he fell from the top most stair to the bottom"*. The White Horse was a good place for him because *"it's on'y a gnat's nip away from our house - anyway the ale ain't all that bad"*. On one occasion, he is beaten up by a group of soldiers after he has left the pub - *"The*

White Horse, Radford

White Horse stood on a corner, and he went out by the main door, watched a trolley bus descend from the station and stop at the opposite corner. "Shall I run, and take it to town?" he asked himself. "No", he answered, without thinking. He heard the conductor's bell and, like a lighted greenhouse growing people, the bus trundled away up the hill. He turned into the darkness of Eddison Road, walked a few yards and heard a movement of heavy feet behind him ... A hundred people were drinking beer or whisky in the White Horse, but the world had shrunk for him to a struggle being decided in the space of a few square yards, and his world was the colour and hue of sombre purple".

As Arthur said one fictional Friday night in 1958, *"Now I can go home, change and tek mysen off to the White Horse for a pint or two"*.

RAINWORTH

ARCHER - *Warsop Lane*

Opened on the 2nd December 1965, this pub is named after the area's connections with Robin Hood and Sherwood Forest.

LURCHER - *Westbrook Drive*

The sign of this pub (opened July 1990) displays the traditional country dog, the Lurcher, after which it is named.

The first pint was handed to Mrs Mavis Smith, former secretary to the chairman and managing director of Hardys and Hansons who was retiring after 44 years service with the brewery.

A plaque inside the pub gives a helpful definition of the breed (or rather, crossbreed) concerned:

"In medieval times the Forest Laws of England were draconian. This meant that a gypsy and his dog were in constant danger, and both went on their business secretly, the dog lurking in cover.

It is thought that greyhound and sheepdog were crossed in an attempt to disguise a hunting-dog - and anyone who was not a nobleman seen with such a dog would be certain to die on the gibbet. The resulting 'Lurcher' (meaning 'a prowler who waits in ambush') was found to be far more intelligent than a pure hound and took to Poaching naturally. Blessed with keen sight and scent, they move in absolute silence, and are quick to perceive and obey the slightest sign from their master, to whom they are invariably faithful."

The author of this information is not known to us, but we are also given to understand that for the foregoing reasons the Lurcher is commonly found as a pet within the encampments of those modern-type gypsies - the *New Age Travellers*.

RAMPTON

EYRE ARMS - *Laneham Street*

Rampton once boasted a fine Tudor Hall built during the reign of Henry VIII but pulled down two centuries later. The Hall was occupied by the Babington family, an heiress of which married Sir Gervase Eyre. Sir Gervase fought for the Royalist cause during the Civil War and was killed "defending Newark Castle for the King", in 1644. He is buried in Rampton Church which is full of monuments to other members of the Eyre family. These included Admiral Sir George Eyre, Sir William Eyre who fought in the Crimean War, and many others.

The pub, which was originally called the *'White Swan'*, is listed in the 1879 Directory.

RANBY

CHEQUERS INN - *Old Blyth Road*

James Brindley's Chesterfield Canal, Nottinghamshire's oldest, was constructed in 1771 and took six years to complete. It links Chesterfield in Derbyshire to the River Trent at West Stockwith.

In 1835, Little Ranby, as the community around the canal was called, had a beerhouse but it was not until 1840 that the *'Chequers Inn'* graced its banks. Known by the singular *'Chequer Inn'* at first, the landlord was Samuel Read, victualler and maltster. The inn took its name from Chequerhouse Farm (on whose land it was built), which stood until the site was required for the new A1 bypass. The *'Chequers'* has a beer garden fronting the canal, with swans adding to the charm of the setting. Inside the pub are a number of photographs of different locations along the canal. Please refer to the *'Chequers'* at Chilwell for further information about the name.

RAVENSHEAD

HUTT - *Nottingham Road*

Though appearing in the 1832 Directory as an inn, the building's history can be traced back much further. It is mentioned in historical documents as early as 1400 - when it is recorded as a hut standing opposite Newstead Abbey gates and used by the keeper of the king's deer in Sherwood Forest. Around 1868 it was converted from an inn into a residence for the chaplain of Mr Webb, the then owner of Newstead Abbey. By 1905 it reopened as an inn (albeit a temperance one) known as the *'Hut'* (with one 't').

The present house is barely 150 years old, but incorporates some of the stone from the original building. It was a former landlord who earlier this century added the extra 't' to the pub's title - he made the change so that visitors would not confuse his house with the various wooden huts that used to stand nearby.

In 1969 the pub underwent extensive refurbishment and was reopened by the former Mayor of Mansfield, Alderman T.S. Martin. A further refurbishment took place in 1995 and included a children's indoor play area.

LITTLE JOHN - *Main Road*

This pub, named after Robin Hood's faithful lieutenant, was acquired by Mansfield Brewery in 1896 for £3,250. It is mentioned in White's Directory (1832) and is the oldest pub in the village. There is a pub of the same name at Hathersage, Derbyshire where John Little's body is said to be buried. Here, in 1784, a grave bearing the initials J.L. was opened and revealed the thighbone of a man who at one time would have been about 8ft tall.

Mentioned in all of the early ballads and legends of Robin Hood, he was nicknamed Little John due to his great height and girth. Known to be shrewd, generous and forgiving, he was a first-class swordsman and archer who had no equal with the quarterstaff.

> 'And Robin Hood in Bernesdale stood,
> And leaned him to a tree,
> And by him stood Little John,
> A good yeoman was he.'
> (from the *Little Geste*, 1500)

SHERWOOD RANGER - *Chapel Lane*

This pub opened in grand style on the 6th May 1971, when two Saladin armoured cars arrived at its entrance to form a guard of honour for Mrs P.J.D. McCraith, wife of Pat McCraith, Honorary Colonel of the Sherwood Rangers Yeomanry. On her arrival to open the house she was formally greeted by a lance-guard comprising the armoured car's crews and two sword orderlies.

The name here symbolises the close connections of Nottinghamshire with the former Sherwood Rangers Yeomanry Cavalry Regiment, which traditionally recruited men from this area over a period of many years. Formed in 1794 in answer to the invasion threat posed by the French, the regiment saw action during the Boer War and earned 13 battle honours during World War I. In July 1940, when it was realised that horses no longer had a place in modern warfare the Rangers became an armoured regiment. Now part of the Territorial Army Volunteer Reserve they are based at the Drill Hall in Carlton.

Though this pub does not display a traditional signboard in the normal sense, it does have a life-size portrait of a Ranger wearing the Newark Troop uniform of 1798 on show in its entrance.

There is another pub with this name at Carlton-in-Lindrick.

RETFORD

ANCHOR - *Carolgate*

Mentioned in the 1832 Directory, the sign of this old house has a religious connotation - a reference to which can be found by referring to the pub of the same name at Gunthorpe.

BLACK BOY - *Moorgate*

Recorded in the 1832 Directory as the 'Black's Head,' this old hostelry has borne its present sign since at least 1869 when it appears in Morris's Directory under its current name.

The sign of the 'Black Boy' is similar in origin to that of the 'Black's Head' - please refer to the pub of this name at Carlton.

BRICK AND TILE - *Moorgate*

The present inn was once owned by the leading brick and tile manufacturer in the district and is located near to the site of a former brickyard. Recorded in the 1832 Directory, this house takes its name from its association with the building trade - brick being a reference to the walls of a house and tiles to the roof.

FLYING SCOTSMAN - *Hallcroft Road*

This former nursing home, maternity home and in turn private mansion, opened as a pub in July 1954. The name is an obvious reference to one of the most famous steam locomotives of all time - the first of Sir Nigel Gresley's Pacific Class to appear after the 1923 formation of the London and North Eastern Railway (LNER). Originally having the engine number 4472, it was once a familiar sight on the nearby railway tracks as it thundered its way from King's Cross, London to Edinburgh. It was purchased as a speculative venture by Retford businessman Frank Peglar, who took it to America. It is now back in Britain and is regularly in steam.

JOINERS INN - *London Road*

Opened on the 27th February 1969 this pub, like many others throughout the country, recalls a local trade - joinery. It stands on the site of the former *'Railway Inn'*, demolished in 1968.

At one time, hostelries were used as a meeting place by men of a particular calling. Here they would hold their union meetings and discuss trade matters.

KING AND MILLER - *North Road*

The first reference to this old inn under its current sign is recorded in a deed of 1842. The document, which also mentions the existence of a corn mill nearby, notes that the occupying licensee at the time was a certain Mr Joseph Harrison.

The name is a reference to a ballad called *The King and Miller of Mansfield* which was written before the time of Edward IV and can be found in the Dodsley Collection at Mansfield Library. Its many stanzas record how a miller called John Cockle gave shelter to his king and was later dubbed a knight for his services - full details of which can be found by referring to the *'Sir John Cockle'* public house at Mansfield.

MARKET HOTEL - *West Carr Road*

This busy pub in the centre of Retford (a market town since the 13th century) was once known locally, and unofficially, as *'The Pig'*. Until 1980, the town cattle market was held in its grounds.

Packet Inn, Retford

NEW SUN - *Spital Hill*

In the 1832 Directory this house is recorded simply as the *'Sun,'* but had changed prior to the production of the 1864 Directory to its current sign.

The sign of the sun was first used to adorn signboards because of its simple visual form - once a means of attracting the mostly-illiterate populace to the presence of the house.

PACKET INN - *Bescoby Street*

This old hostelry appears in the 1832 Directory as a beerhouse. Rebuilt in 1913, it stands near to the Chesterfield Canal and was often used by the crews of the Packet boats that used to tie up nearby - a fact reflected in the colourful sign that adorns this house.

Sherwood Ranger, Retford

SHERWOOD RANGER - *Churchgate*

Formerly the *'Ram Inn,'* this house was renamed in 1894 in honour of the Sherwood Ranger Yeomanry Regiment that was formed in 1794 and based at Retford.

The pictorial signboard seems to offer a differing interpretation of the name here - suggesting that its title recalls the forestry rangers who patrol and maintain the beauty of nearby Sherwood Forest.

TURK'S HEAD - *Grove Street*

Recorded in the 1832 Directory, this house has a sign that became popular after the Crusades - a detailed description of its origin can be found by referring to the pub of the same name at Balderton.

VINE INN - *Churchgate*

The *'Vine'* is a typical 3 storey Georgian building with a large archway indicating its use as a coaching inn in times past. Certainly it was popular with carriers (particularly from Clayworth and Gringley) collecting and delivering in Retford. Even today the archway is the only public entrance, and leads for 85 yards down to the beer garden! One of the upstairs windows used to be bricked up, a common practice to avoid the Window Tax (repealed in 1851). It has become a window again thanks to recent renovations which, in 1992, won a rare award from the Retford Society for the outstanding way in which the work, to both the inside and outside of the inn, had been carried out. See also the *'Vine'* at Sneinton for an explanation of the origin of this name.

Vine Inn, Retford

White Hart, Retford

WHITE HART - *The Square*

This former coaching inn is mentioned in the County Records of Nottinghamshire of 1770-1, although it probably had its first licence some 40 years before that. Three generations of the Dennett family controlled the destiny of this old hostelry for over a century from 1818, and one of its former postboys - John Blagg - could claim almost 50 years of service.

It was Blagg who set his fellow-servants to anxious glances up the road, their eyes agog with intense excitement, as he set out one early morning to attempt the well-nigh impossible task of journeying to York and back within the day - a distance of 110 miles. The staying-power of his horse must have been something to be marvelled at, as much later that day it returned, panting and steaming, to the inn bearing its jubilant rider. Blagg had triumphed. His ride won for him renown, and many travellers and horsemen would visit the inn to share the memory of his remarkable feat, and no doubt to drain a tankard or two of foaming ale.

The pub is now owned by Mansfield Brewery, who purchased it from North Country Breweries, an old Hull brewery, in 1985.

An explanation for the origin of this pub's name can be found by referring to the 'White Hart' at Lenton.

YE OLDE SUN - *Chapelgate*

Formerly just known as *'Old Sun,'* this is one of Retford's oldest inns dating back to the 16th century. An explanation for the origin of the name here can be found by referring to the *'New Sun'* at Retford.

RISE PARK

CHARLES II - *Bestwood Park Drive West*

Opened in November 1968, this pub is known locally as the *Charlie Two*. Years ago, the area in which this pub stands was often visited by various members of the Royal family to hunt - in particular Charles II, who reigned from 1660-1685.

Debonair, dissolute, and extremely selfish, Charles's easy charm made him popular with the people - especially after his return to England from exile. However, he was also capable of the occasional noble gesture - such as granting a charter to the Royal Society, the illustrious members of which have constantly added to this nation's reputation in respect of their scientific achievements.

Apart from the latter, this unkingly monarch is best (or worse) remembered for having a Spanish wife, no legitimate heirs, but any number of mistresses - Nell Gwynn, naturally, in particular.

ROLLESTON

CROWN - *Staythorpe Road*

The *'Crown'* dates from the early years of Queen Victoria's reign, and today is familiar to racegoers who flock to the nearby Southwell course. The pub was famous for an old tree which once grew there. It was known as "the horseshoe tree" and had an opening in its trunk large enough for 2 people to go through. It was thought to bring good luck to newly weds who followed the custom of passing through it together - (see also the *'Crown'* at Beeston for an explanation of the name).

RUDDINGTON

JOLLY FARMERS - *Wilford Road*

Originally a farmhouse dating from the 1750s, it became a licensed alehouse almost a century later, in 1850. The signboard picture is quite appropriate, showing as it does a trio of jolly farmers (and one jolly porker).

Humorous

Squinting Cat, Clipstone

Filly & Firkin, Nottingham

Toby Jug, Carlton

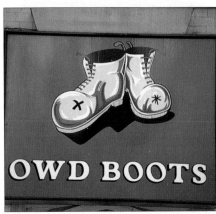

Fletcher & Firkin, Nottingham

Owd Boots, Nottingham

Ye Olde Jug & Glass, Edwinstowe

Dog & Rabbit, Warsop

The Windmill, Gotham

Ye Olde Market, Newark

March Hare, Nottingham

Plate V

Occupations

The Gleaners, Calverton

The Coopers, Mansfield

The Air Hostess, Tollerton

Bricklayers Arms, Ruddington

Smithys, Nottingham

Shepherds Rest, Lower Bagthorpe

Jolly Farmers, Ruddington

The Gardeners, St Anns

Masons Arms, Hucknall

Plate VI

RED HEART - *Easthorpe Street*

This old hostelry began its life, as a farmhouse, in the reign of Charles II, its date of foundation (1674) being shown on three old drawings in the possession of the licensee, all of which depict it as having a thatched roof at that time.

There are at least thirty different examples of pubs throughout the country having their name prefixed with the word *Red* - all the way from *Red Admiral* to *Red Rum* - and the *'Red Heart,'* like most in this unusual company, is unique by name and derivation. It has a wrought-iron sign, with a heart over-painted in red. The heart is said to symbolise that of Mary I (better-known as Mary, Queen of Scots, whose execution in 1587 preceded the reign of her cousin Elizabeth).

Red Heart, Ruddington (c.1930)

In 1558, the French town of Calais (captured by Edward III in 1347) had been handed back to its countrymen, and Mary's grief at this news was such that almost thirty years later, when she realised her death was imminent, she declared (so the legend says) that the word 'Calais' would be found engraved upon her heart.

THREE CROWNS - *Easthorpe Street*

This sign is interpreted in various ways by the sign-painters. In some instances the reference is to the Magi (the three wise men mentioned in the Gospels) who are often called kings and who came to Bethlehem to visit the Christ child. Later signs have added a portrait of James I as history credits him as being the first monarch (in the year 1603) to rule jointly over England, Scotland and Wales.

The sign here at this Free House is the orthodox one showing a row of three royal crowns. According to deeds, the building itself dates from 1762, shortly after the accession of George III.

VICTORIA TAVERN - *Wilford Road*

Evidence of the existence of this former farmhouse can be traced back to 1858 when it is recorded as operating as a beerhouse. At the turn of the century the house was run by a certain William Hicking, a charismatic figure who had no use for a till, preferring to deposit his takings into one of the numerous pockets set about his waistcoat, whilst he bustled about the place humming to himself.

As can be seen from the sign that hangs outside this house it is named in honour of Queen Victoria (1819-1901).

SCROOBY

PILGRIM FATHERS - *Great North Road*

Recorded in the 1832 Directory under its previous sign the *'Saracen's Head,'* this old hostelry was renamed the *'Pilgrim Fathers'* in 1969, following alterations to the building. Further extensions were added in 1989. The gable facing the road once had the datestone 1771 but this is now covered with rendering. The road outside was formerly the turnpike road of 1766, so the inn was clearly built to cater for travellers using it. Until 1906, the main door faced the road.

The inn's name commemorates the Pilgrim Fathers, many of whom came from the Scrooby area, including William Brewster, author of the Mayflower Compact, a democratic constitution leading to the first democratic election of a Governor in the entire history of European colonies.

The son of Scrooby's postmaster, Brewster was an intelligent and perceptive man. Whilst studying at Cambridge University he met the passionate Separatist leader Robert *'Troublechurch'* Browne and became one of his devout followers. When Browne fled to Holland in 1578, Brewster returned to Scrooby a committed Separatist, and became renowned for *'ripping up ye hart and conscience before God.'*

At nearby Babworth Church, Brewster discovered another ex-Cambridge scholar and follower of Browne, Rector Richard Clyfton. Here, Brewster and others worshipped in their own style and were joined in 1602 by the 12 year old William Bradford from Austerfield, who in later years became Governor of the 'Mayflower' colonists in their new settlement.

In late 1606, despite the possible danger from his landlord the Archbishop of York, Brewster set up a second Separatist Church in his home at Scrooby Manor. Formally separated from the Church of England, the Separatist congregation vowed: *'We covenant with God and with one another to walk in His ways made known or to be made known to us, according to our best endeavours, whatsoever it shall cost us, the Lord assisting us.'*

Shortly afterwards, following predictable harassment by his landlord and employer, Brewster was briefly imprisoned in York for his Separatist activities, and together with other Puritans, both from his own village and

Gainsborough, made a decision to leave England. In September 1607 the Scrooby congregation sold all their belongings and travelled to the Lincolnshire port of Boston. Having hired a ship to transport them to Holland they were soon betrayed by its Captain who robbed them and abandoned them downstream from Boston at a creek now known as Scotia Creek. Arrested for attempting to emigrate without permits, they were returned to Boston whereupon they were placed in the Guildhall Cells. A month later, the majority were released and returned to their own parishes, but seven, including Brewster and Clyfton, were detained for a longer period until local sympathisers were able to obtain their freedom.

By August 1608 Brewster and his family, together with a number of other Separatists, had managed to travel to Amsterdam where a number of them, including Richard Clyfton and Thomas Helwys (the squire of Broxtowe Hall, and a Baptist preacher), decided to settle. For a while Brewster was content to print inflammatory religious pamphlets which he then had smuggled back to England, but when King James traced their origin to his press he was forced to become a fugitive once more.

During the Autumn of 1620 a core group of the party, led by Brewster, Bradford and John Carver sailed from Delftshaven, Holland aboard the *Speedwell*. At Southampton they joined the *Mayflower* with its crew and passengers who were emigrating for economic reasons and the two ships set sail for the New World. *The Speedwell* soon proved to be unseaworthy and was forced to dock at Plymouth for repairs. Here, Brewster and his party boarded the *Mayflower*, which later sailed alone from Plymouth carrying these Pilgrims to their new life in North America.

SHELFORD

EARL OF CHESTERFIELD ARMS - *Manor Lane*

Earl of Chesterfield Arms, Shelford

Shelford Manor was the Stanhope family home for many generations. Sir Michael Stanhope, an important man during the reign of Queen Elizabeth I was beheaded on Tower Hill for his involvement in the failed Lady Jane Grey plot. Sir Michael's grandson, Philip was knighted in 1605, made Baron Stanhope of Shelford and then in 1628 was created the 1st Earl of Chesterfield. During the Civil War, the Earl's son, also Philip, unsuccessfully defended Shelford Manor against a Parliamentarian onslaught, and died from wounds received in the battle.

Yet another Philip Stanhope, 4th Earl of Chesterfield is famous, or infamous, for the somewhat scandalous Chesterfield letters, written between father and son, with tragic consequences. The daughter of the 6th Earl of Chesterfield married the 4th Earl of Carnarvon and the Shelford estate eventually passed to this family.

The local inn quite appropriately takes its name from this family's connections with the village. Ironically, part of this inn was once the Primitive Methodist Chapel!

SHERWOOD

QUORN - *Hucknall Road*

This pub was 'converted' from a former Sweets Factory in 1937. Its attractive signboard pictures the famous Quorn Hunt, which in turn is named from the village of Quorn near Loughborough.

ROBIN HOOD - *Mansfield Road*

This old pub, (listed in the 1861 directory) was rebuilt in the 1920s. It stands appropriately close by the '*Sherwood Inn*,' and proclaims a title found in well over a hundred locations elsewhere in the kingdom.

Not surprisingly, therefore, this traditional outlaw and subject of many English ballads yields place only to Nelson and Wellington in the long list of our national heroes immortalised on signboards, and signs in London antedated these names considerably, appearing as from the end of the 16th century. Charles Hindley, in his '*Tavern Anecdotes*' published in 1875, offers the following revealing comment. '*This sign has of late years been very much on the increase, and may to some account be accounted for by the rapid spread of the Ancient Order of Foresters.*'

The first mention of Robin Hood was by William Langland in his alliterative poem '*The Vision of Piers Plowman*' published in 1377. The first published collection of ballads about him was printed by Wynkyn de Worde about 1489. Sir Walter Scott introduced him to a wider audience in his stirring novel '*Ivanhoe*.' The stories concerning his '*Merrie Men*' formed the basis of early dramatic representations and were later amalgamated with the May Day revels of the Morris Dancers.

He is remembered in company with his chief henchman at Arnold - which carries the sign of 'Robin Hood and Little John' - whilst the latter on his own can be seen at Ravenshead. 'Friar Tuck' is also found in Arnold (he is represented at Blidworth as the 'Jolly Friar') as too is 'Maid Marian,' whereas 'Will Scarlet' resides at Hucknall. There was formerly a 'Robin Hood Arms' in the street of that name, but this pub was demolished in September 1972. The short-lived 'Robin Hood Tavern' in Market Street, Nottingham, opened in September 1986 but closed in July 1988 (having occupied the site of the former Classic Cinema, previously the Scala Cinema, and now demolished as part of the "Pearsons" re-development).

Interestingly, this pub at Sherwood is the sole one bearing this name to survive within the city boundary itself.

In June 1984 a regular here, Tony Fukes, spent five and a half hours in the Lounge breaking the World Press-ups Record - doing 6,220 in all!

SHERWOOD - Mansfield Road

The Sherwood Inn was built during the mid-1840s, and stands on the site of a former beerhouse run by a certain Widow Palethorpe. There were stables at the inn, which was strategically placed to serve both locals and travellers on the Mansfield Turnpike road. This house stands on the edge of what was once Sherwood Forest - hence its name. The name 'Sherwood' means 'wood belonging to the shire.' The inn's frontage was extended around 1898, with further additions coming later.

Sherwood Inn, Sherwood (c. 1890)

SHIREOAKS

HEWETT ARMS - Shireoaks Hall Drive

Sir Thomas Hewett, a London merchant, acquired Shireoaks in 1546, his son Henry building the Hall around 1600. Henry's son (another Sir Thomas) was High Sheriff of the county in 1620, while his grandson (a third Sir Thomas) achieved fame as the "Surveyor of Woods North of the Trent" to King William III, and then later (in 1719) as Surveyor General to King George I. It was this Sir Thomas who laid out the extensive gardens which included a unique water garden, still surviving, with a long canal, circular pond and thirty four cascades. Hewett also built the two little pavilion like stable blocks which frame the house on the north side in the distance. The Hewett family remained at Shireoaks Hall until 1811, when it was bought by the Duke of Norfolk who, in 1840, sold it to the 4th Duke of Newcastle.

Yet another stable block and coach house, built around 1714, is now the 'Hewett Arms'. Flanked by two formal ponds, the building was made into 3 cottages in 1914. In 1988 this conversion was removed to reveal the original form of the building, and to provide the ideal setting for a new pub which serves good food and 'real ale'. With so much good fishing nearby, the pub was initially a facility for local anglers but soon attracted many villagers, drawn to it by its charms and atmosphere. With the large breweries undertaking so much "modernisation" of their establishments, the "old fashioned" pub is becoming a rarity. The 'Hewett Arms' however, is a highly successful recreation of the traditional English pub but, with modern overtones provided by the additions of paintings by living artists, this is a also a contemporary pub - the ambience, however, remains "olde worlde".

In so many ways unique, the 'Hewett Arms' attracts architectural historians, anxious to see for themselves, the fascinations of this most interesting of pubs.

SKEGBY

MAYPOLE - Dawgates Lane

This old house (recorded in the 1832 Directory) was styled as the 'White Swan' until its current sign was unveiled on the 28th November 1975.

Even whilst operating under its former title it was still known as the 'Maypole' by the locals - recalling a real maypole that once stood opposite the pub many years ago.

SNEINTON

BATH INN - *Handel Street*

The first baths and wash-houses in Nottingham were founded in 1850 on the corner of nearby Bath Street and Sneinton Market.

BENDIGO - *Thurgarton Street*

Proudly named after the famous Nottingham boxing-preacher, this pub (opened on the 26th July 1957) replaced the *'Old Wrestlers'* as the pride of the district. A statue of the celebrated pugilist stands above the main door entrance, whilst he is commemorated inside the pub by a large oil-painting which shows him erect in southpaw stance (leading with his right!), stripped to the waist for action. Underneath this portrait are the words: 'He fought 14 battles and never was beaten.' The details of these historic bouts (one of which went to 99 rounds!) are listed on a broadsheet of the period which is framed and hung nearby.

William Abednego Thompson was born in 1811 at New Yard, now called Trinity Walk, Nottingham, the youngest of a family of 21, and one of triplets. It requires no profundity of biblical knowledge to realise that his equally unfortunate brothers were named after Shadrach and Meshach! By the time he had become a Champion of the Ring, after beginning his career as a prize-fighter in 1832, his middle name had been shortened by dropping its first letter, and his supporters found it convenient to make further adaptation. After his retirement from the Ring in 1850, he became a heavy drinker, being locked-up no less than 28 times in Nottingham's 'House of Correction' for disorderly conduct and worse. Then came a meeting which altered the whole course of his life. He went to listen to the preaching of Richard Weaver, the converted collier, and was so impressed that he, too, became converted and gave up his drinking habits. As William Thompson, he became a popular preacher, and when sermonising failed he would drive home the truth with his fists.

Bendigo, Sneinton

No doubt the picture conjured-up by these spectacular happenings prompted Sir Arthur Conan Doyle to recall one of them in verse, and the following lines form a vivid extract from 'Bendigo's Sermon' which he wrote (perhaps as a relaxation from Sherlock Holmes' latest adventure?) in the centenary year of the birth of the Thompson Triplets:

> *"But the roughs they went on chaffing and the rumpus it was such,*
> *That the preacher in the pulpit might be speaking Double Dutch,*
> *Till a working man who shouted as he got upon his feet,*
> *'Give us a lead, your reverence, and heave 'em in the street.'*
>
> *Then Bendy turned and said 'O Lord since first I left my sinful ways*
> *Thou knowest that to Thee alone I've given up my days,*
> *But now dear Lord (and here he placed his Bible on the shelf),*
> *I'll take with thy permission, just five minutes for myself.'*
>
> *He vaulted from the pulpit like a Tiger from a den,*
> *They say it was a lovely sight to see him floor his men,*
> *Right and left and left and right straight and true and hard*
> *Till the Ebenezer Chapel looked more like a butcher's yard.*
>
> *Tommy Pratt was on his back a-looking at his toes,*
> *Solly Jones from Perry Bar was feeling for his nose,*
> *Long Connor from the Bull Ring had all that he could do*
> *In raking for his ivories that lay about the pew.*

Jack Ball the fighting Gunsmith was in a peaceful sleep,
Joe Murphy lay across him all tied up in a heap,
Five of them were twisted in a tangle on the floor,
And Ikey Moss de Betting Boss had sprinted for the door.

Five repentant fighting men sitting in a row,
Listening to words of grace from Mister Bendigo
Five repentant fighting men all as good as gold,
Pretty little Baa-lambs gathered to the fold.

And that's the way that Bendy ran his mission in the slum,
And preached the Holy Gospel to the fighting men of Brum,
'The Lord' he said 'has given me a message from on high'
'And if you interrupt Him I will know the reason why.'"

In his 60th year Bendigo rescued three people from drowning in the River Trent, and on another occasion, for a wager, proved his ambidexterity by throwing a half-brick with his left hand over the river near Trent Bridge, a distance of 70 yards. The power of his arm was further demonstrated when another time he threw a cricket ball a distance of 117 yards.

He died in 1880 at his residence in Beeston, and was buried in St Mary's Cemetery, Bath Street, Sneinton, now a Garden of Rest. Here one can see the carved lion which surmounts his grave. The lion itself, symbolic of Bendigo's undoubted courage, has its inscription concluded with these epic lines:

"In Life always brave, fighting like a lion,
In Death like a lamb, tranquil in Zion."

Many citizens of Nottingham who have emigrated to Australia have been surprised to find that in the state of Victoria there is a flourishing city named after this remarkable man, and it is truly astonishing (as Cedric Bonnell said in his fascinating accounts of *'The Lambs of Lambkinville'*) to realise that Bendigo, on Bendigo Creek in Bendigo County, a hundred miles from Melbourne, actually became a city more than a quarter-century before William Abednego Thompson's native town was created such in *letters patent* by Queen Victoria in 1897. How many other citizens of Nottingham have had a city named in their honour, I wonder?

Bendigo's various trophies were for several years on exhibition at the *'Forest Tavern'* on Mansfield Road, together with a portrait of him painted in 1850, the year he became the Champion of All England and then took his retirement.

A local admirer subsequently penned these lines:

"Bold Bendigo is dead and gone, he in the grave does lie:
But praise be given where praise is due: his memory will not die.
At Mr. Beresford's spirit vaults, the far-famed Forest Inn."

It should be explained that this amateur poet really meant the *'Forest Tavern,'* not the *'Forest Inn'* on Alfreton Road - and in order to prevent any lasting confusion this was clearly stated in a footnote beneath the lines of verse. The 'presents' mentioned included some of his fishing prizes and a gold watch presented to him by the sporting landlord of a rival tavern.

EARL MANVERS - *Colwick Road*

The first pub to bear this name stood on Sneinton Hermitage before it was eventually demolished. This present house was built at the turn of the century in its place. At first it was called the *'Manvers Arms'* - and there are others so-named at Cotgrave and Radcliffe-on-Trent.

Earl Manvers himself had his family seat at Thoresby Hall. He was a prominent landowner in the district around Nottingham.

FOX - *Dale Street*

Opened as a public house in 1760, the *'Fox'* used to have three cellars (two of them caves set into the rock), but now it functions with only one.

The name here most likely alludes to the former Lord of the Manor's passion for fox-hunting.

HUCKLEBERRY'S - *Colwick Road*

This pub, then owned by the brewers Warwicks & Richardsons of Newark, started its life in November 1964 under the fanciful title (and a progressively-saucy trio of feline sign-pictures) of the *'Ginger Tom.'* Following the merging of its previous owners into the Courage group, the latter's marketing men decided, in August 1986, to re-christen the pub with

Earl Manvers, Sneinton

111

the 'novel' title it has borne since. This is in keeping, by the way, with the modern itch of brewers in general to try to impart an air of cosy congeniality into their new pubs by giving them a name allied to some celebrity of the past - either fact or fictional, often Dickensian or of Hollywood fame, but invariably relating to the world of literature or films.

'Huckleberry Finn,' like the equally-popular 'Tom Sawyer' and 'Pudd'nhead Wilson,' was a character created by the celebrated American humorist Samuel Langhorne Clemens (1835-1910). Under the subtle pseudonym of 'Mark Twain' - a nautical term relating to the Mississippi river-boats he knew well in his boyhood - he wrote several nostalgic novels that achieved for him a lasting fame. The name 'Mark Twain' was in fact one of the calls used by river pilots when taking soundings, in this case the 2-fathom mark on their lead-line.

JESTER - Sneinton Dale

The unusual name of this pub, opened in November 1967, possibly refers to a certain David Seal, a travelling showman who visited this area in the 1880s. However, tradition suggests that the subject was William Wallett, the eldest of 24 children, who was born at Hull in 1807. He made his first visit to Nottingham in 1848, where he married Sarah Farmer.

Wallet was a man of many accomplishments. An expert horseman and actor, he was chiefly famous for his Shakespearean orations in the circus ring and, at more serious gatherings, for delivering long monologues full of moral and political sentiments, spiced with wit and wisdom, well suited to the Victorian taste. His chief claim to national fame was in performing before Queen Victoria at Windsor Castle on the 19th July 1844, assuming the title of 'Royal Jester' (unofficial, really, since this office lapsed in the reign of James I). The remarkable Wallett appeared in his original role as the Shakespearean clown, and also took along four baby lion cubs from a friend's travelling circus. The show so pleased Her Majesty that he came away with a gold medallion and her permission to bill himself as 'The Queen's Jester.' Before he died in 1892 at his home in Beeston, he had a long and mainly successful career. The tombstone inscribed to him and his wife can be seen in the General Cemetery at Nottingham.

KING WILLIAM IV - Eyre Street

Known locally as the 'King Billy,' this pub was first recorded in the 1832 Directory.

The monarch after whom it is named lived from 1765 to 1837 and succeeded his brother George IV in 1830. Sadly, neither of them showed any kingly capacity, and both died from alcoholic cirrhosis - but despite this, a large number of tavern signs were put up in their honour. Genial and pleasure-loving, 'King Billy' placed no obstacles in the way of government - indeed, the repeal of the Malt Tax in 1830, the year of his accession, was alleged to have happened through his influence - and he remained popular with the majority of his subjects.

Flatteringly styled the 'Sailor King' (the signboard portrays him in splendid nautical uniform), he was present as a Midshipman at the relief of Gibraltar in 1780, served as Captain of a frigate with Nelson in the West Indies five years later. He became a Rear-admiral five years after that - the quickest-ever leap up the promotion ladder to Flag rank in naval history, without any doubt!

Lord Nelson, Sneinton (1933)

LORD NELSON - Thurgarton Street

Known locally as the 'White House,' this pub was originally two cottages which were knocked together when it first started serving ale about 200 years ago. The building itself is thought to be 500 years old. The cellars here have been hollowed out of the sandstone caves beneath it. The 'Lord Nelson' was once known as the 'Hornbuckles', and served as an inn and coaching house on the road to Southwell.

A detailed explanation for the name can be found by referring to the pub of the same name at Arnold.

MAGPIES - Daleside Road

The sign here depicts a pair of these handsome but predatory birds, but the title itself signifies footballers wearing black-and-white kit who play for Notts. County F.C., the oldest soccer club in the Football League, which was established in 1862.

This pub, opened on the 26th April 1957, stands close by the team's ground - and as the club's nickname is 'The Magpies,' the name here is implicit.

MARKET SIDE - Bath Street

Previously called the 'Sir Robert Clifton,' it was re-opened under its current title on the 12th March 1982 by the then Lord Mayor of Nottingham, Councillor John Arnold.

The pub takes its name from its close proximity to Sneinton Market.

QUEEN ADELAIDE - *Windmill Lane*

Opened on the 28th December 1962, this place is the successor to the old pub of the same name in North Street, which closed down just two years earlier. Built on the site of a former building, once occupied by the superintendent of Nottingham's public parks and cemeteries, its name remembers Queen Adelaide, the wife of William IV. The pub has a superb sign bearing her portrait.

In the decade following the Beer Act of 1830, licences proliferated, almost like overnight mushrooms, in the congested courts and thoroughfares of our noble city. In consequence of this, any personage who caught the public fancy was usually 'adopted' by an innkeeper and commemorated accordingly - as occasioned by the royal, though fleeting enough, visit to Nottingham by Adelaide in July of 1840.

Queen Adelaide, Sneinton

Nottingham in medieval times was all too well accustomed to the comings and goings of the monarchy, but royal visitations had dried up for almost a couple of centuries - ever since Charles I raised his ill-fated standard outside the castle in 1642. So the town (we didn't become a city until 1897, remember) was a-buzz with gossip when it became known that the Queen Dowager was to set foot within its boundaries. Truth to tell, Adelaide had no interest in Nottingham whatever, except that it was the terminus of the Midland Counties Railway, which had opened the year previous. She was on her way from Belton House, near Grantham, where she had been visiting Earl and Countess Brownlow, and intended to proceed to Harewood House in Yorkshire. An article appearing in the *Guardian Journal* on 29th December 1962 recalls the occasion of her visit. *"The royal cortege, consisting of three carriages, with an advance and rear-guard of dragoons, rolled across Trent Bridge and along the Flood Road to Leen-side. Reaching Carrington Street, it turned left over the canal bridge and reached the M.C.R. station on the right-hand side of the road. The Station House, as it was then called, had been decorated for the occasion, the Mayor was presented and, amid great enthusiasm, the Queen Dowager and her distinguished retinue took their seats in the train which transported them to Derby and thence by the York and North Midland Railway into Yorkshire."*

A day so memorable that a Sneinton innkeeper put up a new sign which has been perpetuated for well over a century.

Not to be too unkind to Queen Adelaide, the sad fact remains that she was one of those worthy, but stiff-necked, German ladies of exalted birth, whom the sons of George III (there were 9 of them!) were persuaded by the politicians into marrying in the hope that they would provide male heirs to the throne - daughters in those days creating what card players would term a royal abundance.

Born in 1792, the daughter of the Duke of Saxe-Coburg Meiningen, Adelaide was 26 when, in 1818, she married William, the third of George III's nine sons. He was then Duke of Clarence, 53 years of age, and already the father of ten children by the actress Mrs Dorothea Jordan, whom one must inevitably suspect of being even more accommodating than Nell Gwynn where subservience to royalty was concerned! To add to her humiliation, poor Adelaide could only bear him two daughters, both of whom died in infancy - and her unpopularity with the populace was heightened owing to her supposed interference with politics during the agitation over the revolutionary Reform Bill of 1832.

There is another pub with this name at Swingate, near Kimberley.

VINE - *Handel Street*

Mounted beside the curiously-shaped main entrance to this old house is a plaque, which reads :

'One of Nottingham's last examples of a corner door pub. The curved front door opens directly onto the street corner. It has been an inn since 1876. Home Brewery bought it in 1896 when the premises also included stables and a smithy. The structure with its uneven floor has been kept virtually unchanged ever since.'

First appearing in the 14th century, the sign of the *'Vine'* is not so common in Britain today as it once was. It is often a reference to heraldry and the Worshipful Company of Distillers (1638), whose arms show a vine bearing grapes. Vines may also be a reference to wine. In 1720 The Compleat Vintner had this to say of the vine:

Vine, Sneinton

'Without there hangs a noble sign,
Where golden grapes in image shine;
To crown the bush, a little Punch
Gut Bacchus dangling of a bunch,
Sits loftily enthron'd upon
What's called (in miniature) a Tun.'

As well as appearing on the pub's more traditional hanging sign, grapes can be found in abundance here - with a large mural of a vine, laden with fruit, cascading down its outer walls.

WHEATSHEAF - *Sneinton Road*

Formerly the *'New Inn,'* this pub was re-built and opened as the *'Wheatsheaf'* by Home Brewery on the 24th October 1966.

An explanation of the origin of the name here can be found by referring to the pub of the same name at Burton Joyce.

SOUTHWELL

ADMIRAL RODNEY - *King Street*

The *Admiral Rodney* stands on the site of another pub, the *"White Lion"*, demolished in the 1750s. It was named after the admiral whose exploits are listed under the *'Admiral Rodney'* at Wollaton.

BRAMLEY APPLE - *Church Street*

Recorded in the 1832 Directory as the *'George and Dragon,'* this old inn changed its sign to the *'Bramley Apple'* in 1976. This unique new name is aptly portrayed by a large green plastic apple of the said variety, which hangs outside the pub. At the pub's re-opening after refurbishment in 1989, the guests included Newark MP, Mr Richard Alexander

Bramley Apple, Southwell

and Mrs Celia Steven, great-grand-daughter of the man who grew the original Bramley apple tree in Southwell, at a cottage near to where the inn stands. The original tree is still growing *and* bearing fruit! A framed legend inside the pub recalls the event:

'In the garden of a nearby cottage, an apple tree of great history and interest began its life at the beginning of the last century in a plant pot into which the lady of the house set two or three pips from an apple she was eating. The seedlings grew, and two or three were planted in the garden. By the time a Mr. Matthew Bramley purchased the cottage in 1846 the tree was bearing a good crop of apples and one day Mr. Henry Merryweather met the gardener carrying a fine basketful. He went to see Mr. Bramley, who said he had named the apple Bramley's Seedling and told him he could take what grafts he liked. It was at the Royal Horticulture Society's Fruit Committee that the Bramley was first exhibited in 1876. Whilst it may have been possible to count the apples that grew on that first tree, nobody knows the number of trees that have originated from the apple a lady of Southwell ate in the year of Trafalgar.'

Interestingly, when the apple sign outside this pub fell down in March 1981 and had to be removed for repair, some practical joker temporarily replaced it with a papier-mâché apple core!

CROWN HOTEL - *Market Place*

Displaying a sign that shows allegiance to the monarchy, the origins of this old coaching inn can be traced back to a bill of 1770 which was issued to the Steward of the Courts of the Manors of Southwell, Scrooby, Laneham and Askham, an appointee of the Archbishop of York. The bill was paid by the Steward on behalf of a gentleman and his servant who had stayed at the *'Crown'* for a full day that year, and covered *'eating 7s 0d, wine 2s 0d, ale, beer and porter 4s 9d and servant's eating and ale 2s 4d, a total sum of 16s 1d' - a princely sum in those days.*

Betty Arundel, in her excellent booklet *Southwell, A History Walk*, notes that the inn was re-built in 1820 by the innkeeper, William Smith. Until then the first floor overhung the roadway on pillars, with butchers' stalls occupying the space beneath. The old *'Crown'* building even had its own slaughterhouse! The area opposite, adjacent to the *'Saracen's Head'*, was Southwell's original market place.

HEARTY GOOD FELLOW - *Church Street*

The name of this old house (recorded in the 1832 Directory) is adopted from a ballad which was popular during the 1860s. (See pub of the same name in Nottingham).

NEWCASTLE ARMS - *Station Road*

This pub, standing adjacent to the former railway line, now the Southwell Trail, was built in the 1860s. It is not certain as to why the pub is so named, because the Duke of Newcastle did not own land in Southwell. He was however, very much a benefactor of the area and perhaps this name indicates a certain local appreciation.

Hearty Good Fellow, Southwell

REINDEER - *Westgate*

Betty Arundel's researches have revealed that this pub was built in 1827 by George Abbot who, in addition to being the landlord, was also a "coach proprietor, livery stable keeper and veterinary surgeon". The inn does not appear to have had a name until at least forty years after it was built. The 1864 directory lists William Baker of Westgate as a *'letter of horse and gig, omnibus proprietor and agent to Railway Company'*. In 1872, William Baker was at *'The Reindeer'*, described then as a 'posting house', and the first occasion it is referred to by this name. Betty Arundel says that *'The Reindeer'* was an important coaching inn with stable accommodation for about 20 horses. Some of the stable buildings still survive although today serving other purposes.

Newcastle Arms, Southwell (c. 1900)

SARACEN'S HEAD - *Market Place*

Historically, this former coaching inn, is one of Nottinghamshire's most notable hostelries. Evidence in the form of a Deed (dated 20th October 1396) records the sale of an existing building on the site, by the then Archbishop of York, Thomas Arundel to John and Margaret Fysher. Tradition dates the building back almost to the time of the Norman Conquest in 1066 and, over the years, a number of Kings and Noblemen are reputed to have stayed here, but there is no certainty that it was actually an inn.

It is likely that the old building was demolished, and the present day *Saracen's Head* built on the same site. We know from tree ring dating that the oldest timbers date from 1430. Timbers from a different part of the inn date from 1460 thus indicating that extensions were added in that year. It is quite possible that this new building was known as the *'Saracen's Head'*.

On 5th May 1646, an event occurred within the walls of this hostelry, which was to ensure its place in history. At seven o'clock that morning, following his escape from Oxford, King Charles I arrived with his faithful companion Dr Hudson. Weary after an all-night ride, he rested a while, ate and then left for Kelham where he surrendered to the Scottish General, Sir David Leslie. That was the end of Charles as a free man. In January 1647, the Scots handed him over to the Parliamentarians. After a period in captivity, the King was eventually tried and later beheaded at Whitehall on 30th January 1649.

A verse was written by the Right Reverend Selwyn, then Bishop of New Zealand, who stayed at the *'Saracen's Head'* on 5th March 1858. In spite of his good accommodation he passed a sleepless night and wrote a poem which alludes to King Charles's unhappy stay. It includes the following verses:

1. 'I cannot rest - for on this spot
   Where I have made my bed,
   O'erwearied with the strife of state,
   A king hath laid his head.

2. Thy sacred head, ill-fated Charles,
   Hath lain where now I lie;
   And thou has passed, in Southwell Inn
   As sleepless night as I.

3. I cannot rest - for o'er my mind
   Come thronging full and fast,
   The stories of the olden time,
   The visions of the past.

4. 'Twas here he rested
   Ere he raised his standard for the fight;
   Here he called on Heaven to help his cause,
   My God, defend the right!

5. Here gather'd round him
   All the flow'r of England' chivalry;
   And here the vanquished Monarch
   Closed his days of liberty.

6. I cannot rest - for Cromwell's horse
   Are neighing in mine ear;
   E'en in the Holy House of God
   Their ringing hoofs I hear.'

Saracen's Head, Southwell (c. 1900)

A later visitor to Southwell was Lord Byron, who stayed at his mother's house on Burgage Green. On one of his visits, he wrote his well-known epitaph on John Adams of Southwell, a carrier who operated his business from the inn and who had died of drunkenness:

*John Adams lies here, of the Parish of Southwell
A Carrier who carried his can to his mouth well;
He carried so much and he carried so fast
He could carry no more - so was carried at last.
For the liquor he drank, being too much for one,
He could not carry off - so is now carri-on!*

It is a widely-held belief that the inn was known as the 'Kings Arms' when King Charles I visited it in 1646 but there appears to be little documentary evidence to support this. Dr Thoroton in his 1677 'History of Nottinghamshire' writes that "there is in Southwell a chief inn now, and long since, called the Saracen's Head". Noble families whose members had taken part in the Crusades often included a Saracen's Head as part of their arms, it then being transferred to inn signs in the normal way. During the reign of Richard Coeur de Leon (Richard I), many inns displayed the Saracen's Head. Richard Shilton in his 'History of Southwell' (1818) describes how the proprietor in 1797, William Hind, discovered beneath an old sign of the *Saracens Head*, a square stone set into the wall, on which were carved the Kings Arms and the date 1693. Shilton indicates that *both* titles might have been in use at the same time when the stone was placed in the wall. A mystery not yet fully explained!

In the 1840s the *'Saracen's Head'* was described as a 'commercial inn, posting house and excise office'.

A television crew from Yorkshire Television arrived at the *'Saracen's Head'* in 1969 to film a scene for the series *'How We Used To Live.'* For the episode a coach-and-four, supposedly transporting passengers on a journey from York to London, was driven into the courtyard of the inn, where it was greeted by an actress posing as a buxom landlady.

In 1978, the exterior stucco, which had covererd the building for nearly 300 years, was removed to reveal the superb half-timbered frontage we see today.

Saracen's Head, Southwell

WHEATSHEAF - *King Street*

This pub, which has been selling ale since 1799, stands adjacent to the present day Market Place. The building has undergone considerable alterations in recent years, as Betty Arundel notes in her *Southwell, A History Walk*. She also relates that when the innkeeper during the 1820s, Richard Revill, died, his body and coffin supposedly "weighed 5 cwts"! An explanation for the origin of the name can be found by referring to the *'Wheatsheaf'* at Burton Joyce.

ST. ANNS

BEACON - *Blue Bell Hill Road*

Opened on the 19th June 1974, this pub's lofty position no doubt gave rise to its name. Outside, its sign displays a warning beacon being lit to warn of a naval invasion (possibly the Spanish Armada).

An explanation for the origin of the name can be found by referring to the *'Beacon'* at Aspley.

CHASE - *Robin Hood Chase*

Opened on the 5th October 1973, its name was chosen due to its proximity to the tree-lined Robin Hood Chase. This pub replaced the *'Garden Gate Inn'* (closed on 4th October 1973) which used to stand nearby.

DAME AGNES MELLERS - *Woodborough Road*

This pub, with its notable name, opened in June 1973, but it had been preceded by another hostelry, which closed in 1968, called *'Dame Agnes'* in the street of that name, now no more.

On the death of her husband, Richard Mellers, a wealthy Nottingham bell-founder and former Mayor, Dame Agnes Mellers (from whom this pub takes its name) became what was known as a vowess, which mean that she resolved to remain a widow for the rest of her life. As part of her vow she also decided to devote her energy and fortune to good works.

A woman of her word, many poor people in the district benefited from her generosity. The dearest wish of Dame Agnes' heart, though, was to found a school for boys. She knew exactly the kind of school she wished to see. It was to be a place where boys would receive the finest education available. Importantly, the boys' curriculum would have to include Latin and sound religious training, and they should be brought up to be honest and useful citizens.

It was not an easy matter to found such a school. Whilst Dames Agnes had plenty of good will and money, she soon found out that she also needed to obtain Royal Assent.

It is at times like this, that it is very convenient to know people in the right places. Being highly-respected and well-connected, Dame Agnes was fortunate in having Sir Thomas Lovell as a friend. Not only Governor of Nottingham Castle, Sir Thomas was also Speaker of the House of Commons and thus a very powerful man. Through his influence, she received the long-awaited document from King Henry VIII, granting her permission to found her school.

A considerable amount of money, even in those days, was required to endow such a school, so Dame Agnes opened a subscription list. Her own name was at the head, followed by her two sons, themselves prominent businessmen in the city. Others contributed and the scheme was launched.

In her will (she died in 1514) Dame Agnes instituted an annual obit (death anniversary) in St Mary's Church to herself and her late husband. To secure the attendance of the Mayor, she granted him a payment of 6d, to each Alderman 4d, and to the Mayor's Clerk and Sergeants 2d. To this she added a grant of 2/- for bread, cheese and ale. This may strike us as frugal fare for the dignitaries of the town, but it was then general - tea and coffee were unknown, and bread and cheese a standing dish.

With regard to the school officials, she made a curious ordinance, one from which we may glean that the morals of our ancestors were no better than our own. It was that they should abstain from drinking, from making and using potations (strong liquor) and from attending cock-fights - either by themselves, or in company with their wives, or with any of the tavern hostesses. This rule was not to be absolute, but the exceptions were not to be more than one or two in the year, one of which was doubtless the great Annual (Goose) Fair, a regular short season of carnival (in those times it was literally a Nine Days' Wonder) always stimulated by the provision of drinking-booths.

Dame Agnes would be proud to see how her dream has been fulfilled, and in what high respect her school (founded in 1513) is held. Boys have gone out from Nottingham High School to fill important positions in many countries of the world.

GARDENERS - *Wells Road*

Opened in April 1962, this pub was built on a site formerly spanned by an old single-track railway bridge. Part of an abutment from the bridge was used as a wall for its cellar. When built, the pub overlooked nearby allotments - prompting the name, the *'Gardeners.'* This name was changed in October 1982 to the *'Hoe Down'* (a subtle image-transference to a Barn Dance?) but reverted in August 1989. The *'Gardeners'* stands on the site of the old St Ann's Well (refer to the *'Wishing Well'* for further details).

Gardeners, St Ann's

LORD ALCESTER - *St Matthias Road*

Built in the late 1880s, this pub was named after a former Commander-in-Chief of the Mediterranean Fleet, Admiral Seymour. In 1882 he was raised to the peerage as the 1st Baron Alcester for his efficiency in persuading Arabi Pasha, the Egyptian ruler to repay his country's outstanding debts to Britain. Diplomacy having failed, this was achieved by the simple expedient of bombarding the port of Alexandria until a large white flag hoisted ashore signalled that the stubborn Pasha was now ready and willing to pay up.

Curiously enough, an unexploded bomb was found in the rafters of this pub when alterations were being made in 1978 - but it was carried out by the builders and made safe!

PEVERIL - *Beacon Hill Rise*

This name refers to William de Peverel, a bastard son of William the Conqueror, who was ordered by his father in 1068 to build a castle on the precipitous rock on the outskirts of Nottingham town. Peverel became the Castle's first governor. Originally a wooden fortress, it was later re-built in stone by King Henry I. This was burned down, however, and in turn was resurrected by Henry II, who gave Nottingham its first charter in 1155.

The pub itself, opened in December 1975, is a successor to the former *'Peveril'* (closed in February 1974) which stood on the corner of Gordon Road and Pym Street.

ST ANN'S INN - *Shelton Street*

Like the area in which it stands, this pub (opened in July 1973) is named after St Anne (50BC - 50AD), the wife of St Joachim and mother of the Blessed Virgin Mary. St Anne, whose feast day is the 26th July, is the patron saint of carpenters.

SYCAMORE - *Hungerhill Road*

Opened on the 12th November 1971 by the then Sheriff of Nottingham, Councillor Bernard Bateman, this was the second new pub to be opened in St Anns following redevelopment of the area (the *'Westminster Abbey'* being the first). It replaced the old house of the same name which stood, as its name implies, on Sycamore Road - thus perpetuating its name.

WELCOME INN - *St Anns Well Road*

The title of this pub, when it opened in November 1984 as the *'Pint And Pot',* was deliberately ambiguous, referring as it did to the joint activities once available within - drinking at the bar and potting at the twelve snooker tables away from it! In the latter sense it compared with the pub at Bestwood named 'Potters' (qv).

By February 1994 the pub had been reduced to two snooker tables and the brewers, deciding that its title was no longer apt, opted to run a Name-a-Pub Competition amongst its patrons - the current title being chosen as the winning entry - a reference to the warmth and friendliness of its regulars.

WESTMINSTER ABBEY - *St Anns Well Road*

The original pub of this name was demolished (together with more than fifty others) as part of the St Ann's area development during the 1970s. This, its successor, was opened on a nearby site in September 1971, and preserves the uniqueness of this name as applied to a public-house.

It would be readily assumed, no doubt, that the majority of our monarchs have been wed (as well as crowned) in the real Westminster Abbey. In fact since King Henry I's marriage in 1100, the first truly royal wedding to follow in this place was that of the present Queen Mother in 1923 - since when the nation has celebrated first the wedding in 1947 and then the coronation in 1953 of her elder daughter Elizabeth, our present Queen, both in this same historic building.

WISHING WELL - *Cardinal Close*

Opened in August 1978 by the then Lord Mayor, Councillor Oscar Watkinson, this pub reflects the history of the former *'St Ann's Well'* pub on the road of the same name. The latter building was shown on Cherry's map (see the *'Aviary'*, Trent Bridge for details) and also listed on Sessions Rolls of 1822-1824. According to legend, the water in the well on the premises of this former ancient tavern possessed certain healing properties, being famous for curing practically everything - from painful gout to lack of amorous potential.

According to Richard Iliffe of the Nottingham Historical Film Unit, it was first recorded as a resort for pilgrims seeking cures as early as 1409, and during the 17th and 18th centuries the area had become a well-patronised spa where visitors would be entertained by musicians and dancers. In 1824, however, the drunken and unseemly orgies at the place had attracted the official attention of the magistrates and its licence was withdrawn. Moreover, the place in due course was turned into a Temperance Tea Garden - with disastrous results to its popularity!

The celebrated Well was demolished and covered over during the construction of the Nottingham Suburban Railway in August 1887. It had stood on the site of the bridge carrying the line over Wells Road, and a plaque marking this site can be seen high up on the side wall of the *'Gardeners'* pub nearby (qv).

The old *'St Ann's Well'* pub was the very last to be demolished under the massive Redevelopment Scheme for the area (it closed in August 1976) - and it was replaced exactly two years later, under a different (but related) name, by the present house.

Wishing Well, St Ann's

STAPLEFORD

CHEQUERS INN - *Nottingham Road*

Very little appears to be known about the history of this pub, which stands at a place known locally as 'The Roach', a name which goes back to Napoleonic times when French prisoners of war camped there. They were engaged on road building, and because of the amount of rock they encountered they continually made reference to 'les roches' (the rocks).

The earliest listing for this pub is in White's Directory of 1864 when the landlord was William Randall, but it could well have existed several decades before that. It is said that, after the Charge of the Light Brigade, during the Crimean War, Scots Guards came back to drink at the *'Chequers'*, but there is no evidence to confirm this. The building appears to be mid-19th century, and probably replaced, or incorporated, an older building which stood on the site. By 1922, it was listed as the "Chequers Hotel".

For further information about the name, please refer to the *'Chequers'* at Chilwell.

FEATHERS TAVERN - *Church Street*

This name is a reference to the plume of three ostrich feathers first adopted by the 'Black Prince,' known as such because of the colour of his armour. He was Edward, Prince of Wales (1330-1376), the eldest son of Edward III - and the insignia by which this title was recognised is the same as that which belongs to the present Prince of Wales, together with its motto *'Ich dien'* (meaning 'I serve').

The underlying significance of such a name is one of allegiance. It is fairly common in other parts of the country, but for some reason it is not found elsewhere in Nottinghamshire.

HAPPY MAN - *Hickings Lane*

The happy man shown on the attractive, double-faced, sign outside this pub is Admiral Sir John Warren, Bt., the girl of his choice is a general's daughter named Caroline Clavering, whom he met at a party in 1780. They have been on public view since June 1955, by courtesy of Hardys and Hansons Brewery.

According to the romantic story, Sir John was suddenly transfixed by one of Cupid's arrows whilst sitting opposite Miss Clavering at table, and proceeded to express the ardent nature of his sentiments by writing a message to her in French, then the socially-acceptable medium of communication in High Society, within the outline of a heart he had drawn on a sheet of paper. The words, depicted quite clearly on the inn-sign, were as follows: *'Si vous croyez ce coeur digne de vous et si vous daigner l'accepter, vous me ferez le plus heureux des hommes'*. This can be translated as, 'If this heart is worthy of you and you deign to accept it, you will make me the happiest of men.' He then folded the paper and passed it across the table to Miss Clavering, who fortunately by this time had caught Cupid's arrow on the rebound. She read it, looked up, smiled demurely and replied in English, *'Then you shall be happy!'* Their wedding took place soon afterwards, and the pair lived happily together for over forty years until the gallant Admiral's death in 1822. A memorial tablet to his life and work can be seen in St Mary's Church, Attenborough.

Happy Man sign, Stapleford

Sir John's middle name was an unusual one. He is commemorated in full by the *'Sir John Borlase Warren'* at Canning Circus, Nottingham - although in fact for many years his middle name here was incorrectly spelled Borlace. Other local pubs which perpetuate his name are the *'Warren Arms'* in Stapleford and, over the border in Derbyshire, the *'Sir John Warren'* which appears at both Ilkeston and Loscoe.

Born in 1753, Sir John served the city as an MP for twelve years and lived at Stapleford Hall - serving also as a county magistrate. During the struggles at sea against the French he was a conspicuously successful officer under both Nelson and Howe (he was promoted to full Admiral in 1810) and later during the Napoleonic Wars he was appointed Commander-in-Chief of America and the West Indies.

According to the biographical study of the *'Men of Nottingham and Notts.'* by Robert Mellors, Sir John was 'courageous, active, skilful, generous, courteous and affable' - but just how much of this was due to his wife, the records do not relate! Lady Caroline Warren survived her husband by eighteen years, and died in 1840. She was keenly interested in matters of education, and in addition to a school at Toton she also built and endowed schools in Stapleford.

HORSE AND JOCKEY - *Nottingham Road*

This pub is the one of the oldest buildings in Stapleford, dating back quite possibly to 1790, according to local records. Its former patrons include Sir John Borlase Warren, squire of Stapleford Hall, whose coach was once a regular sight outside the pub. He owned one racehorse 'Old Careless' which he entered in Nottingham Races and elsewhere, with some success. The horse was always ridden by the same man, Jockey Towle, who lived close to Stapleford Hall.

During the 1970s its rooms were given appropriate names associated with horse-racing, such as *Tattersall's, Tattenham Corner* and *The Paddock*. Its public toilets followed suit - those for women and those for men being designated as The Royal Enclosure and The Winning Post respectively. A dead-heat between Ascot and Epsom, evidently!

JAGUAR - *Hickings Lane*

Opened on the 5th August 1965, this pub has a name that is almost unique, a 'partner' for it can be found in Coventry, not far from the gates of the internationally-known motor manufacturers.

Those patrons who enquired the reason for their 'local' having such a strange name were told that the brewery architects had suggested some variation from the usual run of wildlife, and had borrowed a big cat idea from the South American jungle.

MAGPIE - *Toton Lane*

Opened on the 19th April 1956, this pub's signboard features a colourful picture of the bird that according to the Bible, refused to enter Noah's Ark.

Having started life with the simple name of 'pye' or 'pie,' this long-tailed bird with black and white plumage reputedly collects objects. Due to its antics it became known as the 'maggoty pye', which was later abbreviated to Magpie. This epithet is preserved in the following Nursery Rhyme, which also happens to mention ale:

'Round about, round about
Maggoty Pie,
My father loves good ale
And so do I.'

MAN OF IRON - *Pasture Road*

The name of this house, complete with its signboard's depiction of a furnace-man at work, is a reference to the nearby Stanton Ironworks.

Once a former working-men's club called the *'Grosvenor'*, this pub was opened on the 19th March 1965 by Councillor M. Challenger, then vice-chairman of the Beeston and Stapleford Urban District Council.

OLD CROSS - *Church Street*

First appearing in White's 1853 Directory as an unnamed beerhouse before being mentioned in the 1864 County Directory under its current title, this old pub takes its name from the ancient Saxon cross which stands opposite in St Helen's Churchyard. The cross is ten feet high and has been ascribed to the period of King Canute, i.e. early 11th century. The weather-beaten carvings that adorn it include one which probably represents the symbol of St Luke - it is a horned figure with wings, treading on a serpent. How the cross came to be erected is a mystery - at one time it used to stand in the road outside the church, and near to the pub, but was re-sited in the churchyard earlier this century.

PAVILION - *Derby Road*

The *'Pavilion'* is one of the county's newest pubs, built in 1988, and very much a product of the time - a very lively place with the younger visitor in mind. Although the sign depicts what appears to be a bandstand in a park, no one, not even Mansfield Brewery, is quite sure why this pub should be so named. Perhaps its shape being similar to a cricket pavilion may provide an answer.

WARREN ARMS - *Derby Road*

A listed building, this old inn dates back to at least 1726 and is one of the oldest licensed

Old Cross, Stapleford

premises in Stapleford. Like the sign of the *'Happy Man'* (qv), the name here recalls the town's association with the Warren family of Stapleford Hall. In 1992 the brewery considered changing the pub's name to *'Lloyds'* with the intention of transforming it into a so-called fun-pub, but local folk and the town council steadfastly refused to allow Ansells to break its links with its famous namesake Sir John Borlase Warren.

STAUNTON-IN-THE-VALE

STAUNTON ARMS - *Main Street*

This pub certainly dates from the early 1800s, and may possibly be older than that. Until 1978, it was part of the Staunton Estate (it was originally built to serve the estate workers), and had a 6 day license. The grandfather and great grandfather of Edmund Staunton, who resides at the Hall today, were both vicars of the local church and would not allow the pub to open on Sundays. Since 1978, the inn has been in private hands and now opens every day.

The Staunton name is one which, in Nottinghamshire, goes back over 900 years to the days when Sir Mauger Staunton defended Belvoir Castle against William the Conqueror. A family tree inside the pub traces the descendents of Geoffrey de Staunton who lived about 1230 AD. Many of his descendants are buried in the nearby village church which stands adjacent to the Hall. This is still occupied by members of the Staunton family, thus making them probably the oldest family in the country still to occupy the ancestral estate from which they take their name.

An oil painting in the pub shows Sir William Staunton, a typical Cavalier who fought for King Charles I in the Civil War. This painting is a copy of the original which hangs in Staunton Hall, which came under fire from the Roundheads, forcing Sir William's wife and family to flee to London. Several large holes in the front door were caused by cannon fire during this raid.

Staunton Arms, Staunton-in-the-Vale

During the 1940s, the pub's roof was replaced by German prisoners of war, who were then working on the estate as farm labourers. The pub was then an ordinary beerhouse, popular with quarrymen working in the limestone and gypsum quarries nearby. Some of these men are no doubt to be found in the large collection of family photographs, some going back as far as 1869, displayed on the walls.

In 1991, the pub received a Royal Visit from Princess Anne who was in Staunton to plant a tree.

The inn once had a sign depicting the Arms of the Staunton family. This has long since gone, but it is expected that a replacement sign will be put up in the near future.

STOKE BARDOLPH

FERRY BOAT - *Stoke Lane*

Over the years this pub's position next to the River Trent, has led to it being flooded on a number of occasions. During the bleak winter of 1947 the river burst its banks and swept into the building, and in 1977 the waters were once again seeping into its cellars after violent storms had caused the river to swell.

It was during the early 1970s that the owners of the house, Nottingham City Council, leased it to Greenalls Brewery on the condition that the building was demolished and the site redeveloped. In 1991, after major building work and refurbishment by the brewery, the City

Ferry Boat, Stoke Bardolph (1886)

Council removed the demolition clause and this old hostelry (mentioned in the 1832 Directory) was saved. During the latter part of the 19th century the building was used as the background for a photograph of the South Notts. Hunt which was published in *Punch* in 1886.

The name here is a reference to a ferry that once transported passengers across the river to Shelford and operated from the river-bank in front of this pub. The last known ferryman was a Mr George Chambers, whose fare for the trip was 6d per person, or 7d for those who had a bicycle.

STRELLEY

Broad Oak, Strelley

BROAD OAK - *Main Street*

'Broad' here can be interpreted as 'spreading,' but this venerable village inn takes its name not from the tree outside the building but from the original tree in the Broad Oak plantation behind nearby Strelley Hall.

After more than 200 years as part of the estate, the inn itself was sold by auction in September 1962. Before that it was one of the few inns still operating under a six-day licence, closing on Sundays and such days as Christmas Day and Good Friday, in common with almost all licensed houses on private estates that were tied in this way.

When it was sold, the *'Broad Oak'*

became the property of the People's Refreshment and Holidays Association (PRHA) and after due renovation, was sold in turn to Hardys and Hansons. The latter re-opened the place under a new licence in March 1967, when the 'Sunday Rush' proved quite phenomenal - naturally enough, it could be said, as this was the first time such an event had taken place since the premises had been originally licensed in 1811.

That eminent County historian Arthur Mee records in his writings, *'Strelley lies off the beaten track, an unspoiled village with luxuriant lanes and a wealth of trees. From Norman days to Charles the Second there was an unbroken line of Strelleys in this place which gave them a name and a home, and it was their boast that twelve successive generations were knighted. They were renowned for their service to county and country, and were among the biggest landowners in Notts.'*

These words were written in 1938, and the account mentions Ralph Edge, to whom the estate was sold in 1678, and in the hands of whose family it remained until 1962. He was three times Mayor of Nottingham.

It is recorded in the village church that Strelley itself is one of the few places entered in the famous *Domesday Book* (1068 AD) whose population over the intervening centuries has kept fairly constant to the present day, seldom exceeding a total of one hundred people.

This area was important for coal-mining as far back as the 15th century, and the Guinness Book of Records states that *'between 1603 and 1615 waggons running on wooden rails were used to convey coal at Wollaton - thus being the earliest railway in Britain.'* This of course is a reference to the horse-drawn trucks built to carry coal from the Strelley pits to a land-wharf serving Wollaton Hall (completed in 1588).

ROSE - *Strelley Road*

Opened on the 25th April 1958, this house replaced a former pub of the same name which used to stand in Mill Street, Basford (the latter house being demolished to make way for a road widening scheme).

A heraldic national symbol, the *'Rose'* in its various forms is a fairly common name for a pub.

STURTON-LE-STEEPLE

REINDEER - *Church Street*

For many 19th century years, Sturton-le-Steeple had four inns, the *'Blacksmiths Arms'*, the *'Crown'*, the *'Fox and Hounds'* and the *'Stag'*. The *'Stag'* was run by Robert Moore in 1888. Seven years later it was in the hands of Mrs Hannah Moore, victualler and farmer, one assumes after her husband's death. Interestingly the *'Stag'* died too, but was reincarnated as the *'Reindeer'*! The other inns had all disappeared by 1925. The *'Reindeer'* has been much extended and stands by a small pool, in the shadow of the great tower of Sturton Church.

Reindeer, Sturton-le-Steeple

SUTTON BONINGTON

KINGS HEAD - *Main Street*

The *'Kings Head'* is a very common sign throughout the country, with other Nottinghamshire examples to be found at Mansfield, Collingham and Worksop. Usually King Henry VIII is featured on the sign, or sometimes it is the playing card version of the King. At Sutton Bonington the chosen monarch appears to be King George III. In 1881, the landlord was Thomas Pierrepoint, and there were occasions when his relative, the hangman Pierrepoint came to Sutton Bonington to visit. It is said that the villagers would leave the pub whenever he walked in.

SUTTON-IN-ASHFIELD

APOLLO - Mansfield Road

Recorded in Kelly's 1855 Directory as the 'Odd Fellows Lodge,' this old hostelry, opened in 1832, was acquired by Mansfield Brewery in 1893.

In early use the sign of 'Apollo' derived from heraldry and features on the arms of the Apothecaries. Representing manhood in all its perfection, Apollo was thought by the ancient Greeks to be the god who brought about and cured plagues.

CARDINAL - Sutton Junction

Opened in April 1968, the name here commemorates the visit of Cardinal Wolsey to the area in 1530. Prominently on display in the entrance hall of this pub, the following legend recalls the event:

"History records that Cardinal Wolsey, appointed Archbishop of York in 1514, was never formally installed in this office at York Minster. After some years journeying to and fro between his various palaces such as Peterborough and Southwell, he started his journey to York in 1530 in preparation for his installation as Archbishop. It is interesting to note that at this time he was at odds with Henry VIII, having spoken against the divorce of the King and Queen Catherine. Consequent on this disagreement, the king ordered his arrest for treason. Having reached his palace at Scrooby (near present-day Bawtry) the King's Guard arrested him, and he started his journey to London, presumably by pack-horse, to stand trial. The route followed the ancient track known as the 'The Great Way,' through Sherwood Forest, and this is thought to have run nearby - along the present Coxmoor Road, which lies a quarter-of-a-mile northeast of this house. Record has it that the Cardinal spent a night at the home of the Earl of Shrewsbury, whose mansion Kirkby Hardwick still exists and lies some three-quarters of a mile to the south-west of this spot. By this time the Cardinal was ill with dysentery, and his journey ended prematurely at Leicester Abbey - where he died before he could be called to account."

CART AND HORSE - Station Road

Mentioned in the 1832 Directory, this old house was acquired by Mansfield Brewery in 1883.

The whimsical circular signboard that hangs outside this house depicts a horse pushing a cart laden with produce whilst its driver lays asleep on his seat. The name appears to derive from the Latin phrase 'Currus bovem trahit praepostere,' meaning that someone is doing things in the wrong logical order - putting the cart before the horse.

DENMAN'S HEAD - Market Place

Built around 1750 as the 'King's Head,' this inn changed its sign to the current title in 1820 to honour Lord Denman's and Lord Brougham's successful defence that year of Queen Caroline (wife of George IV) against a government charge of adultery.

Thomas Denman (1779-1854) was born in London. Educated at Eton and St John's College, Cambridge, he later became an eminent English judge. Prior to his becoming Lord Chief Justice in 1830, he served as Whig MP for Wareham and Nottingham between 1818-26. Raised to the peerage in 1834 as the 1st Baron Denman, he retired from the bench in 1850.

During the 1760s a 'Friendly Society' was held at this pub, and a 6d fine was imposed on any of its members who cursed or swore or failed to attend church. A hefty sum, given that sickness benefit in those days was only 3/- per week and Death Benefit amounted to only one guinea.

DEVONSHIRE ARMS - High Pavement

Mentioned in the 1853 Directory under its current sign, this house was acquired by Mansfield Brewery in 1894.

It takes its name from the Dukes of Devonshire, who, together with the Dukes of Newcastle, were for many generations owners of several large estates in Nottinghamshire.

MAPPLEWELLS - Alfreton Road

The current house, opened in December 1963, replaced an old 19th century inn of the same name which had been acquired by Mansfield Brewery in 1880.

The name is a reference to a series of wells that once stood nearby and which are remembered in the following verses written at Sutton-in-Ashfield in 1847 by Spencer T. Hall in his poem 'The Upland Hamlet':

'A change has come o'er all the town;
The Cotton-works in ruin stand,
And Unwin's hall is coming down.
Although to last for ages plann'd
Cowpasture hills are levell'd low,
And Maple-wells are all closed in;
The Forest-side few flowers can
show - Its streets grow thick, its
woods grown thin ...'

OLD BLUE BELL - *Lammas Road*

Built around 1730, this is the oldest hostelry in Sutton-in-Ashfield. Originally styled as the *'Blue Bell,'* it changed its name to its present title in 1992.

During the ministry of the Reverend William Goodacre (1820-1859) the inn hosted the meetings of the 'Bright Eyed Club', where the vicar would read the weekly broadsheets to his parishioners to keep them abreast of the news.

In 1817, the pub itself would certainly have been in the news. When Elizabeth Shepherd was murdered on Sutton Forest, her killer Charles Rotheram was brought here by the officers of Justice to attend the inquest.

Before being acquired by Mansfield Brewery in 1880, the *'Blue Bell'* was kept for many years by the Evans family. The will of Isaac Evans, proved in November 1825, reveals an interesting perception into the tools of the brewing trade in those days. The brew house contained a cast iron boiler, cover and underworks, mash tubs, hop sieves, a square

Old Blue Bell, Sutton-in-Ashfield

cooler, round tubs and water buckets. The bar contained an array of jars and mugs, plus a copper ale warmer and iron candlesticks. The club room came equipped with tables, chairs, forms, and perhaps most importantly - four spittoons!

An explanation for the origin of the name here can be found by referring to the *'Blue Bell'* at Nottingham.

OVAL - *The Oval, Carsic Estate*

Built by Mansfield Brewery in 1961 to serve a new estate in the area, the name of this pub could easily be misinterpreted as being a reference to the famous Kennington Oval in London SE11, home of Surrey CCC and a regular Test Match venue, especially as its circular signboard appears to support this notion with its cartoon-style depiction of a scene from a cricket match. In fact, the *'Oval'* takes its name from something far less inspiring - namely, the shape of the road on which it stands.

SNIPE - *Alfreton Road*

Opened in November 1992, this new pub is named after the heraldic bird which appeared on the former coat of arms of Sutton-in-Ashfield. The *"gules, a snipe argent, gorged with a crown"*, is the Official Seal of the Sutton in Ashfield Urban District Council and appears on the Arms of the Snittertons, of Snitterton, Derbyshire, who were said to have held the Manor of Sutton in 1066.

STAFF OF LIFE - *West End*

The historical background to this pub (opened on the 29th April 1968) reveals most interestingly why bread - rather than beer, as some loyal swillers still insist - should be regarded as the *'staff of life.'*

The old hostelry which this pub replaced was first occupied by a certain James Crofts in 1832. Crofts was also the miller in Sutton and had a baker's shop adjoining the premises. In a yard behind the old house stood a windmill, and its foundations can still be seen. Until 1940 the pub had been looked after by a succession of eleven landlords - an average of a decade apiece - but Mr Sam Sadler, who then took over its running, remained as landlord for 27 years, until October 1967, when the new building was partly completed and the old premises had to be demolished so that work could proceed.

SUTTON-ON-TRENT

LORD NELSON INN - *Main Street*

Even village inns, more usually called the 'Plough', 'Blacksmith's Arms' and similar rural names, honour Nelson, the most famous of English admirals. This inn was serving ale in the days of Trafalgar when Nelson was a national hero (see *'Lord Nelson'* at Arnold for further details). Other *'Lord Nelson'* inns can be found at North Muskham and Besthorpe.

NAGS HEAD - *Old Great North Road*

At one time, the road outside the 'Nags Head' was the main highway from London to the north. The inn catered for those who travelled along it, including the stage coach passengers and no doubt the highwaymen as well. A nag was a small riding horse or pony, and early signs depicting them probably indicated that they could be hired from the inn.

Nags Head, Sutton-on-Trent

TEVERSAL

CARNARVON ARMS - *Fackley Road*

The 'Carnarvon Arms', a former coaching inn, is thought to be around 400 years old, and was originally known as the 'Cross Keys'. It acquired its present name between 1869 and 1872. Surrounded by the hustle and bustle of modern times, Teversal remains a delightfully 'olde world' village, typically Derbyshire in character and appearance,

Carnarvon Arms, Teversal

but geographically in Nottinghamshire. The church is an intriguing place, with the old fashioned box pews, squire's pew and a vast collection of monuments and hatchments. Many of these are to the Molyneux family, Lords of the Manor until the estate passed, by marriage, to the Earls of Carnarvon in whose hands it remained until 1929.

The 5th Earl of Carnarvon achieved fame as the archaeologist who, with Howard Carter, tracked down the tomb of Tutenkhamun in 1922. Legend tells of a curse which would befall anyone who opened the tomb - only months after the amazing find, Lord Carnarvon was bitten by a mosquito and died.

It is widely believed, locally, that Teversal is the fictional home of D.H. Lawrence's Lady Chatterley (it is known as 'Tevershall' in the novel), and that, for a time, the author actually lived in the village, even writing some of the book there. The woodlands close to the Hardwick Hall estate are reputedly the fictional meeting place of Lady Chatterley and Mellors, the gamekeeper. Certainly the walk at the back of the manor house is as described in the book, the gamekeeper's cottage is a mile from the manor and the former Silverhill Colliery could be 'Tevershall' pit. It has to be said that both Eastwood and Eckington in Derbyshire also lay claim to being the locations Lawrence had in mind, but the people of Teversal know more besides!

A unique feature of the 'Carnarvon Arms' is the amazing 'ship room' - it is all wood, built like an old galleon with portholes, slanting walls, as in a ship, and with old barrels for seats. The room was the landlord's private accommodation until 1936, when the pub's owners, the People's Refreshment and Holidays Association, created this fascinating nautical feature.

To heighten further this pub's claims to fame, it is reputedly the most haunted pub in the county - with *lots* of ghosts!

THURGARTON

COACH AND HORSES - *Main Street*

This former coaching inn was built around 1801. Its sign is a common one and has been in use in Britain since the 17th century when stagecoaches became a popular mode of transport. In 1780 the first stagecoach on the Southwell line is known to have pounded a route past this house - no doubt giving rise to its name.

RED LION - *Southwell Road*

Though sporting the most common of all pub names, this old hostelry (recorded in the 1832 Directory) became the scene of a most uncommon crime on the 31st August 1936. The landlady at that time, Sarah Ellen Clarke was found murdered in her bedroom and her cat, which had been drowned by someone weighting it down with a 1lb weight round its neck, was discovered in a water-trough at the front of the inn.

Red Lion, Thurgarton

An explanation for the origin of this pub's name can be found by referring to the '*Red Lion*' at Costock. Other villages having inns with this name are Walesby and Treswell.

TOLLERTON

AIR HOSTESS - *Stanstead Avenue*

This pub, opened December 1966, takes its name from its position, not far away from Nottingham's civil airport. At its opening, two real air-hostesses were flown up specially from Birmingham Airport to lend a touch of glamour to the occasion, which took place a week before Christmas that year.

The arresting figure of an air-hostess framed by the signboard is made of glass fibre (adorned with gold leaf) and its creator has been tactful enough not to link her with any particular airline - only the letters 'BE' being visible on her uniform bag.

TIGER MOTH - *Tollerton Airport*

This former wartime mess hall, sited on the edge of Tollerton Airfield, was opened as a pub in January 1982. Some five weeks later, on the 1st April 1982, an electrical fault caused a fire in the roof of the building and firemen, supported by several volunteers, had to rescue seven aircraft from an adjoining maintenance hanger used by the Sherwood Flying Club. The pub was rebuilt in 1983 and boasts an unusual interior created with beams from a 300-year-old Norfolk barn.

In 1995, there was a further revamp, with a beer garden and boules alley being added. The name was changed from the '*Inn at Tollerton*' to the present one honouring the vintage Tiger Moth aeroplane which belongs to airfield operator Derek Leatherland. It was he who flew the aeroplane overhead on 3rd August 1995, the day of the official re-opening. The pub is run by Labatts who are also the 1995/96 sponsors of Nottingham Forest Football Club, so it was appropriate that star player Neil Webb should have pulled the first pint.

The pub also boasts a members' flight deck, a room for pilots and aviation enthusiasts, and must be unique in having its own computerised flight planning system.

The old sign depicted a Hurricane - no doubt a reference to the wartime use of this airfield for aircraft repairs. The new sign, of course, now shows the Tiger Moth.

TOP VALLEY

DUKE OF ST ALBANS - *Bewcastle Road*

The ducal title of this pub (opened on the 30th June 1983) relates to Charles Beauclerk, the elder of the two illegitimate sons borne to King Charles II by his mistress Nell Gwynn. According to legend, his father created him the first Duke of St. Albans when his mother threatened to throw him out of the window (as a baby) - adding for good measure a thousand acres of his favourite hunting-grounds.

The 10th Duke built Bestwood Lodge last century, and Bestwood Park passed out of the hands of the ducal family in 1938 - being partly bought by both Nottingham Corporation and Nottinghamshire County Council. The Lodge itself was taken over by the Army during the Second World War and they continued to occupy it until it became a hotel. The core of Bestwood Park is in fact owned by the County Council, and is run by them jointly with Gedling Borough Council as a country park. The outer parts of the estate were sold for housing.

This pub's name was arrived at via public competition, the lucky person, Mrs Joan Ducker, winning a holiday for two in Spain. For the brewers, Bass Worthington, it was their first venture into this area - and they were keen to promote the 'family emphasis' of their newest pub in a big way, both within and without, as far as children were concerned.

There was formerly a city pub of this same name situated in Sherwood Street, and claimed to be the smallest pub in Nottingham. It dated from 1927 but closed in March 1963.

ROYAL HUNT - *Top Valley Way*

Opened in June 1978, the name here clearly follows the lead given by the other local pubs in the area, by relating to the royal hunting-parties once staged hereabouts by Charles II and others.

TOTON

OTHER SIDE OF THE MOON - *Sandown Road*

Opened in December 1959, this pub was originally to have been styled the 'Welcome,' but after the Russian 'Sputnik' had then gone aloft and attracted such enormous publicity, Hardys and Hansons decided to commemorate the historic occasion by choosing a more topical theme. They followed it seven years later with their 'Man In Space' at Eastwood.

The interior of the Toton pub was 'decorated' with autographed photographs and cartoons (including pictures of Lunar III's canine passengers) which appeared in the national Press at that time.

The original sign, which depicted a full moon bisected by a rocket has been replaced, sadly, by a mere lettered board.

TROWELL

FESTIVAL INN - *Ilkeston Road*

The site on which this pub now stands is part of an estate on which a working farm known as Church Farm was situated at the time of purchase. The estate was bought around 1948, later being re-sold for the proposed building of an inn to be called the 'Stuart Arms.' However, a licence was not granted, and after Trowell had been appointed the Festival Village in 1951, the original purchasers of the estate, the Festival Inn Company Limited, bought it back again with a view to building the 'Festival Inn.' Some three attempts later, a licence was granted and the pub's construction began in 1952.

Opened in March 1955, the name of this pub, owned since September 1993 by Tom Cobleigh, reflects Trowell's success in the 1951 Festival of Britain year when it was selected as typifying an English village. The inn was almost completely rebuilt in 1995.

TUXFORD

NEWCASTLE ARMS - *Market Place*

An inn has stood on this site since the 1400s. Then it was the 'Crown' "chiefly bylded of tymber" with a thatched roof. Margaret, sister of Henry VIII, stayed there in 1503 on the way to Scotland to marry James IV, King of Scotland. The 'Crown' was eventually destroyed by a great fire which ravaged Tuxford in 1701. Apart from the church and the old grammar school, little survived. When rebuilt, the inn took the name 'Red Lion' and acquired the reputation of being one of the most comfortable coaching inns on the Great North Road. The stage coach era brought prosperity to Tuxford which had nine public houses catering for travellers, including the 'Black Horse' and the 'Sun' in the Market Place, the 'Blue Bell', 'Coach and Horses', 'Fox' and 'Reindeer' on Eldon Street, with the 'King William IV' on Mill Hill. Stage coaches bearing fanciful names - 'Express', 'Rockingham', 'Wellington' and 'Amity' - provided a service to major towns including London, York, Leeds and Edinburgh. Fictional Jeanie Deans, heroine of Sir Walter Scott's novel 'Heart of Midlothian' overslept in a four poster bed at the 'Red Lion'. A regular visitor was the young William Gladstone, then MP for Newark who would ride to Tuxford to catch the 'London Flyer' stage coach.

The coming of the Great Northern Railway in the 1840s spelt the end of the coaching era resulting in deserted turnpike roads, little used inns and empty stables.

The 'Red Lion' became the 'Newcastle Arms' in 1828, one of a number of Nottinghamshire inns to honour Henry Pelham Clinton (1785-1851), the 4th Duke of Newcastle under Lyme, who inherited his title at the tender age of 10. He lived at Clumber and was a major landowner in the county.

UNDERWOOD

SANDHILLS TAVERN - *Mansfield Road*

This pub, opened on the 27th April 1939, was built as a replacement for a former house of the same name that once stood nearby.

The original pub, which used to brew its own ale up until 1939, was built around 1800. It was kept by three generations of the Gill family, the last landlord being Jarvis Gill.

The name derives from the pub's close proximity to a number of fields at Felley, which at one time were covered with sand.

Newcastle Arms, Tuxford

UPTON

French Horn, Upton

CROSS KEYS - *Main Street*

This very popular 300 year old pub was originally a farmhouse, with a dovecote which has now been converted into the restaurant. Inside you find beams and brasses, real fires and a room containing carved pews from a Newark church. For an explanation of the name, please refer to the 'Cross Keys' at Burton Joyce.

FRENCH HORN - *Main Street*

The date on the front of the *French Horn* pub says 1803 and as it is listed under this name in the 1832 directory, it is reasonable to assume it has always been an inn. The musical instrument shown on the sign is perhaps misleading, as the modern French Horn with its three valves did not come into use until the 1840s. In France the instrument was called the *'cor de chasse'* or 'hunting horn'. The Knights of old enjoyed the 'chase' with their hunting horns in their hands, and the instrument was often used on shields and coats of arms. Many pub names are derived from heraldry and this is possibly one of them!

WALKERINGHAM

BRICKMAKERS ARMS - *Caves Lane*

Walkeringham was one of a number of villages in the north of the county, including Everton, Gringley, Hayton and Misterton, to have its own brickworks. This industry, on which generations of local people relied for employment, continued until 1956 when the last bricks were fired and the kilns then allowed to go cold. Some Walkeringham bricks were used in the village itself (this inn may possibly have been built with them), but most were transported along the Chesterfield Canal by horsedrawn barge to West Stockwith and the River Trent.

This early 19th century inn, which once incorporated a sweet shop (now the pool room) has expanded considerably in recent years, with 3 adjoining cottages and a barn being converted into hotel accommodation.

THREE HORSESHOES - *High Street*

As one might expect from the name of this village inn, a farrier's shop once stood close by. In fact in the early 1800s, the local farrier, John Fenton, was also the innkeeper. His son, also John Fenton, was born in 1832 and eventually took over both roles from his father. In 1860 a local farmer was shot dead in the village and John junior, church-going and apparently law-abiding, was subsequently charged with his murder. Despite consistently protesting his innocence he was executed at Nottingham in August of that year. He was the last person to be publicly hanged in the town. John Fenton's ghost supposedly continues to haunt the inn - the present landlord's dog can vouch for this!

The sign typically portrays the farrier at work, shoeing a horse, with the three remaining horseshoes ready on the anvil.

WARSOP

DOG AND RABBIT - *Sherwood Street*

For over 150 years this old hostelry (mentioned in the 1832 Directory) was run by five successive generations of the Wilkinson family. The Wilkinsons were succeeded by Mr George Tattersall in 1871, and upon his death in 1893 his wife became the first female licensee in the county.

The name probably refers to the sport of rabbit coursing, which is practised using a breed of dog called a whippet - an image which has certainly been captured on the pub's colourful and humorous signboard which depicts a rabbit eluding the dog by scooting between its legs.

HARE AND HOUNDS - *Church Street*

Recorded in the 1832 Directory, this old house witnessed one of the most moving events ever to occur in Market Warsop.

When John Stubbins, the son of a Warsop sawyer and a corporal in the Dragoon Guards, found himself in the midst of the Battle of Waterloo, he only narrowly evaded death when a French sabre meant for him cut off the ear of his mount instead. Upon the defeat of the French, John was promoted to sergeant and retired from the regiment the following year, taking with him a medal and a present of £20 for his part in the victory. Some two years later a detachment from his old regiment rode through the village of Warsop and drew up outside the *Hare and Hounds*. Among them was a one-eared horse - the one that John Stubbins had ridden so gallantly at Waterloo. It is said that the entire village turned out to witness the emotional reunion of the local hero and his noble steed.

Hare and Hounds, Warsop

Most likely the name of this house relates to the traditional sport, in this area, of hare-hunting.

SWALLOWS - *Cottage Lane*

Opened in 1957, this pub's name does not refer, as you might at first suppose, to the thirsty nature of the local population - but to the little feathered friends which have a habit of nesting hereabouts.

TALBOT - *High Street*

The present house was built over a century ago on the site of a former coaching inn. It takes its name from a breed of hound (usually white, and now extinct) that was formerly used for tracking and hunting. With its large ears and heavy jaws, it had remarkable powers of scent and was the ancestor of the modern-day foxhounds and staghounds. The *Talbot* is also the crest of the Earls of Shrewsbury (whose family name is Talbot), and it is often found as a sign in places where they have, or have had, possessions.

WATNALL

QUEENS HEAD - *Main Road*

This former coaching inn, once owned by the Rolleston family of nearby Watnall Hall, is thought to be some 300 years old. Around the turn of the century it was given as a gift by Colonel Sir Lancelot Rolleston to his former batman Joe Haywood as a 'thank you' for saving his life, after he had been wounded during the Boer War. Haywood became a popular landlord and for a while the pub became known as 'Joe Haywood's.'

Now owned by Home Brewery (Scottish and Newcastle), this pub is still a popular resort.

The distinctive sign outside this house appears to depict a youthful Queen Elizabeth I - a very popular monarch whose features appear on the signboards of many a pub sporting this title.

WELLOW

DURHAM OX - *Newark Road*

The original sections of this house (mentioned in the 1832 Directory) are to be found at the rear, and are several hundred years old.

At one time the pub had its own resident ghost, in the guise of a small woman or child wearing a cloak, which used to roam the stairs and bump and bang in the study. When one night, landlady Sandra Jackson was startled by the apparition as it brushed past her, she screamed so loudly that she terrified everyone in the pub - including it seems the ghost - which has not been seen since.

An explanation for the origin of this pub's name can be found by referring to the *'Durham Ox'* at Beeston.

Durham Ox, Wellow

OLDE RED LION - *Eakring Road*

An advertising leaflet for this old hostelry gives an interesting insight into its history. It reads:

'The Olde Red Lion itself is situated between the village Green and St Swithin's and is a traditional English Pub, lovingly restored but retaining its olde world charm and hospitality. It dates back to 1600 when it was a one room pub and a row of farm labourers' cottages. On an early lease which can be found in the Cottages Bar, you can see that in 1827 The Olde Red Lion was leased to the landlord for a princely sum of one peppercorn per annum! Each room has its own character and contains many of the original features ...'

On the village Green opposite the pub stands a permanent maypole - the only surviving one of its kind in the county. The existence of the Wellow maypole can be traced back as far as 1856, though on the 9th May 1860 a new one had to be erected - the old one having been deliberately damaged by revellers who had attended a drinking spree a few weeks earlier. In 1887, to celebrate Queen Victoria's Jubilee, a splendid new pole with three cross-pieces near its summit, painted decorations and a seat around its base, was donated by Sir John Savile of Rufford. This was replaced in 1923 by a new 60 foot pole which itself lasted until 1937 when an examination revealed that it was unsafe and had to be shortened. Reduced in height to 20 feet, this pole remained in use until 1950 when a new maypole was purchased from the Rufford Estate. Made of larch, this pole hosted many a celebration until it was damaged by a storm in 1966 and had to be removed and sold for firewood. A new larch pole was erected, and despite problems due to the wood being unseasoned, remained in place until 1976. The current 60 foot tubular steel pole was built in 1977, and each year on the former Whit Monday (now Spring Bank Holiday) the 'Gypsies Tent,' the 'Single Plait' and the 'Spiders Web' are just some of the traditional dances that are still performed around it - a sight well worth a visit.

The origin of this inn's name can be found by referring to the *'Red Lion'* at Costock.

WEST BRIDGFORD

LARWOOD AND VOCE TAVERN - *Fox Road*

This pub stands within the confines of the Nottinghamshire County Cricket Club, and a wonderful view across the whole ground can be seen from its Bar windows. It was opened in the summer of 1985 (to coincide with the Third Test v Australia) by Reg Simpson, former Club captain and England opening batsman. Among the memorabilia is a large framed photograph of Larwood and Voce taken together when they were invited to attend the Centenary Test in 1977.

Harold Larwood (see entry for the *'Larwood'* at Annesley Woodhouse) and Bill Voce were the spearhead of England's pace attack in the so-called 'Bodyline Tour' of 1932-33, in which the MCC team, captained by Douglas Jardine, won the legendary *'Ashes'* during that notorious series of matches against Australia. They have always been regarded as the finest pair of fast bowlers England has ever produced, both at county and national level. Larwood was born in 1904 and died in 1995 in Sydney, Australia, to where he and his family emigrated in 1950. His comrade Voce, was born in 1909 and died in 1984.

The original sign, showing a set of stumps with a cricket ball at the centre, was later changed to portray a batsman ducking beneath a 'bouncer' whilst surrounded by a strong legside 'trap.' Nowadays the tavern is also advertised by a board on which the portrait of each hero is shown. This is specially erected behind a Stand in Radcliffe Road, together with a large arrow which directs strangers to nearby Fox Road.

MANOR HOUSE - *Albert Road*

The smart sign board outside this pub depicts West Bridgford Hall, a large Georgian house of 1770 built by the Musters who were then the Lords of the Manor. It stands in the park to the rear of the *'Manor House'*, and is where Mary Chaworth (Byron's sweetheart) is said to have met Mr Musters, whom she later married. The Hall was leased to Lewis Haymann in 1840. He was head of the Lace Market firm of Haymann & Alexander, and Mayor of Nottingham in 1857. The Haymann family eventually bought the Hall and occupied it until 1924. West Bridgford Urban District Council bought the property and grounds and it has remained as Council offices since.

The pub at one time was a private club, the *'Manor Club'*, but during the 1980s it became known as the *'Manor House'* and now opens to the general public.

Manor House sign, West Bridgford

OLD COLONIAL - *Compton Acres*

Opened in December 1993, this newly-built public-house derives its name by reference to an old colleague of the managing director of the brewery company (Tom Cobleigh PLC of Mansfield) who had his early origins out in India.

SOUTH NOTTS HUSSARS - *Greythorn Drive*

There was a most colourful ceremony at this pub's official opening in December 1965. Trumpeters and Lancemen of the South Notts Hussars and a number of ex-members of the regiment were present when the ceremonial key was handed over by brewery chairman Mr. James Shipstone to Sir William Barber, Honorary Colonel of the 307th South Notts Hussars Yeomanry Field Regiment RA (TA).

In former days there had always been a close association between Shipstone's brewery and the regiment. When the British Expeditionary Force was being assembled for France at the outbreak of World War I and the need for horses became paramount, transport requisitions came into force whereby farmers, coal-merchants, brewers and so on were required to provide what they could.

The Star Brewery at Basford was naturally in a position to supply some of the best animals for this patriotic purpose, and in fact many of Shipstone's men enlisted in the Yeomanry, together with the horses under their charge. This link of comradeship was perpetuated in one way or another right up to the late 1980s when, for a year or so, the present masters (Greenalls of Warrington, who took over Shipstones in 1978) apparently severed the brewery's long-standing connection with the Military in favour of more topographical detail. This caused the *Hussars* to disappear temporarily from the title - and with it the imposing inn-sign featuring the mounted horseman in his uniform of 1900.

At the time of the pub's opening, the Regiment loaned items of equipment and uniforms to be displayed within the premises - and even the flooring bore the regimental colours in attractive tiles of red, yellow and blue. Incorporated in the wall-panelling were framed oil-paintings, reproduced locally from the originals, which depicted mounted Hussars in various types of uniform between 1794 (the year of their foundation) and 1855, the year which saw the fall of Sebastopol and the end of the Crimean War. A record of battle-honours from the South African war(s) onwards was also on view, together with the scroll giving the Regiment the Freedom of the City of Nottingham in 1946. But sadly, all these splendid aspects of military memorabilia are now all gone.

South Notts Hussars, West Bridgford

The South Notts Hussars were formed originally in 1794 at a time when events across the Channel, after the French Revolution, suggested to the Civil Power at home that a strengthening of militia might come in more useful. Just over a century later the South Notts Hussars became the first 'Terriers' of Yeomanry to set foot on foreign soil when they disembarked in South Africa to engage in the Boer War. In World War II they remained as one of only three units of Yeomanry who could claim the title of 'Royal Horse Artillery'. All in all, they represented a distinguished record of service down the years from a very professional array of amateurs!

The word *Hussar* (given in dictionary terms as *'a light-armed cavalry soldier'*) originally denoted a soldier (Huzzar) of the national cavalry of Hungary. Until about 1807 their counterparts in the British Army were known as 'Light Dragoons,' but then some of them became *Hussars* - a term not fully accepted by the Army authorities until 1841.

It was the fashion-conscious Prince Regent (later George IV) whose influence led to the British Cavalry wearing some of the most striking apparel ever devised for them, during this period. The uniform of a Lancer cost between £200 and £300 - but a Hussar had to spend up to £400 on his full-dress uniform. (One can't help speculating what it would cost him today!).

By the way, many of us can recall with nostalgia the once-familiar sight of Shipstone's dray-horses that clumped around the city years ago providing, as a journalist friend once dryly remarked, 'beer for the pubs and piles of steaming dung for avid gardeners . . .' The last pair of these horses, Victor and Luke, made their final run from the Star brewery to the *'Carlton Hotel'* in Hyson Green, on the 24th January, 1979.

Test Match, West Bridgford

TEST MATCH - *Gordon Road*

It might be thought that the reason for this name is self-evident (bearing in mind the proximity of the pub to the Trent Bridge Cricket Ground) - but in fact the name originally had more of a legal connection than a cricketing one. For no less than 44 years before the building was finally accomplished in 1938, the West Bridgford Defence Association had waged a stubborn battle against the granting of a licence - as indeed they had done in the case of the *'Wolds'* (*'Quinceys'* since 1992 but reverted back to the *'Wolds'* in 1995) on Loughborough Road, completed for Shipstone's Brewery about the same time. This was in the days when only a 'hotel' was deemed respectable enough to fit into West Bridgford society (the *'Trent Bridge Inn'* then being within the city boundary) and the climate of local opinion was unfavourable to ale on sale under any pretext whatsoever.

When eventually the Kimberley Brewery obtained permission from the licensing magistrates at Shire Hall to put up the 'Hotel,' their chairman, clearly relieved that the long protracted struggle was at last over, was heard to remark "that it had been as hard to win as a 'Test' against Australia!" The place was badly damaged by fire in February 1979, but subsequently restored to its previous opulence - so suggestive of Palm Court (without the orchestral Trio) and its comfortable aura of excellence. The fine set of colour-prints reproduced from the MCC Collection is to be admired, as are the striking wall-murals executed in oils by Leonard Huskinson, the Nottinghamshire artist, in what is called 'Gresaille monochrome'. The first of these shows those cricketing giants of the past George Parr and William Clarke standing together on a wicket which is pitched in the old meadows, with the castle and its rock in the background.

The second mural, which is on top of the first flight of stairs leading from the main hall, is a decorative trophy in honour of an assortment of cricketing regalia. But the third mural, portraying the legendary urn in which repose those famous 'Ashes,' is a real eye-opener. Like the famous painting of the violin, hanging from the cupboard-door, at Chatsworth House, it is a superb example of the technique known to the French as 'trompe d'oeil'.

At the foot of the staircase another cricketing phenomenon is on display - this being one of the celebrated tea-towel replicas as sold at Lords, representing in the most skilful detail the gallant twelve (yes, twelve) who went out to Australia in 1863/4. Led by George Parr himself, the team included Dr. E.M. Grace (elder brother of the famous Dr W.G. Grace) and the redoubtable Julius Caesar - one of twelve Caesars who once appeared together and played for Surrey - and they returned to these shores undefeated. Perhaps the unanimous choice of beards or sideburns had something to do with it?

Outside this Grade II Listed building is a pair of signboards on a special plinth. Both depict a close-up of the wicket, with exciting games in progress.

TRENT BRIDGE INN - *Radcliffe Road*

The visitor here cannot help being impressed by the brewery's logo (prominently displayed on its walls together with the usual globe) as 'The world-renowned Trent Bridge Inn' - signifying of course that the fame of this old hostelry as 'The T.B.I.' has spread far and wide to all parts of the cricketing world - to India, Pakistan, Sri Lanka, the West Indies, New Zealand, and 'Down Under' especially. Test matches have been played at the Trent Bridge cricket ground since 1899. William Clarke, former landlord of the *'Bell'* on Angel Row (qv), came here to marry the widow Mary Chapman of this inn. He laid out a cricket 'square' in the 'back garden' in 1838. William Clarke was probably the last man to play cricket in a *white* tall hat (everyone else wore a black one) on the Trent Bridge Cricket Ground he formed and lived to see famous all over England. Born in 1798, he became first Captain, and then Secretary, of the All-England XI before George Parr succeeded to these offices. During this time he remained landlord of the T.B.I. from 1838 until 1854. He died in 1856.

In the first County Directory of 1832 the pub was referred to simply as the *'Bridge'*. It thus predates the establishment of the present County Cricket Ground, and in fact refers to the bridge over the nearby River Trent. A new bridge was built in 1871 to replace the dilapidated stone one which was then 950 years old. Part of this old bridge can still be seen in the traffic island opposite the T.B.I.

The original inn stood on a site in front of the present building, with the boundary between the City of Nottingham and the county, running right through the middle. In the 19th century when the Micklethorn Jury 'beat the bounds' each year (see the *'Old General'*, Nottingham for further details of this event), it is said that they entered the inn through one of the windows, followed the boundary through the building, and left through one of the doors, stopping of course for liquid refreshment en route!

The new Trent Bridge Inn was completed in 1890, and only then was the old inn demolished.

Today, the T.B.I. naturally contains much cricketing memorabilia as well as a lending library.

Old and New Trent Bridge Inns, West Bridgford (1890)

WEST LEAKE

STAR INN - *Melton Lane*

This former farmhouse has been serving ale since the early part of the 18th century. Now owned by the Bass Brewery, it was formerly part of the Derbyshire based Offiler's Brewery.

It is known locally as the *'Leake Pit House'*, a name that is said to have originated back in the days of cock fighting when the birds were put to fight in a cock-pit behind the pub. More likely, though, is that it was given this unusual name due to its location. 19th century farmers, merchants and coal dealers used to visit a wharf on the River Soar at Kegworth with their horse-drawn carts to collect coal from the many barges that moored there, and on their return journey they would stop off at the 'Star' to give themselves and their animals a breather. A flagon of ale for themselves and water for their horses led to the inn becoming known as the *'Coal-pit House,'* which was later abbreviated to *'Pit House.'*

Star, West Leake

WEST STOCKWITH

WATERFRONT INN - *The Marina*

When the Chesterfield Canal was built in the 1770s, it joined the River Trent at West Stockwith Basin. It was here that nearly 3000 men worked at various trades associated with canal and river life.

The village of West Stockwith once had 13 inns to cater for the demands of this very thirsty workforce. The *'Crown'*, contemporary with the canal itself, was one of these. It retained this name until 1989 when, after closing temporarily for refurbishment, it re-opened with its new image as the *'Waterfront Inn'*. It is an integral part of the life of the new Marina, transformed from the old 'Basin' during the past couple of years, and designed to cater for the modern day pleasure boat enthusiasts and tourists who call at West Stockwith to enjoy the leisure facilities it has to offer.

WIDMERPOOL

PULLMAN INN - *Kinoulton Lane*

In June 1966 this unusual village pub took over from the local railway station (closed not long before in March of 1965, under the so-called Beeching axe) and has purposely inherited some of the latter's memorabilia - the

Pullman Inn, Widmerpool

former Waiting-Room windows, for starters, and the ability to seat 'passengers' in a former train carriage.

The place was originally 'run' by an Australian lady who called it the *'Schooner'* - in memory of the large measure of sherry she was accustomed to - but in 1976 it became the *'Pullman,'* and in this 'guise' added a new flavour altogether.

Other pubs of this name (but not within this county) echo the example of the railway coach built to luxurious standards by, and named after the Pullman Carriage Works, Illinois, USA. Such saloon and sleeping-car coaches were designed by George Pullman (1831-1897) of Chicago.

WILFORD

FERRY INN - *Main Road*

This historic old inn was first mentioned in County Records in 1787. In the 14th century a section of the present hostelry was a farmhouse, and the king at the time (probably Edward III) issued a charter granting permission for the operation of a boat ferry. The proceeds from the ferry fees were to go towards the upkeep of the original 10th-century Trent Bridge, a mile downstream. When the provision of a river-crossing at this point resulted in a road passing close to the farmhouse, some far-sighted person converted the premises into a place of refreshment.

During the vogue for coffee-houses in the 18th century, the inn became the *'Old Wilford Coffee Tavern'*, but eventually it was named the *'Punch Bowl'* - probably when this was the symbol of Whig supremacy in Parliament and landlords were eager to please their principal patrons in order to retain their licence. The 1858 Directory records the inn as the *'Punch Bowl,'* but in 1860 indicates, without giving a reason, its re-naming as the 'Ferry.' In those days the Ferry House (as it was popularly known) was one of the best-patronised 'resorts' in all Nottingham and district - and cherry-eating seems to have been for some obscure reason quite a speciality, notably during the first week of July. There is a painting in the Castle Art Gallery by John Holland, dated 1863, which shows a boat-load of passengers being towed over the river. A crowd of ladies wearing crinolines, and gentlemen in top hats, are waiting their turn, whilst the vendors of cherries are clearly doing a brisk trade.

Robert Mellors, in his chronicles of *'Wilford - Then and Now'* (published in 1914) records some notable incidents concerning the ferry crossings. The most tragic of these was on the 31st July 1784, when a small wherry was being used while the ferry-boat itself was laid up for repair. *"In the forenoon, being market day, eleven men and women got into the boat at once, when the wind was blowing a gale, and the river unusually high and rapid. In the middle of the stream the boat became unmanageable, was forced against the ferry-chain and upset, while all the passengers were thrown into the river. Six of them were able to swim, or with difficulty saved themselves, but a further six, the ferryman being one, were drowned."*

Mellors narrates another accident as follows: *"In July 1819, on a Sunday evening, a party had been to Ruddington feast, and on their return called at the 'Punch Bowl,' where they drank excessively. At half-past ten they obtained a ticket to ferry fifteen over the river. When halfway across an altercation ensued. The ferryman foolishly fastened a hook in the chain, a sudden jerk followed, and John Good fell into the water to drown, leaving a wife and seven children to mourn his loss."*

The building once served as a mortuary for people such as those mentioned, drowned in the river. One of the seats, still in use today, is said to have been used as a slab on which the bodies were laid out.

Wollaton records show that in 1593, a messenger from Wollaton Hall entered in his expenses sheet: *'ferryla at Wylford, being sent to Sir Jarvis (Clifton), a halfpenny.'*

During the latter part of the 18th century, when a Mr William Carver was the innkeeper, a local Friendly Society formed in 1787 held its meetings here, Rule 13 of which specified: *'There shall be taken as many twopences as there are members on the roll: taken for, paid for, and spent in liquor.'* Rule 41 stated that every member should attend the Parish Church (or some other place of public worship) to hear Divine Service or Sermons, *'and if any member neglects to do so on four successive Sundays, unless prevented by something lawful, he shall for every offence forfeit one shilling - or be excluded.'*

In 1796, a Female Society was formed and met here also, but unlike their male counterparts, the women attending did not seem to have had the privilege of drinking the health of absentees with the money accrued from profits!

In passing, it may be stated that Wilford has the honour of having been the most-painted and best-illustrated village in the entire County. In contrast to the tragic events already described by Robert Mellors, a writer styling himself as 'Timon,' soliloquising on the pleasant country scene in the year 1866, paints a most appealing picture in these words:-

"About 300 yards the other side of the ferry is the comfortable and truly rural Hostelry with its Terpsichorean platform, behind which the lads and lasses of old Nottingham do the polka to the dulcet strains of a string band every Monday evening throughout the summer, for the small charge of three pence: and where artisans and some of the better class sit on rough benches to drink beer, eat Colwick cheese, and smoke."

Incidentally, the 'Ferry Inn' had a thatched roof until the war years, tiles being substituted when it was found impossible to locate a thatcher for the repair work needed.

Good news for cyclists and pedestrians wanting to cross the River Trent came in April 1982 when the 'new' Wilford Bridge was officially opened to form part of the cycle route linking Clifton and Nottingham city centre. The old toll bridge was first opened in 1870 and closed in 1974.

The ferry-boat itself made its final crossing on September 18th, 1864.

MAYPOLE - *Wilford Lane*

Opened in December 1968, the sign here is an attractive one of children dancing gaily round the maypole. However, local history reveals that there has never been a maypole on the village green - not in living memory, at any rate - and it seems that Home Brewery were perhaps thinking of the portable maypole to be seen operating on the green at Clifton, only a few miles away, in the early 1950s.

WOLLATON

ADMIRAL RODNEY - *Wollaton Road*

This old inn was first mentioned in County Records in 1796. It probably owes its existence to a contemporary Lord Middleton who often played host at Wollaton Hall to his old school-friend Admiral Rodney (1719-1792). When part of the Middleton Estate, the pub was a Free House with a Six-Day Licence and brewed its own beer. It was sold, together with most of the estate, in 1924, and was acquired by Home Brewery. At that time it was a basic village 'local' - red brick with a slate roof and a passage down the middle - price £4,500 for the lot, and let to a lucky Arthur Hodgkinson (as the first tenant) for the princely sum of £52 per annum! It is worthy of note that the 1841 Census mentioned a later pub in Wollaton as being on the Trowell Road. This was the *'King's Head,'* with John and Hannah Burton as licensees. It lasted until 1864.

George Brydges (later Lord Rodney) was born into an old Somerset family. His parents decided that he should start his Navy career under the 'patronage' system, whereby carefully-selected boys of birth and breeding were sent to sea to 'learn the ropes' under royal sponsorship. He entered the Royal Navy (like Nelson, Jellicoe and Mountbatten after him) at the tender age of twelve, and his career for the next forty years, as listed in the Dictionary of National Biography, shows a formidable record of successes. In 1742 he was promoted to Post-Captain, an unusually rapid advancement for a young man of only 22. In 1763 he was promoted Admiral, and the following year he was created a Baronet. There followed a few years ashore and he was, at one time, MP for Northampton. In 1771 he was recalled to active service and sent out to Jamaica as Commander-in-Chief of the West Indies station.

In 1774 he returned to England, and as a period of peace had intervened between Britannia and her enemies, he was put on half-pay, together with so many other senior officers. Due to his extravagant tastes he ran up a fearsome amount of credit and in fact was forced to live in Paris between 1775-78 in order to alleviate his difficulties. His

regaining of power and authority was due to the War of American Independence, during which period England was also at war with France, Holland and Spain! When the British forces under General Burgoyne had to surrender to the Americans in 1777, this single act had convinced the French that now was the time to avenge their humiliations during the Seven Years' War and within six months they had signed an alliance with the USA which once again brought them into conflict with the British at sea.

Ironically, Sir George Rodney was ineligible for high command at this critical time, because of the embarrassing nature of his financial circumstances. During 1779 the centre of the naval war was clearly shifting across the Atlantic,

Admiral Rodney, Wollaton

and it was becoming obvious that the main clash with the French would occur in the Caribbean. Fortunately for Sir George, and for England, too, as it turned out, he managed somehow to liquidate his debts in time to meet the national crisis. He was promptly recalled to active service as Commander-in-Chief, West Indies, having been reappointed full Admiral in 1778, taking command after his arrival at Barbados. Three months later he fought an indecisive engagement with French naval forces in the Battle of Martinique.

The historic 'Battle of the Saints,' however, was the one which set the seal on his reputation as a tactician - taking its name from the little group of islets called Les Saintes, adjacent to the island of Dominica. The date, April 12th 1782, was memorable for the fact that the British carronades - a new type of gun mounted on the upper decks - did tremendous damage to the French fleet and demoralised some of the enemy crews to such an extent that they surrendered without firing a shot.

Rodney's decisive victory freed the West Indies from French domination, it enabled a satisfactory peace treaty to be signed after the American Revolution and it led to his being raised to the peerage as 1st Baron Rodney of Rodney Stoke in the county of Somerset. Moreover, the bizarre sequel to the victory provides one of naval history's most farcical chapters. A change of administration had taken place in Whitehall the month before the battle took place and the new Government had decided to supersede Rodney in his command. His relief, Sir Hugh Pigot, sailed from Plymouth on the 17th May, the very day on which the frigate *Andromache* arrived with the Admiral's triumphant despatches. Too late, frantic efforts were made to recall Pigot, who was already on his way to Jamaica, and Rodney returned home to find himself a national hero, with Authority seeking to amend its blunders by pouring honours on his head. The strategic nature of his recent naval triumph had now been fully realised, and he received the thanks of a remorseful Parliament. An entry in the Nottingham Date Book of 20th May 1782 records the town's ovations: *'All the customary displays of popular delight were indulged in, and at night there was a very brilliant and general illumination.'*

More tangible tokens of the nation's gratitude were accorded to the victorious Admiral in the shape of a peerage and a pension of £2,000 a year - and his immortality was assured by having his likeness put on canvas by the two foremost portrait artists of the day, Reynolds and Gainsborough. Nowadays, of course, he yields place only to the peerless Nelson in popularity among our inn-sign Admirals, of whom the present writers have confirmed a total of 40 such to be found throughout the nation (see also entries for 'Admiral Duncan' and 'Lord Alcester').

A similar if less intense air of excitement was apparent forty-six years on, when the first horse-drawn bus to ply between Ilkeston and Nottingham pulled into the courtyard at the rear of this inn in order to pick up passengers from Wollaton on its maiden journey in the year 1828.

Across this same courtyard is a double-storey building with a large barn above, approached by well-worn external steps. Until the village school was built in 1841, the barn served as a school-room, and later became the headquarters of the Wollaton Rural Library. The barn was also used as a meeting-place for the Village Institute, as well as being the village morgue!

In present times the courtyard has seen the advent of a camera crew from ITV, who made it their headquarters for a period during the summer of 1994, for the filming of a second series of the popular cricket-comedy *Outside Edge,* which focused on different aspects of Wollaton's sporting activities - in particular at the Bowling Club, the Tennis Club and, of course, the Cricket Club.

GONDOLA - *Wollaton Vale*

The location of this pub, opened in June 1970 at the top end of the Vale opposite Firbeck School, is still referred to by older folk as Balloon Woods - and in turn named after the so-called 'Balloon Houses', demolished in 1925, which used to stand where there is now a busy five-ways traffic junction. They are marked on Ellis's map of Notts. dated 1825, and there was a Balloon Plantation nearby as early as 1856. What cannot be agreed upon, though, is just why those 'Balloon Houses' were given their name in the first place, but there remain at least three possibilities:

 – A balloon in one of its ascents from the Forest passed over the site the day on which building was completed.
 – This was the site of an actual ballooning ascent/descent.
 – There was a field nearby in which experimental work on a ballooning project was carried out.

It seems that Nottingham failed to get in the forefront of balloon aviation on a national level when the first-ever attempt in this direction locally was made on the old Forest racecourse on July 4th, 1785 - it failed ignominiously. The unlucky genius was a certain Mr Cracknell (misquoted freely as 'Crackpot') who had visions of emulating a much-publicised ascent made at Versailles two years earlier by a Frenchman who carried a sheep as his passenger.

Mr Cracknell's on-the-spot efforts to control his output of hydrogen lasted from noon until evening - and after a seven-hour wait the large crowd finally lost patience, surged forward, and cut the cords. Even after the balloon had been borne aloft and disappeared their sense of frustration was still not vented. They proceeded to rough-house the unfortunate balloonist and smash all his apparatus. The balloon itself eventually came down in Lincolnshire, near Horncastle, apparently inconveniencing the pastoral pursuits of some farm labourers, who tore it to ribbons with their pitchforks and set fire to the remains. An inglorious episode from start to finish, indeed, and one which dampened the ardour of any prospective balloonists in Nottingham for almost thirty years.

However, on 1st November 1813, a Mr. Sadler made a successful ascent from Canal Wharf (he landed at Stamford), and exactly ten years later his son went up in a balloon from Castle Yard, carefully observed by 2,000 fee-paying patrons from prepared vantage points, and watched at a greater distance by a huge crowd of an estimated 70,000.

These spectacular efforts set the scene for popular invasion of the new medium in transport, and after a Mr Green had demonstrated an easy solo ascent from the Market Place in 1826, '*a number of ladies and gentlemen for the consideration of half-a-guinea apiece were gratified with ascents to a considerable height - and after enjoying the prospect from their giddy elevation were pulled down again by means of ropes attached to the car.*'

An even bolder spirit, a Mr Saywell, paid Green 25 guineas for the privilege of soaring with him as far as Edwalton at a height of over 2,000 feet. An hour or so later they returned in triumph to the city centre, bringing the balloon back with them atop a handsome chaise and pair!

Fifty years later there was a balloon field situated in the Arboretum, and a public outcry ensued when the Parks Committee decided in 1884 to turn the site into tennis courts. Two years previously the intrepid and legendary Colonel Burnaby (qv) had ballooned himself across the English Channel - much to the amazement of the French peasantry and the glorification of his own regiment.

Wollaton, of course, is a long way from Venice, but readers will recall that when balloons were in their heyday, the basket (elongated in shape) in which the passengers travelled was, in fact, called a gondola. This theme is echoed through all this pub's public rooms. Downstairs, in the main lounge, the gondola theme is repeated in the ceiling, which represents the bottom edge of a balloon basket. Prints of balloons, including the original one of 1785 piloted by the Montgolfier brothers, are visible everywhere - and the shape of the pub itself is of course circular.

Perhaps it should be added that quite nearby is a pub which, when opened in October 1957, was called the '*Balloon.*' Like its neighbour the '*Gondola*', it had an eye-catching pictorial signboard - but this was changed to one of heraldic design when, in December 1985 (having passed through the control of four different breweries), it was renamed as the '*Wollaton Arms.*'

Cricket & Transport

Cricket Players, Hyson Green

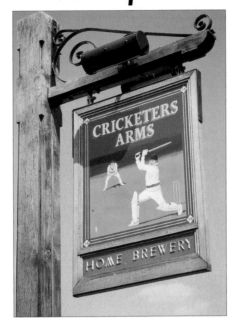

Cricketers Arms, Kirkby-in-Ashfield

Old Cricket Players, Nottingham

Larwood & Voce, Trent Bridge

Tiger Moth, Tollerton

Narrow Boat, Nottingham

Three Bridges, Nottingham

Ferry Inn, Wilford

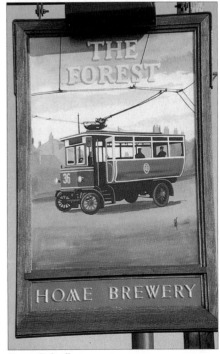

Forest, Bulwell

Gondola, Wollaton

Plate VII

Miscellany

The Beacon, St. Anns

Dixies Arms, Lower Bagthorpe

Old Volunteer, Carlton

Arboretum Manor, Nottingham

The Mill, Nottingham

Red Heart, Ruddington

Chesterfield Arms, Gedling

Welcome Inn, St. Anns

St. Ann's Inn, Nottingham

Plate VIII

HEMLOCK STONE - *Bramcote Lane*

The sign of this pub, opened in April 1959, depicts a strange-looking object resembling a meteorite. The rock itself, from which this pub takes its name, stands well back from the road (on Coventry Lane) just inside the Bramcote boundary and only about a mile away from this house. This often-discussed and ancient phenomenon is, according to geologists, a mass of red sandstone whose summit is more or less protected by layers of a harder formation i.e. barium sulphate, which defies the action of frost, rain, sun and wind alike. Its curious shape was formed after countless centuries of weathering. It is 30 feet high, 70 feet in girth, and is said to

Hemlock Stone, Wollaton

weigh over 200 tons. Holland Walker, F.R.S.A. says in his writings that at one time it was thought that *Hemlock* could be equated with *Cromlech* (the name for those mysterious stone circles of unknown antiquity and usage) and that therefore the Stone itself was once a Druid altar. Be that as it may ... but the nearest *'Druid's Tavern'* happens to be on the High Street in Arnold!

ROEBUCK - *Trowell Road*

This pub was opened in February 1972 as the *'Deep Cellar,'* but its present title dates from September 1986. The original sign was good enough to deserve closer examination, but its successor - or rather, successors - are even more enterprising. These consist of a 'swinger' sign adjacent to the main road, a wall-fixture sign facing the side road, and a fibreglass figure of the animal mounted alongside the front door. Such a varied trio of inn-signia shows a touch of real enterprise and distinction!

WHEELHOUSE - *Russell Drive*

Circular in shape and opened in December 1965, this pub was recently renovated, including a new sign with nautical overtones, and presumably now has even more success with steering potential patrons in the right direction!

Willoughby Arms, Wollaton

WILLOUGHBY ARMS - *Lambourne Drive*

Opened in August 1956, this pub's name is synonymous with that of the family who were Lords of the Manor at Wollaton for many centuries. In October 1982 the name was unaccountably changed to the *'Greenhouse,'* perhaps as a reminder of the fame enjoyed by the Camellia House at Wollaton Hall nearby, established by Lord Middleton in 1823 to house his fabulous collection of camellias. This is claimed to be one of the first examples seen in this country of a glass structure supported entirely by cast iron.

Quite unexpectedly, the pub's name reverted back to its original title in September 1988, together with a suitably heraldic design on its signboard.

WOODBOROUGH

FOUR BELLS - *Main Street*

The association between Church and Inn is well over a thousand years old, and during much of this time the two have been very good friends. In fact, the close connection between the ancient monasteries and the evolution of the national beverage points to the influence exercised by the Church at large upon the English habit of beer drinking. Many of our oldest inns were attached to monastic houses for the purpose of accommodating pilgrims, and in this way acquired a semi-religious character. No doubt this is the reason why, in England, the pub became as universal as a place of worship.

The bells represented on the signboard of this pub are situated in the belfry of the nearby church of St Swithun's. A manuscript history of Woodborough Church, compiled in one copious volume by W.E. Buckland, vicar from 1891-1896, reveals the following facts.

The four bells were all probably cast at the same time by Henry Oldfield, head of a Nottingham firm which turned out bells for a period of four generations during the 16th and 17th centuries. According to Phillimore's article in 'Old Nottinghamshire,' the versatile Henry was of ill-repute with his neighbours in the time of Elizabeth I, but 'his handiwork is excellent, and the letters, stops and borders used in the inscription of his bells, display high artistic feeling.'

The treble bell carries the inscription 'GOD SAVE OUR QVEENE.' The second bell, before its recasting by Taylors of Loughborough in 1886, was inscribed 'GOD SAVE HIS CHURCH.' The third bell, probably the oldest of the quartet, has initials inscribed, and the largest, the tenor

Four Bells, Woodborough

bell weighing at least 12½ cwt., bears the date 1680 following the words 'DONUS SANTIS SWITHUNIS CAROLUS LAWCOCK ESQ' (translated from the Latin as 'a gift in honour of St Swithun by Charles Lawcock'). This tenor bell cracked in 1896, and on examination at the Taylor Foundry, it was thought to have been recast once before at an earlier date.

That vastly informative and entertaining book 'The History of Signboards' by Larwood & Hotten (first published in 1866) points out that the Bell is one of the most commmon inn-signs of all, and was used (vide Chaucer) as early as the 14th century. Most probably bells were set up as signs on account of our national fondness for bell-ringing, which procured for our country the name of 'the ringing island,' and made Handel say that the bell must be our national instrument! There are reckoned to be close on 500 of this name in England, excluding all supplementaries such as Bluebells, Ring O'Bells, etc. Paul Hentzer, a German traveller who visited this country between 1596 and 1600, has been quoted as saying: 'the English are very fond of noises that fill the air, such as firing of cannon, beating of drums, and especially the ringing of bells - so much so that it is quite common for a number of them to go up into some belfry, and ring bells for hours together for the sake of exercise ...'

The pub itself, designed in an attractive Tudor style, replaced a pub of the same name in 1926.

WORKSOP

BOUNDARY - *Potter Street*

This pub is so named because it is situated on the old boundary between Worksop town and the old 19th century hamlet of Radford which merged into Worksop as building went along Retford Road towards Manton. In 1985, regulars were surprised to see their new pub sign depicting a cricketer fielding the ball on the boundary which of course misses the significance of the name.

FLAMINGO - *Kilton Hill*

Until zoos were introduced into this country (London's Regent's Park Zoo was opened in 1826) most of us had never seen a flamingo or even knew what colour they were, apart from pictures in books. Although the ones in captivity are usually pink in colour, they can be bright red. The one depicted on the signboard of this pub, opened in 1948, is of the pink variety, but in fact the name of the house doesn't come from the tropical long-legged bird at all. It refers to a racehorse once owned by the Farr family, former owners of Home Brewery, who had a stud at Worksop Manor.

FRENCH HORN - *Potter Street*

Adapted from a malt-kiln, the original house of this name which had stood on this site since the latter part of the 18th century, was replaced by the current building around 1906. The former inn was much smaller than its successor and used to stand next door to a small saddler's shop once occupied by a generation of the Preston family. During the re-building, this shop was demolished to allow the pub to be expanded.

The sign, though depicting the musical instrument of the brass family, most likely derives from the drinking horns that were once used for the quaffing of ale. For an alternative explanation of the name, please refer to the pub of the same name at Upton.

FROG AND NIGHTGOWN - *Carlton Road*

Opened in January 1978, this pub's name is somewhat unusual. Ted Ray used to end his radio show, the popular BBC series 'Raise A Laugh,' by saying that 'he was off to the *Frog and Nightgown*.' The latter was a real inn situated in Old Kent Road, London, and the pub here takes its name from this famous counterpart.

In 1983 a competition was run to re-name this pub and for a brief period it was restyled as the '*Cavendish,*' reverting to its former name some two years later.

GREENDALE OAK - *Norfolk Street*

The history of this old hostelry, together with an explanation for its name, is recorded on a plaque that hangs on a wall situated in the main bar area. It reads:

"The '*Greendale Oak*' is situated in the middle of Norfolk Street. In 1790, the actual building was built to house textile workers who toiled in one of Worksop's first factories on Lead Hill. It must have been located over one of the wells for which the street was famous. The Hooson brothers of Park Brewery, Sheffield and the Union Maltings, Eastgate were the owners of this inn in 1873. Various real-ale accolades have been lavished on this Stone's house. In 1912 the Hooson's sold out to Ind Coope. The Lascelles Directory of 1846 lists this inn with its very traditional sign taken from the Duke of Portland's wager with the Earl of Oxford. This hung on a bet that a coach-and-four could be driven through the trunk of this ancient tree which stood in Welbeck Park. Pigot's Directory of 1822 does not mention the '*Greendale Oak,*' Worksop, so that we may conclude that the conversion of two houses into one took place after the Beerhouse Act in 1830, which encouraged such an arrangement. Modern interior decorations have added to its charisma. It was rated at £19 in 1872 and had one unfortunate brush with the law. On the 8th October 1884, for a Public Order offence, the licensee George Askew was fined forty shillings and disqualified from holding a licence. He was keeping a brothel. Four months later he was replaced."

INNINGS - *Prospect Hill*

Opened in March 1975 by former England opener Geoffrey Boycott, this pub's name pays tribute to local cricketing hero Edwin (Ted) Boaler Alletson (1884-1963).

The son of a wheelwright, Alletson was born on the Duke of Portland's estate at Welbeck in 1884 and began his county cricketing career with Nottinghamshire in 1906. During the Great War he served in the Royal Garrison Artillery, and later went to live at Worksop to work at Manton Colliery.

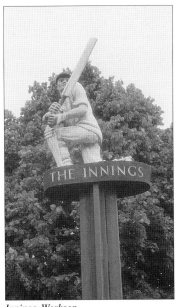

Innings, Worksop

It was on the 20th May, 1911 at Hove that Ted earned himself a place in the annals of cricketing history by playing a hurricane *innings* for Notts against Sussex. Having batted first, his side managed only 238 runs. When the home side replied with 414, Notts were hard-pressed to save the game and were struggling, having lost seven wickets for 185 - only nine runs ahead. It was at this juncture that Ted entered the crease. A powerfully built man of 15½ stones with an arm span of 6ft 6inches, he was a good all-rounder - a good fielder and a medium-pace bowler. In what was to become an historic *innings*, Ted slaughtered the Sussex bowling attack. In a fifty minute period before the lunch interval he struck 47 runs, including two sixes - but Notts also lost two wickets. With only one Notts wicket left standing when play resumed, no-one could have foreseen what was to happen next.

Some three minutes after the restart Alletson drove a four to bring about his half-century, but still Notts were in trouble. Wielding his 2lb 3oz bat like a man possessed, Ted began to strike the ball with the velocity of a shell from a cannon. One immense drive flew right out of the arena and smashed through the pavilion window, sending broken glass and shattered beer mugs about the room. Another drive sent the ball thudding into the soft wood of a new stand pillar (the ball having to be removed later using a chisel). The fielders began to scatter, but still Ted did not relent. With a hammer-blow he sent another ball crashing over the entrance gate into the street beyond, where it was picked up by a small boy, who was later found playing with it on the beach. Such was the ferocity of his assault on the bowling that the match was repeatedly interrupted by the bemused umpires whilst they searched the precincts of the pavilion for a new ball with which to play - Alletson having already struck five of them out of the ground.

When he was eventually caught on the boundary, Ted had scored 189 runs, the last 142 of which he had struck in a mere 40 minutes! In the end, Sussex who at one stage looked certain to win the game, were lucky to save it. They were still 24 runs in arrears with only two wickets left when stumps and the match were drawn.

Interestingly, Alletson's inclusion in the Notts side for this particular game had been a touch-and-go affair, as he was suffering from a sprained wrist. One wonders what his contribution might have been had he been fully-fit? Incredibly, it was the only century he ever scored in first class cricket.

For a month after its opening, this pub had on loan from Gunn & Moore, of Nottingham, the very bat that Alletson used to play this famous *innings*. Though this is no longer on display, outside the pub there is a fine statue of the cricketer himself wielding his bat. A cricket ball, of course, is nowhere in sight - but then you wouldn't expect it to be with Ted batting!

KING EDWARD VII HOTEL - *Ryton Street*

Purchased by Mansfield Brewery from Whitbread in 1992, this pub honours King Edward VII who reigned from 1901-1910. Built during his reign in 1903, it was designed to draw custom from the nearby cattle market - a tradition that continues today.

Though it stands at the junction of Ryton Street and Watson Road, the only entrance to it is from the former street. This lack of accessibility is not due to neglect on the part of the architects, but rather in accordance with the wishes of one Sir Henry Watson who decreed that there should be no business premises sited on Watson Road.

At one time customers could leave their horses in purpose-built stables at the rear of the hotel, but these have long since disappeared. Due to its inability to meet new fire regulations in 1978, this hostelry ceased to accommodate guests. Before that a number of well-known personalities who usually played at what was the Regal Cinema stayed here, including a youthful Jimmy Tarbuck.

MILL HOUSE - *Newcastle Avenue*

This former flour mill, a Grade II listed building, was opened as a pub on the 16th December 1988 by Joshua Tetleys. The mill's former owner Mrs Sheila Beard, having travelled from her home in Guernsey to Worksop, pulled the first pint.

Included in this hostelry's design are a number of the original features of the mill, including the old slate roof tiles and external brickwork.

ODDFELLOWS ARMS - *Netherton Road*

Once a meeting place for the "Friendly Societies" and early trade unions, this pub has seen some changes since it was first built in 1852. The present day tap room is a converted cottage which was added on to the pub. The Independent Order of Oddfellows was a secret benevolent society which is said to derive its name from a remark made about the founding members.

Old Ship, Worksop (c. 1930)

OLD SHIP - *Bridge Street*

Legend has it that this, the oldest pub in Worksop, contains a number of wooden beams that came from ships which took part in the Battle of Trafalgar - hence its name. Folklore also has it that the 'Old Ship' is connected to the Welbeck estate via a secret passage and that it contains a hidden recess where priests used to hide. Whether this is true or not is open to debate. One thing that is certain, however, is that the pub still contains a framed drawing of the building in former days which shows it was a much larger establishment. It was presented to a previous innkeeper by a satisfied guest signing himself Charles Tracher, and who stayed here in 1841.

Around 1993 the pub underwent a brief change of name to the 'Tut 'N' Shive' before returning to its present title in April 1995.

SHIREOAKS INN - *Westgate*

In 1873 this former beerhouse was owned by George Swann and his wife Sarah, of Wales Church, near Shireoaks. In 1881 it was sold to the newly-formed Worksop and Retford Brewery Company and continued to operate as a beerhouse until 1896 when its name emerges in the local Directories as the 'Shireoaks Inn.'

In 1978, having been taken over by Whitbreads, the pub was closed for economic reasons. In 1987 it reopened under its original guise - a name that no doubt reflects the origins of the original licensee and his wife, on the outskirts of the nearby village of Shireoaks. Shireoaks itself takes its name from the "Shire Oak" which once stood where the three counties of Nottinghamshire, Derbyshire and South Yorkshire meet.

THREE-LEGGED STOOL - *Raymoth Lane*

The name of this pub (opened in November 1978) was chosen by NALGO clerk, Dianne Neal, the winner of a North Country Breweries competition to choose a name for their new house.

The name - a reference to the stool on which farm-hands sit to milk cattle - reflects the pub's former use as an old Northern Dairies milk depot, and before that a barn. Many of the old beams and much of the original stonework from the old building were retained in its design, which comes complete with a suspended gallery to add to its rustic charm.

UNICORN - *Bridge Street*

This house was first licensed as a pub in 1813. The sign of the *'Unicorn'* is usually an heraldic reference. Two unicorns support the royal arms of Scotland, and when James VI of Scotland became James I of England, one of these legendary creatures displaced the Welsh dragon on the English royal arms. A unicorn also features in the arms of the Worshipful Company of Goldsmiths (1327), the Worshipful Company of Wax Chandlers (1483) and the Worshipful Company of Apothecaries (1617).

Whilst the fabulous one-horned horse can only be witnessed on the pub's colourful signboard outside, the house has a more gripping tale to tell.

It is said, that many years ago, in tunnels that are believed to have existed beneath the pub for over a century, a monk was killed. The legend says that he died when one of these tunnels collapsed and was set alight. Now, whenever a smell of burning is detected in the pub, his ghostly apparition appears!

WYSALL

PLOUGH - *Keyworth Road*

The Plough was originally 4 separate cottages, built over 300 years ago. They were converted in the 19th century into this cosy inn with the low ceilings and oak beams - the typical old fashioned village pub. Like many other 'Plough Inns', there is an old plough attached to the wall over the doorway.

ZOUCH

ROSE AND CROWN - *Main Street*

This 19th century pub, once called the *'Bull's Head'*, is squeezed between the main road and the Zouch cut (an arm of the canal). The *'Rose and Crown'* is a most common sign, found all over the country, and indicates loyalty to both England and the monarch.

Rose and Crown, Zouch

ROYALTY AND THE PEERAGE

It is fascinating to think that Nottinghamshire should have had so many pubs named after members of the royal family or the peerage - some easily identifiable, but others needing a sharp shuffle through the Dictionary of National Biography - umpteen volumes, and let's hope that we can pick the right one!

Alfred the Great (located in Alfred Street, Nottingham, until June 1973) was a fair enough choice - although his noble deeds as the nation's lawgiver, and his foresight in founding the English Navy, were completely ruined by his single act of carelessness in somebody else's kitchen - but what about *King Edgar* (in Peashill Road, St Ann's, until May 1971)? Not many realise that his chief counsellor was St Dunstan, and that he became the first monarch of All England. As for the *King of the French* (Woolpack Lane, Nottingham, closed in December 1947) one can only conjecture vainly 'which king?' And 'what French?' Then there was the *Empress Eugene* in Alfred Street, Nottingham, who was lost to view (and rightly so, with a name like that) in November 1959 - she was Napoleon III's wife and visited Queen Victoria in 1855.

The popular sailor-king *William IV* still holds court in Sneinton and Mansfield, whilst his wife *Queen Adelaide* has *her* attention divided between Sneinton and Kimberley. The **Princess Royal** drew the curtains in Northumberland Street, Nottingham, in March 1966, likewise **Prince Leopold** in Moffatt Street in July 1971. He was the youngest son of good Queen Victoria, who sent him to perform the opening of the old University College in June, 1881. As for **Queen Elizabeth** (presumably in honour of Good Queen Bess, as the premises were rebuilt in 1928), she is still tucked away in Bottle Lane, Nottingham and remembered as one of our most respected and successful sovereigns. This could never be said of **Charles II,** who is 'featured' in Brownlow Drive at Rise Park.

As for **King John** (Carrington Street, Nottingham), the less said about *him*, the better! Just that after his brother Richard I received a fatal wound whilst fighting the French in 1199, he reigned until his own death, from dysentery, took place in Newark Castle in 1216 - only months following his deposition by the Barons.

A sinister, scheming villain (as no doubt Robin Hood would wholeheartedly agree) King John's one saving grace was to grant, under compulsion, England's great bulwark of liberty, the Magna Carta.

We have several distinguished Dukes by name: a pair of **Cambridges** at Clarence Street and Woodborough Road, Nottingham, respectively (he was Commander-in-Chief of the British Army between 1856 and 1890); a single **Devonshire** in Carlton Road, Nottingham; a brace of **Newcastles** in Kirkewhite Street, Nottingham (closed in April 1975) and Whitemoor Road, Basford; and a **Duke of St Albans** on Bestwood Park Drive whose predecessor-by-name in Sherwood Street, Nottingham departed in March 1963. The **Duke of Wellington** is still remembered in Kirkby-in-Ashfield, as he once was in Manvers Street, Colwick (closed in December 1946), and Mill Gate, Newark (closed in 1933). The **Duke of Cumberland** who commanded the English troops at the Battle of Culloden in 1746, and whose cruelties earned him the nickname 'Butcher,' once stood in Middle Gate, Newark until its closure in 1989, under its new sign, **Kirrages**.

The belted Earls are represented, in Carlton Road, Nottingham, by a member of the famous **Howe** family whose seat was at Langar; this was Richard, the gallant Admiral, whose brother William defeated the Americans at Bunker Hill in the War of Independence. At nearby Granby, also in the Vale of Belvoir, there is (naturally enough) another successful general in the person of the **Marquis of Granby**, who can also be found in Hoveringham. He is supported by his pair of fellow-peers in Radford, who can be found in Salisbury Street and Ortzen Street respectively. The first of these is the **Marquis of Lorne**, a courtesy title of the Duke of Argyll who, in 1871, married Princess Louise, fourth daughter of Queen Victoria. The second is the **Marquis of Waterford**, a courtesy title of Field-Marshal Earl Roberts, who was awarded his Victoria Cross in 1858 for his achievements during the Indian Mutiny. As for the **Marquis of Hastings**, he vanished from Marple Street off Alfred Street North, Nottingham in November, 1955.

Next come seven noble Lords, headed by the peerless **Nelson**. He has several dedications - in Carlton Street and Thurgarton Street, Nottingham; Percy Street, Basford; Front Street, Arnold; Nottingham Road, Eastwood and Sellars Wood Drive, Bulwell - although vacating Mitchell Street in December 1947 and Balderton Gate, Newark in 1914.

Lord Raglan at Newthorpe Common is remembered for his victory over the Russians at the Heights of Alma in 1854 during the Crimean campaign. **Lord Roberts** in Broad Street, Nottingham (i.e. Earl Roberts, - publicans in the Victorian era were noticeably prone to consider all peers of the realm as 'Lords') won immortal fame for his successful march at the head of 10,000 troops from Kabul to Kandahar to secure victory in the Afghanistan campaign of 1880. **Lord Alcester** in St. Matthias Road, Nottingham received his peerage (i.e. as the former Admiral Seymour) for the fleet bombardment of Alexandria in 1882 - which persuaded Arabi Pasha, the Egyptian ruler, to pay his long-standing debts to the British government. The more peace-loving **Lord Belper** disappeared from Robin Hood Street, Nottingham in December 1958.

Lord Alcester, Nottingham

The **Lord Lincoln** which once stood proudly in Mill Gate, Newark until closed in 1907, was named in honour of Henry Pelham Alexander Pelham Clinton (6th Duke of Newcastle) who was Newark's MP from 1857-1859, and from 1865-1868.

The present **Byron's** in North Church Street, Nottingham presumably possesses a mateyness implicit in its truncated title which is so beloved by many brewers these days - thus making the **Lord Byron** at Hucknall and Mansfield appear really old-fashioned. We should also have included those local landowners **Earl Manvers** on Colwick Road and the **Earl Of Chesterfield** at Carlton, with their counterparts in the ranks of the peerage.

In addition to this long line of royalty and aristocracy we also have in our county a short but imposing list of famous edifices bearing a connection with many of them. The **Crystal Palace** in Clumber Street, Nottingham (closed March 1981) and also in Manvers Street (closed April 1963); the **Dover Castle** in Denman Street, Radford;

the (Nottingham) **Castle** in Lower Parliament Street, Nottingham; the **Windsor Castle** at Carlton and also in Sneinton Road, Nottingham (closed December 1940); the **Newstead Abbey** in St Alban's Road, Bulwell, and - believe it or not - the **Westminster Abbey** at St.Ann's.

SOLDIERS ON PARADE

Adjutant White (Hungerhill Road, St Anns) was named after a Radford man called Jonathan White. There is a commemorative bust of him in the grounds of Nottingham Castle, and outside the main Museum entrance is a plaque which records the following:

'On this terrace the first Drill of the Robin Hood Rifles commenced at 6 o'clock am Monday, 30th May 1859, under the instruction of Sgt. Major J. White, the first Adjutant of the Battalion (Captain and afterwards Major).'

The historical background to this pronouncement is worthy of recall. For some time past there had been a threat to Britain of an invasion by Napoleon III of France - so it was decided to form a corps of volunteers throughout the land to supplement the regular army. This happened similarly with the advent of World War II, the strengthening of the Territorial Reserve and the formation of 'Dad's Army'. These volunteers would train as Riflemen, and each town and county would have at least one Corps, being organised by their respective lords-lieutenant.

The Lord Lieutenant of Nottingham at that time was the Duke of Newcastle, and he employed as his agent an architect named T.C. Hine. The latter and his friends met to discuss the formation of a volunteer unit for Nottingham, and the name of the 'Robin Hood Rifles' was chosen, together with that of the redoubtable 'Jonty' White as instructor. Permission was given by the Duke to use his castle grounds for drill, the castle itself having been sacked by the Reform Bill rioters in 1831.

Robert Mellors records in his book *Men of Notts* that *'as a Drill-Master, Jonathon White developed into a man without affectation, a strict disciplinarian, rendering steady continuity of service'* - whilst according to a writer in the *Nottingham Datebook 'it would have been impossible to secure a better man. As early as his 19th year he was raised to the rank of Sergeant and had seen brilliant service in India, where his personal character, soldierly zeal and gallantry had extorted the most splendid encomiums.'*

After that initial parade on the Castle terrace which consisted of only six men, White's recruiting was so successful that on the occasion of the Robin Hood Rifle's first field-day, which took place just three months later in front of the Mayor's residence, there was a muster of 400 men - and so great was the interest among the general public that 5,000 of them were admitted by ticket to watch the manoeuvres. By the following year, 1860, the Robin Hood Rifles had made such phenomenal progress that a London newspaper referred to them as 'the crack corps of England'. In 1866, one thousand members of all ranks of the Battalion, dressed in their now-famous Lincoln green, attended the Royal Review in Hyde Park, at which Her Majesty announced her pleasure to approve the promotion of Sergeant-Major White to the rank of Captain.

These volunteer trainees came from all walks of life and were enthusiastic to learn the basic military skills. They would parade at the Castle at six o'clock in the morning, perform 1½ hours of drill and then proceed to their usual day's work. It became customary for the sons of wealthy local families to take a commission in the 'Robins'. Great importance was always laid on marksmanship, a tradition that was to extend over many generations of the Nottingham Volunteers.

When he finally resigned in 1879, with the rank of Major, 'Jonty' White was presented with an annuity for himself and his wife of £200. He died in May 1889 and, of his funeral, the *Nottingham Daily Guardian* reported that 'more than 50,000 townsfolk crowded the route to the General Cemetery and 20,000 more found their way into the burial grounds itself. He was buried with full military honours.'

In 1908 the Robin Hood Rifles became the 7th (Robin Hood) Battalion of the Sherwood Foresters. The glorious history of this regiment came to a conclusion at the end of the 1960s when they amalgamated with the Worcestershire Regiment, Princess Anne becoming their Colonel-in-Chief.

His dates: 1804-1889. Pub closure, February 1970.

Colonel Hutchinson (Castle Terrace, Nottingham) was named after a Puritan, soldier and regicide.

The pub itself was situated near to the spot where Charles I in 1642 raised his Standard to begin the Civil War against Parliament, a wall-plaque placed on Standard Hill commemorates this historic event. When Cromwell's troops seized the Castle, its garrison came under the command of a local man, Colonel John Hutchinson, who defended it against the Royalist army until the king surrendered his throne in 1646 and the war was over. He himself was in periodic conflict with his fellow-townsfolk who were, in the main, supporters of Cromwell. When the latter was away in Scotland following the beheading of the king in 1649 for treason, Colonel Hutchinson somehow managed to obtain the permission of the State Council to destroy the Castle - one theory being that he so hated the place, that he caused it to be demolished in order to get his own back for the seven miserable years he'd had to spend in it. After this, the first Duke of Newcastle cleared away the ruins, and transformed what was left into a ducal palace.

Ironically, as it turned out, the garrison at the Castle had been awarded £1,000 by Parliament for holding Nottingham Town against the Royalists. Whilst the Civil War still ensued, Colonel Hutchinson refused the Duke of Newcastle's offer of £10,000 *and* the gift of the castle itself if he would switch sides and become a Royalist. His reply, was that if the Duke *really* wanted the castle then he must wade the moat to get it, through a river of blood ...

Not long after this, Hutchinson sat as one of the judges at the trial of King Charles and became one of the signatories to this unfortunate monarch's death-warrant.

His dates: 1615-1664. Pub closure, January 1956.

Colonel Burnaby (Hartley Road, Radford) was by profession a cavalry officer - but somehow he also found time to become a seasoned adventurer, balloonist, diplomat, linguist, global campaigner and military correspondent of the *Times*, plus horseman most extraordinary. Frederick Gustavus Burnaby became a national hero following his hazardous 300-mile ride across the frozen Steppes from Kazala to Khiva (USSR) in 1875, and was made Colonel of his regiment (the Royal Horse Guards) in 1881. Four years later he joined the Nile Expedition as second-in-command to General Wolseley. In the attempt to relieve General Gordon at Khartoum, he was killed by an Arab spear-thrust in the skirmish at Abou Klea, a fitting and epic finale to a military career without parallel. Burnaby Street (off Vernon Road, Basford) is named in his honour.

His dates: 1842-1885.

Garibaldi (Cathcart Street, St Anns) was a famous Italian soldier and patriot, remembered especially for his spectacular conquest of Sicily and Naples in 1860, formerly held by Austria, with his thousand-strong volunteer army of 'Red Shirts.'

In 1864, Giuseppe Garibaldi visited London to be presented with the Freedom of the City, and was received with tremendous enthusiasm. There was once a pub in Bridlesmith Gate, Nottingham named after him, just before World War I, and another stood in Alfred Street South about the same time.

His dates: 1807-1882. Pub closure, January 1972.

General Cathcart (Cathcart Street, St Anns) was the Aide-de-camp to Wellington at Waterloo. Sir George survived this battle, but much later in his Army career he was killed at Inkerman during the Crimean campaign.

His dates: 1794-1854. Pub closure, January 1972.

General Gordon (London Road, Nottingham) was in many ways the most remarkable of all Britain's military leaders and administrators. After distinguished service in the Crimea, China and India he became governor of Egyptian Sudan from 1877-1880, but five years later his self-sacrificial career ended with an Arab spear-thrust (as depicted so graphically by a contemporary war-artist) whilst defending Khartoum against the forces of the 'Mad Mahdi.'

Completely indifferent to praise or reward and possessing a supreme contempt for money, Charles George Gordon's whole being was dominated by a strong and inflexible Christian faith. Not least among his contributions to the community was the founding of the Gordon (orphan) Boys' Homes. In any other country he probably would have become President of the Republic and, equally probably, assassinated by one of those misguided fanatics who from time to time have cut short the lives of such men as Lincoln, Gandhi and Kennedy. His dates: 1833-1885. This pub's name was changed to the **Old Tracks** early in 1992 (referring to the nearby railway line) but it closed not long afterwards.

General Havelock was one of the heroes of the campaign to suppress the infamous Indian Mutiny. He died of cholera soon after his troops liberated Lucknow. Sir Henry's last words to his son were: "See how a Christian can die!"

Nottingham pubs bearing his name used to stand in Ronald Street, Radford (closed in August 1971) and St Ann's Well Road, St Anns (closed in December 1973) - but he is still on view at Annesley Woodhouse.

His dates: 1795-1857.

The Hero of Waterloo (Hutchinson Street, off Alfred Street, Nottingham). Surprisingly, this pub's name referred not to the Duke of Wellington, but to one of his Lifeguardsmen, John Shaw, who was born in 1789 at a farmhouse near the village of Wollaton and is buried in the churchyard at Cossall, not far away. To quote from Arthur Mee's 'Nottinghamshire':

"It is strange to find in this little churchyard of Cossall reminders of three wars. One is to 13 lads of the village who died for peace; another is to one who served all through the Crimean War; the third is a marble monument with helmet, cuirass, and crossed swords to three men who fought at Waterloo. Of these one lies buried here; the other two fell gloriously in the fight, and the daring deeds of valour of John Shaw the Lifeguardsman have given him a place among the brave for all time, and a lasting memory, in the words of Scott:

'Nor 'mongst her humbler sons shall Shaw e'er die,
Immortal deeds defy mortality.'"

A giant of physical strength, it is said that he put out of action eight Frenchmen, refusing to retire from the field to have his wounds dressed, and only stopped fighting when he fell from sheer exhaustion. Pub closure, November 1970.

Napoleon (St Ann's Well Road, St Anns) was named after the French emperor, about whom, so many books have already been written.
His dates: 1769-1821. Pub closure, October 1972.

Oliver Cromwell (St Ann's Well Road, St Anns) was no lover of pomp or titles, but for all that he became Lord Protector of the Commonwealth of England, Scotland and Ireland, following the defeat and execution of Charles I. Opinions of him vary widely, though his military genius was not in doubt any more than his personal strength of character, his sense of religious toleration, and his strong foreign policy. As the head of the Parliamentarian Army, his victories over the Royalist forces were at Edgehill, Marston Moor, Naseby and Worcester. Given Newark's staunch Royalist allegiance during the Civil War, it is perhaps surprising to discover that the *'Oliver Cromwell Tavern'* once stood in Barnby Gate until its closure in 1931.
His dates: 1599-1658. Pub closure, February 1972.

ALL THOSE NOBLE KNIGHTS

At one time, Nottingham was unique in possessing among its pub names a more varied collection of Knights of the Realm than any other city in the kingdom, London included. Because of massive property redevelopment in the 1970s most of these names belong to the past, but their proud tradition can be reflected in the following potted biographies which represent the pride of our nation long ago. Moreover - and uniquely - one unexpected female can be added to this imposing list, for, in the words from a well-known Musical, there is *nothing* like a DAME!

First, alphabetically, is ***Sir Richard Arkwright*** (Arkwright Street) who, with his spinning-frame, gave a great impetus to industrial activity in the 18th century. In fact, Nottingham saw the first cotton-mill built in England, in 1769. It stood on the site now occupied by the pub in Hockley named the ***Mill*** in its honour.
His dates: 1732-1792. Pub closure, December 1974.

Sir Colin Campbell (Robin Hood Street) made his reputation as a Field-Marshal, and was Commander-in-Chief, India during the infamous Mutiny of 1857. He became the first Baron Clyde - and the ***Lord Clyde*** pub, which still stands at Kimberley, is named after him.
His dates: 1792-1863. Pub closure, July 1972.

Sir Robert Clifton (Bath Street) was the last baronet of his family. Having lost most of his estates through losses on the 'Turf,' he opened the Clifton collieries in the hope of retrieving his fortunes. The pub itself was renamed as the ***Market Side*** in January 1982.

Sir Thomas Denman (Greyfriar Gate) was an eminent judge who became Lord Chief Justice in 1832. He was Nottingham's MP from 1818-1826. Sutton-in-Ashfield still remembers him by a pub called the ***Denman's Head***.
His dates: 1779-1854. Pub closure, May 1965.

Sir John Franklin (Kirkewhite Street), navigator and arctic explorer, served at Trafalgar and was later sent to trace the coastline of North America. In 1845 he commanded an expedition to discover the legendary 'North-West Passage' leading to the Pacific Ocean, but never returned.
His dates: 1786-1847. Pub closure, February 1974.

Sir Rowland Hill (Hungerhill Road) originated the penny postal system which became the envy of the world after its appearance in 1840. Nowadays this revolutionary idea is just as incredible as it was then!
His dates: 1795-1879. Pub closure, April 1969.

Sir Charles Napier (1782-1853) can still be found in North Sherwood Street, Nottingham. He was the general whose troops were responsible for quelling the Chartist riots in the north of England during 1839, including the one which took place on the Forest on August 12th of that year. According to a contemporary, Sir Charles Napier was "brave to rashness; ready alike with tongue, pen and sword; quarrelsome with his superiors, but beloved by his soldiers" - a paragon indeed!

Sir Isaac Newton (Howard Street) in his day was Europe's foremost mathematician and is still regarded as one of the world's great men of science. He was born near Grantham, where there is a pub honouring his name.
His dates: 1642-1727. Pub closure, August 1971.

Sir Robert Peel (Manvers Street) was twice Prime Minister, but is best remembered for his Act in 1829, when Home Secretary, which established the London police force. Early members of that force were known as 'Peelers' but, as they spread nationwide, 'on the beat' they were universally recognised as 'Bobbies' (i.e. 'Bobby's men'). Two other Nottingham pubs named after him once stood in St James's Street (closed December 1943) and Carlton Road (closed December 1962).

His dates: 1788-1850. Licence lapsed April 1995.

For all-round eminence, in Tudor times at any rate, **Sir Walter Raleigh** took some beating - scholar, sailor, soldier and statesman combined. He was responsible for the colonising of Virginia and, through the introduction of tobacco into England, for making Player's please so many. Potatoes, too! He can be found, inevitably, in Raleigh Street, Radford, but bicycles cannot really be attributed to his undoubted genius - Queen Bess would never have approved.

His dates: 1552-1618.

Sir John Borlase Warren who daily surveys the dizzy scene at Canning Circus, was a local admiral who gained fame in the Napoleonic wars. His story, as the *Happy Man* of Stapleford, is recounted elsewhere within these pages.

His dates: 1753-1822.

In Denman Street, Radford is the popular **Sir Garnet Wolseley**, the Field-Marshal who was appointed Commander-in-Chief of the British Army at the turn of the century. Perhaps the most widely-travelled of all Victoria's generals, he was certainly one of the most influential, not only as regards victories abroad but as a military reformer at home. A brilliant organiser, his skills as a master-planner and communicator became a national byword (as in the phrase 'It's all Sir Garnet' - implying maximum efficiency). His grateful queen raised him to the peerage as Viscount Wolsely. Another pub bearing his name could be found in Gordon Road, Sneinton until its closure in December 1959.

His dates: 1833-1913.

Dame Agnes Mellers (Woodborough Road) is the only lady of this particular title to be found within the whole realm of Inn-Signia - and the only woman (apart from queens) to be honoured in this fashion within our own county. The widow of a prominent burgess and bell-founder, she was, in 1513, the benefactress of a 'Free School' which later became the Nottingham High School for Boys, which has had many famous pupils including writers D.H. Lawrence and Geoffrey Trease, and politician Kenneth Clarke.

SIGNS OF THE TIMES

When the long-awaited legislation introducing flexible pub hours arrived in August 1988, the anti-alcohol lobby prophesied that England and Wales would be awash with booze and drunks. However, their worst fears, as was the case in Scotland previously, have not been realised. Most drinkers have responded to 'civilised opening hours' in a sensible and sober fashion, as CAMRA has often reported.

Nevertheless, one fear expressed by CAMRA has been underscored since the law changed - too many brewers are taking the opportunity to change the nature of many of their pubs. In Nottingham, for example, Ansells lost no time in converting three city-centre pubs into all-day bars. Called 'Disco Nitespots', these pubs have been re-christened **'Butler's'** (formerly the *'Prince Albert'* when opened in April 1972 as this brewery's first pub in Nottingham), **'Cairo's'** (before that the *'Bodega'* - the Spanish word for a 'wine shop' - for many a long year), and **'Nico's'** (replacing the *'Princess,'* its name for the past seven years and which itself took over from the old *'Parliament House'* listed in the 1869 Directory). The brewers themselves explained, having renamed all three during 1988, that 'the emphasis is now on music to attract young people.'

All this, of course, is part of a disturbing nationwide trend to alter the traditional nature of our public-houses and to concentrate on 'Theme' bars that will attract the young and better-off. August 1993 saw a special report in a Nottingham newspaper, over a banner headline entitled *Battle To Save The 'Local'*, which described the fear of many local landlords that the traditional pub is on the way out - to make way for Euro-style cafés. The licensees' anxiety is increased by claims from the Brewers' Society that 10,000 pubs (that's one in six) will disappear by the end of the present decade ...

In a forthright leader-comment on these 'Signs of the Times', made by the Nottingham branch of CAMRA in the Autumn issue 1992 of their local magazine, readers were reminded that:

'The traditional British pub should be one of our most treasured institutions. It is envied the world over - and faithful replicas can be found in almost every major city around the globe. The model is invariably the same, but its success cannot be denied. Popular with homesick ex-Pats and locals alike as a convivial, social venue, the great British pub has attained a virtually unrivalled level of international recognition. And yet with a degree of perversity almost worthy of a Nobel Prize, the custodians of our pubs - principally the major breweries and big freehouse chains - far from seeking to preserve their essential character,

seem hell-bent on transforming as many as possible into Euro-café Bars or Americanised fast food diners with silly names'. The CAMRA writer cites the opening in late 1991 of the former *'Wolds Hotel'* in West Bridgford as one of the most grotesque examples of such pub desecration - *'Behind a ridiculous name,* **Quincey's***, and a hideous exterior of pink neon tubes and lurid green astro-turf, lies a soulless, gimmick-ridden eatery offering little evidence of its origins and fundamental pub character. No wonder there are rumours of disquiet amongst the local populace ...'*

This sturdy diatribe concludes as follows: *'Public bars, Snugs and Tap rooms have been phased out as pubs are 'upgraded' in favour of a boring, one-room uniformity, and with them have gone traditional pub games such as cribbage, darts and dominoes. A whole section of the community is effectively being disenfranchised in this way as the powers-that-be chase a perceived more-affluent, younger and trendy (yet still-gullible) clientele. This is not to argue against change or progress in favour of some sort of moth-balled stereotype. But change and progress should enhance the inherent qualities of the traditional British pub, not destroy them ...'*

City Trading House, Nottingham

The present writers, whilst agreeing with the foregoing wholeheartedly, ponder on the fact that all three of the Nottingham city-centre café bars mentioned earlier were renamed after a relatively short reign as such - one to a traditional name and the others to distinctly unconventional titles. *'Nico's* in Upper Parliament Street changed to the **Cask and Bottle** in November 1993, *'Cairo's'* to **Rosie O'Brien's Pumphouse** in Pelham Street in May 1994, and a few days previously *'Butler's'* in Lower Parliament Street just as mysteriously became **Levers Invention** with its *'Nevada Bar'*.

Subsequent research has so far failed to reveal the identity of the original *Rosie O'Brien*, who has a namesake in Derby and can possibly claim kinship with a certain *Rosie O'Grady* in Whitby and elsewhere. Although, disappointingly, there is no plaque in the pub to this effect, the name *Levers Invention* relates to the net-weaving machine (itself a modification and improvement to the twist lace machine produced by John Heathcote from Belper in 1809) invented by a Sutton-in-Ashfield man, John Leavers, in 1813. A plaque in his honour can be seen on a wall behind the *'Sir John Borlase Warren'* at Canning Circus, and marks the site where he invented his machine in the attic of his house in St Helens Street. The *Nevada Bar*, with its subtle suggestion of Las Vegas, is the pub's inevitably Americanised invitation to the younger set to flock downstairs ...

Mention should also be made of certain other oddly-named establishments within Nottingham's central area such as the *Café Royal* in Market Street, which before its opening as a Bar in November 1985 constituted, via its imposing-looking edifice, a branch of Martins, and later Barclays, Bank. This surprising change in public esteem was followed by the conversion, further down the street, of the former *Black Boy Berni* to the **City Trading House**. This made its appearance in March 1989 operating on a split-level basis - one half downstairs complemented by the other half, the **Old Orleans** Restaurant and Bar, upstairs. The corporate entity of this unusually-named establishment is self-described upon enquiry as a 'Young Person's Pub.'

Continuing towards the city centre, we find in The Poultry on the site of the former *'Exchange Hotel'* (built in 1724, rebuilt 1929, and renamed in 1932 from its 1844 sign of the *'Poultry'*), a premise opened as a Wine Bar in December 1983 under the curious title of **Pumps**. This seeming irrelevancy was explained by the sight of a pair of illuminated 'Petrol Pumps' standing guard on the forecourt - but these were later removed.

Ledgers, Nottingham

On Middle Pavement a pub was opened in December 1975 named quite relevantly (in fact, quite imaginatively, judging by present-day standards) as the *'Bench and Bar'* - since the Shire Hall Law Courts then stood nearby on High Pavement. However, in January 1989 its name was changed to *'Mr. Bailey's Emporium'* and then in March 1994 to *'Metzo's Café Bar'*. In December 1994 it became simply the **Café Metz**.

In August 1983 a pub in Shakespeare Street called the *'Clinton Arms'* (referring to a family name of the Dukes of Newcastle) was renamed **'Russell's'**. The reference this time was to Jane Russell, a statuesque Hollywood 'pin-up' who first burst into prominence in that much-publicised film *'The Outlaw'* in 1947. The Press blurb at the pub's reopening read as follows: *'No expense has been spared in recreating the atmosphere of a Transatlantic 1930s cocktail bar ...'*

Quite near the old Victoria Station clock-tower at the bottom end of Mansfield Road is a pub bearing the name of **Ledgers**. The building was originally named the *'Mansfield Arms,'* and dates from 1894. The title lasted until December 1973 when it changed to the *'Regent.'* After a decade it changed again, in December 1983, to the preposterous *'Blueberry's'* - in which the 'blue' theme was exploited to the full - a textured blue ceiling, blue bar and blue carpet . . . even the furnishings and most of the furniture carried this colour, but thankfully, not the beer itself! The pub has existed as **Ledgers** since December 1988 and now houses an array of artefacts to support the rather Dickensian nature of the present name. Enough said . . .

Just up the road, on the same side, is an establishment which called itself **Bobby Brown's Cafe** - it too suffered changes. It stood next door to the real BBC on Mansfield Road, i.e. Radio Nottingham. It acquired its tea-for-two name in September 1989, but its license lapsed in April 1995. Originally the 'Roebuck,' it was successively 'Old Moore's Tavern' (March 1981) and the 'Empire' (in October 1985). What more can one say, except that, if it reopened, its next title may well become the Chameleon?

At 154 Alfreton Road is an old pub which, until June 1993, could call itself the 'Cricketer's Arms.' As from then, however, it has taken a flying leap away from our national summer sport into the arms of its avoirdupois-orientated owner Ronald George Goodbill, and can now be referred to respectfully as **Defatrons**. Get it? Like it or not, one must confess that it really is a name with a difference . . .

As from April 1992, those passing by the **Tom Hoskins** in Queen's Bridge Road may indeed have pondered over the latest renaming of these premises, which date back to 1887. (In fact, the Leicester pub of this name opened in 1984 next door to the old family brewery founded by Tom Hoskins himself). This house, formerly called the 'Grove,' was rebuilt in 1937 in Art Deco style. Sandwiched between the new Meadows area and the city, however, it gradually slid downhill - despite, or perhaps because of, the brewery's attempts at converting it into a pseudo-Transatlantic disco-bar. It became firstly the 'Miami Bar' and then 'Ziggy's Bar' in September 1988, before in a final attempt to regain credibility its name reverted a month later to the 'Grove.' CAMRA's succinct comment: 'What a (yet another) Whitbread flop it turned out to be!' Also added for good measure was - 'Now, thankfully, the pub is in more responsible hands. Hoskins, the small independent brewery from Leicester, have taken over the reins, bringing their company's beers to Nottingham for the first time on a permanent basis . . .'

This chapter would not be complete without reference to an ancient and honourable pub which in its last phase of life suffered various misfortunes and renamings before it had the final indignity first of being boarded-up and then being sold-off to a restaurant chain.

As from February 1985 it was generally considered that Nottingham's own 'Thingymajigs And Wotsits' was easily the most bizarre (and pointless) naming (or in this case renaming) of any pub in the land. The advertising feature in the Nottingham Trader at that time said it all: "A touch of class comes to Basford this week with the opening of Thingymajigs Speakeasy and Wotsits Lounge Bar - in the former Windmill Bar fun pub at the junction of Valley Road and Radford Road. The names may be whimsical, but there's nothing light-hearted about the way that the owner Chris King has transformed the premises, leased from Shipstones . . ." and so on and on, to the delight no doubt of all those who were prepared to rejoice in such Americanisation ('Speakeasy,' indeed!) ('Traditional-style,' really?) . . .

Actually, the pub in question started life as the 'Shoulder of Mutton' (being listed as such in the 1822 Directory as an Alehouse) - a title fairly common in that Georgian era when the landlord was able to combine a secondary occupation such as Butcher or Baker with his chief job of tavern host or village innkeeper.

Eventually, in 1981, and for no apparent reason after almost 160 years, this weather-beaten old stalwart became the 'Windmill Bar' (the brewery strangely forgetting that they'd already built a new 'Windmill' down Alfreton Road at the end of 1966) before being curiously transmogrified into 'Thingymajigs and Wotsits' early in 1985. A final fling under yet another name in 1989 brought it to what one might truly call the end of the line. . . In all the time since 1822, this unfortunate Alehouse/Pub never possessed a pictorial signboard, so far as is known, to the day of its demise. To be fair Shipstones, via their new masters Greenalls, have of late been replacing their old signs with some handsome new eye-catchers. The final chapter of its long history came about with the decision on the part of the brewery in 1989 to rename the pub, for the last time, as the 'Rocket'. The landlord told me that he wasn't informed why, but agreed with me that the latest name probably related to the nearby railway line.

Not long afterwards, the 'Rocket' itself was exhausted by the odds against it. It finally closed for business in October 1992, and in its place arose the latest outlet in the great Eaterie Empire of McDonalds.

PUBS OF THE PAST

The term 'Public House' is believed to have first appeared in a report made to a Select Committee sitting in Parliament in 1854. From then on it came into indiscriminate use for all conditions and sorts of licensed premises. The important piece of legislation called the Wine & Beerhouse Act was passed in 1869, which seems to suggest that alehouses or beerhouses were still referred to as such, so possibly the term 'pub' gradually evolved in the decade to follow, when so many of the old taverns passed into the hands of the brewers. Alehouses themselves seem to have been more or less 'switched', in generic terms, to beerhouses with the passing of the Duke of Wellington's government's Beerhouse Act of 1830 (the previous statute on the subject, in 1828, had been named the Alehouse Act).

Our own selected Pubs of the Past belong to two categories - those whose social activities took place well before the present century but still exist, and those whose existence from the post-War era can be recalled in living memory. There are, of course, many others!

BEEHIVE - *formerly in Beck Street, Nottingham*

Like the famous '*Beehive*' pub in Grantham - which still has a real hive wedged in the branches of the tree outside, thus giving it a truly 'living sign' - this pub was similarly distinguished. The hive was inhabited by bees, which 'roamed' among the clover of neighbouring fields.

CROCUS - *formerly in Goodhead Street, The Meadows*

Robert Mellors, that indefatigable local historian, has recorded that, in the 1850s, millions of crocuses were growing in the North Wilford meadows. 'The Meadows' district was then within the parish of Wilford, which itself was brought within the City boundaries in 1952.

"They constituted," he wrote, "*a sight of such beauty such as no-one who had seen them could ever forget.*" In his most informative booklet '*Wilford, Then And Now*' which was published in his ninetieth year, in 1914, he philosophised as follows:

"*But why mourn over lost flowers? The places where they grew are occupied by houses, and the houses are full of children: and the children are more beautiful, and of greater value than the flowers.*

This pub, closed in December 1975, took its name from these flowers.

DOG AND BEAR - *formerly in Bridlesmith Gate, Nottingham*

This was one of the city's oldest inns. It was mentioned in Borough Records of 1733, and was rebuilt in 1876. The name itself was associated with the 17th-century municipal 'sport' of bear-baiting, since the Mayor and Corporation held an annual Bear-Baiting Day at Weekday Cross. The keeper of the bears resided in what was known as Bearward Lane, renamed Mount Street in 1810. There the municipal bear-pit was situated for the benefit of the mayor, his aldermen and burgesses. The last public spectacle of bear-baiting took place on the Forest in 1840, less than a decade before this revolting 'sport' was declared illegal by national statute in 1849.

It must be remembered that, in so-called Merrie England, the feelings of animals was generally disregarded, and it was considered a legitimate pastime to tether a helpless creature to a post (whether bull, bear or badger) and set fierce dogs upon it. All classes of society patronised these affairs, seeing nothing wrong in so doing. Baiting in fact enjoyed official approval, from the monarch downwards.

In the days when Nottingham Castle was a royal residence, its courts would often witness bear-baiting, with stands being erected for the accommodation of the ladies and others of high degree. Usually, the bears themselves would be trained and looked after by professional 'bearwards,' who travelled the country to participate in scattered meetings. The bears belonging to the Castle, however, were reserved for exclusive patronage. The license has been transferred to the *Court* (qv), the Dog and Bear has now been refurbished as shops.

DOVE AND RAINBOW - *formerly in Parliament Street, Nottingham*

This pub commemorated the old Nottingham dyeing trade which had its headquarters in Lister Gate, the ancient thoroughfare of the Dyers. The '*Mistery Play Of The Deluge*' was performed every Whitsuntide by the Guild of London Dyers, whose trade sign was the '*Dove And Rainbow.*'

FRANK'S REST - *formerly in Ragnall, nr. Retford*

This has to be one of the most curious public houses ever to have existed in Nottinghamshire, and was no doubt one of the smallest hostelries to be found anywhere in Britain before its closure in 1987. Only about ten people at a time could enter this single-roomed pub, which at one time also contained a three-piece suite, a piano and a table. The house had a beer licence thought to date back to before 1869, and in its latter days sold only bottled beer or cider to passing motorists or local landworkers.

GREYHOUND - *formerly in Mansfield*

This old house was demolished to make way for the Four Seasons Centre. In former days it was a noted meeting place for Mansfield tradesmen and, for many years, gooseberry shows were held here annually. Between 1872 and 1877 the landlord was a Mr Joseph Wildsmith, during whose tenancy the local Horticultural Society was formed at this house.

The name is a reference to the Dukes of Newcastle, whose heraldic emblem is the greyhound.

HORNE'S CASTLE - *formerly in Short Hill, Hollowstone, Sneinton*

Closed in 1948, this was one of those public-houses, the meaning of whose name is now unknown to the general public. It recalls the life and doings of an unpleasant old reprobate who dates from the eighteenth century. In 1729 the tavern was the residence of William Andrew Horne - "Esquire" as his contemporaries addressed him - who, in addition to being a wealthy man, was a real bad character. At one time or another he seems to have committed most known crimes, including that of Murder.

His brother, who knew his guilty secret, offered not to denounce him if he would lend him £5 so that he could make his way to Liverpool and emigrate. "I'll chance it!" was Horne's sardonic reply. For years afterwards there was a saying among elderly townspeople when confronted with a personal decision, "I'll chance it - like Horne did his neck!"

Horne escaped the consequences of his misdeeds until old age, when he was condemned to death for the murder which he'd committed many years before. In accordance with the custom of the times, and befitting a townsman of wealth and property, he was removed from the dock to his own house (and quite literally Castle). From there he was driven by his own coachman to the place of execution on Gallows Hill (see entry for the 'Nag's Head' on Mansfield Road, Nottingham) where he was hanged. Afterwards, his body was placed on view for the public at his late residence.

Horne passed from life in a disgruntled state of mind, for it appears that he was accustomed to eating plum pudding exactly at noon on his birthday. As he was officially due to be hanged during the forenoon, his grievance was that the authorities refused to postpone his fate until after twelve o'clock - and so he was deprived of his favourite dessert.

MALT CROSS HALL -
formerly in St. James Street, Nottingham

In 1877 this four-storey building was opened as a Music-hall, functioning jointly as a public-house and taking the name associating it with the old Malt Cross situated between Sheep Lane nearby (now Market Street) and the Chapel Bar (which had been demolished in 1804). An ice-skating rink was also envisaged here in the basement, but got no approval from the licensing authorities. It lost its licence in 1880 due to unlawful goings-on upon the premises, was once again opened, but again lost its licence in 1914.

In more recent times it was once again reopened as a pub called the 'Old Malt Cross' - but it had only a short reign, from October 1983 to December 1986. The building still exists as 'The Potter's House,' a flourishing eating-and-meeting place run by a Christian group of various denominations. The premises are still graced by part of the original Music-hall stage and the upstairs gallery.

It is worth noting in this same context that the 'Malt House' pub (a Free House in Victoria Street, Nottingham) originally opened in February 1977 and was reopened under new management in February 1986.

Malt House, Nottingham

MILTON'S HEAD - *formerly in Milton Street, Nottingham*

Opened in 1781 and - like the name of the street - honoured by its name England's premier Epic poet, John Milton (d. 1674). At its opening, this pub was ablaze with coloured lamps in celebration of Admiral Rodney's success against the Dutch. It was closed in December 1969 and demolished in order to prepare the way for the Victoria Centre, where a new pub of the same name was opened in July 1974. However, the latter house lost its Head in 1988, and its entirety in 1993!

The pub called the 'Old Milton's Head' which stood in Derby Road, Nottingham opposite the present car showrooms, closed down in January 1945.

NOAH'S ARK - *formerly in Coalpit Lane, Hockley, Nottingham*

This name was possibly a satirical reflection on the mixed crowd which gathered there - not to actually escape the 'Heavy Wet' (as in the case of the animals in the Great Deluge) but in order to obtain some of it! 'Heavy Wet' was in fact a slang name for the famous strong brew known as London Porter, the successor of 'Entire' and predecessor of 'Stout.' 'Porter' originated in London around 1730, and by 1800 was probably the most popular beer in England until it was overtaken by the 'Pale Ales' from Burton-on-Trent. However, in recent years some brewing companies have revived it.

OLD CORNER PIN - *formerly in Clumber Street, Nottingham*

On this site (at the junction of Clumber Street and Parliament Street) the last maypole in the city of Nottingham was put up in 1745 and taken down in 1780. It consisted of the finest fir tree in Nuthall Park and was presented by Sir Charles Sedley in his hour of political triumph, having been returned as M.P. for the town of Nottingham after an exciting parliamentary election. The tree was removed - reason unknown - by a certain Overseer of Highways, who must indeed have been a most churlish fellow.

About the same time, this old tavern's name was mentioned in a popular London ballad which began in rather beguiling fashion with these words:

"When first I saw Miss Bailey
'Twas on a Saturday:
At the 'Corner Pin' she was drinking gin,
And smoking a yard of clay."

The prowess of the bibulous Miss Bailey at skittles is not recorded - but those addicted to this once-universal game are well aware that the corner-pins are the most difficult to strike. In all probability the regulars here would have been adept in the skittles alley when this house, closed in 1989, was in its heyday.

Cherry's map (see 'The Aviary', Trent Bridge, for details) shows this hostelry as the 'George' at the top of Cow Lane, which became Clumber Street in 1811. By the end of the century the inn had been renamed the 'Horse And Groom.' Still in a strategic position, and following redevelopment, the 'Old Corner Pin' has now become the bearer of an even more-notable title, the (Walt) Disney Store!

OLD ECLIPSE INN - *formerly in West Gate, Mansfield*

This old inn used to host the Swainmote Dinner, a court held three times a year before verderers (forestry officers having charge of plants and venison) by the stewards of the court. It was so-called because the swains (peasants) were the jurymen.

The pub itself took its name from a racehorse which was born during an eclipse of the sun in 1763. The horse became a great champion and sired countless others.

PEGGERS - *Southwell Road, Sneinton*

This old pub was listed in the County Directory of 1832 as the 'Fox and Grapes' - a fairly common sign years ago attributable to Aesop's well-known fable, which in turn led to the expression 'sour grapes'.

The pub was, over a long period, identified by the nickname of *The Pretty Windows* - because of its tall, intricately-designed coloured windows, later replaced by ones less consipicuous. However, it later became well known for another, more sinister reason. During the early hours of Sunday, September 8th 1963 the landlord at that time, George Wilson, was savagely stabbed to death on the pavement outside after taking his dog for a walk. This crime became known as 'The Pretty Windows Murder' - and it remains unsolved.

The pub acquired the name 'Peggers' in December 1986, in token of the fact that many of its 'regulars' remembered so well when it used to be a 'Pegger's Paradise', that is, for the local poachers, especially those who went out after rabbits. In the words of a certain Ted Jeffreys spoken yesteryear... *'They used to go out after them rabbits of a summer's evenin' about 6 o'clock, and be back about 9 with the 40 or 50 rabbits they'd shot. They'd stick 'em on the spikes outside and the housewives would come by later and pick 'em, leaving their tanners (sixpences) on the windowsill. And a long time back, there used to be a big stove in the Vaults. People 'd go in the market, buy a couple o' stone of mussels and cook 'em over the stove. Luvly!'...*

The pub used to have unusual opening hours because it served the needs of the Sneinton Wholesale Market. The pub closed in 1995 when the Wholesale Market moved to Meadow Lane.

SPREAD EAGLE - *formerly in Long Row, Nottingham*

This was a popular rendezvous for the market tradesmen and local farmers, who would meet there to settle their accounts and stay for refreshment. At one time a tame eagle was kept in the inn-yard chained to a post, where it was fed with corn thrown to it by sundry agricultural customers. The premises, which were close to where 'Yates's Wine Lodge' now stands, were demolished in 1865 to make room for road-widening.

The *Nottingham Date Book* records that on 28th April 1852, a man named Stevenson, living in Millstone Lane, brought his wife into the Market Place with a new rope around her neck and offered her for sale at a spot near to the sheep pens. "Here is my good woman for sale," he announced. "I shall put her up for two shillings and sixpence - and the rope itself is worth sixpence!"

The unfortunate woman was eventually bought for a shilling by a man named Burrows and . . . *'they all repaired to the Spread Eagle to sign articles of agreement, the lady being the only party to sign her own name.'*

STAR AND GARTER - *formerly in Narrow Marsh, Nottingham*

This pub's name recalled the fatal duel between the 5th Lord Byron and Mr Chaworth of Annesley Hall, which took place at the 'Star and Garter' in Pall Mall, London on the 26th January 1765. Their quarrel occurred during a meeting of the Nottinghamshire Club held at this London tavern, which they had both attended. The duel was fought by the light of a small tallow candle in an upstairs room, behind a closed door guarded by the two men acting as supporters. Only two passes were made. Mr Chaworth thrust his blade harmlessly through his Lordship's waistcoat, whilst Byron shortened his own sword and almost transfixed poor Mr Chaworth, who died the following day.

WAGGON AND COALS - *formerly in Bridge Street, Mansfield*

During the 18th century this house was known as the 'Waggon And Load Of Coals.' When it was sold in 1781, together with a house that adjoined it, the premises comprised a malt kiln, six stables, outbuildings and a large coal yard. It took its name from this once thriving coal business.

ACKNOWLEDGEMENTS

We would like to offer our grateful thanks to the following:

John Bartle (Tenanted Sales Manager - Mansfield Brewery PLC)
Ian Brown (Nottinghamshire County Council)
Joan Bryan
Rodney Cousins
P. S. Forster (Property Manager - Scottish & Newcastle (Trent Inns Ltd.))
R. W. D. Hanson (Chairman & Managing Director - Hardys & Hansons PLC)
Derek Mapp (Managing Director - Tom Cobleigh PLC)
Denis Tennent (Estates Manager - Whitbread Brewery)
Tim Warner (Local Studies Librarian - Newark Library)
Judy Willis (Licensing Records Office)
The Basford Local History Society
The Inn Sign Society (c/o The Secretary, 18 Dunlin Avenue, Newton-le-Willows, Merseyside WA12 9RF)
The Newark Advertiser
The Nottingham Branch of CAMRA
The Nottingham Evening Post
The Nottingham Topic
The Sneinton Voice
The Staff of the Local Studies Library (Angel Row, Nottingham)

and many others who have helped to make this book possible.

We would also like to extend a special thank you to all those publicans throughout the county whom we have had the pleasure of meeting, and talking to, during our researches for this publication. Thank you for your patience and for quenching our thirst for knowledge.

© Photography by:

Brian J. Curtis
Ian Brown, LRPS
Trevor Clayton (Images)
Nic Broomhead

Archive photographs courtesy of the Local Studies Library, Angel Row, Nottingham.

BIBLIOGRAPHY

The following publications have been consulted during the preparation of this book:

Arundel, Betty *Southwell, A History Walk* (1988)
Bartholomew, Claude *The Leen Valley* (1983)
Bradbury, D. J. *Secrets of Sherwood* (Wheel Publications, 1987)
Brewer, E. Cobham *The Dictionary of Phrase & Fable* (Galley Press, 1981)
Bristow, Philip *The Mansfield Brew* (Navigator Publishing Ltd., 1976)
Bruce, George *Kimberley Ale - Hardys & Hansons 1832-1982* (Henry Melland Ltd.)
Bryson, Emrys *Owd Yer Tight* (Ray Palmer Ltd., 1967)
Coleman, Arthur *Eastwood Through Bygone Ages* (1972)
Cousins, Rodney *Newark Inns & Public Houses* (Nottinghamshire County Council, 1991)
Delderfield, Eric R. *British Inn Signs & Their Stories* (Short Run Press Ltd., 1965)
Dunkling, Leslie & Wright, Gordon *A Dictionary of Pub Names* (Routledge & Kegan Paul, 1987)
Fooks, Peter *Pub Walks in Nottinghamshire* (Countryside Books, 1993)
Greenwood, Douglas *Who's Buried Where in England* (Constable & Company Ltd., 1990)
Hackwood, Frederick W. *Inns, Ales and Drinking Customs of Old England* (Bracken Books Ltd., 1985)
Howatt, Polly *Tales of Old Nottinghamshire* (Countryside Books)
Hutchinson *Dictionary of Biography* (Helicon Publishing Ltd., 1994)
Iliffe, Richard & Baguley, Wilfred *Victorian Nottingham* (Volumes Four and Twelve): *A Story in Pictures*
   (Nottingham Historical Film Unit, 1974)
Innes-Smith, Robert *The Dukeries & Sherwood Forest* (1984)
Lambley, Terry *Nottingham A Place of Execution* (Terry Lambley, 1981)
Larwood, Jacob & Hotten, John Camden *The History of Signboards* (Blaketon Hall Ltd.)
Lindley, Luther *History of Sutton-in-Ashfield* (J. H. Hall & Sons Ltd., 1983)
Magnusson, Magnus & Goring, Rosemary *Chambers Biographical Dictionary* (W & R Chambers Ltd., 1990)
Mayfield, Pat *Legends of Nottinghamshire* (Dalesman Paperbacks, 1976)
Mee, Arthur *The King's England - Nottinghamshire* (The King's England Press, 1970)
Mellors, Robert *Wilford - Then and Now*
Minnitt, Bernard A. *A Trentside Narrative* (1986)
Ottewell, David *Nottinghamshire Inns & Pubs* (Reflections of a Bygone Age, 1990)
Pigot's *1822 Directory*
Sutton, John F. *The Date Book of Nottingham 1750-1850*
Tresidder, R. S. *Nottingham Pubs* (Nottingham Civic Society, 1980)
White's *Directory of Nottinghamshire 1832*
White's *Directory of Nottinghamshire 1844*
White's *Directory of Nottinghamshire 1853*
Wright's *Directory of Nottingham 1874*

Various press cuttings from the Local Studies Library, Angel Row, Nottingham.

INDEX OF TOWNS AND VILLAGES

INDEX OF INNS AND PUBS

(Main entries are shown in **bold** typeface, illustrations are indicated by *italics*)

157

City Trading House, Nottingham, 149, *149*
Clifton Bridge, Clifton, 30
Clifton Grove, Meadows, 68
Clinton Arms, Newark, 71
Clinton Arms, Nottingham, 149
Clinton Arms, Radford, 100
Clock, Hyson Green, 50, *50*
Coach and Horses, Eastwood, 37
Coach and Horses, Nottingham, 80, *80,* 81
Coach and Horses, Thurgarton, 127
Coach and Horses, Tuxford, 128
Coachmakers Arms, St Anns, 81
Cock Inn, Balderton, 7
Cock 'n' Bull, Bulwell, 19
Cocked Hat, Aspley, 6
Colliers Arms, Cinderhill, 28
Colonel Burnaby, Radford, 100, 146
Colonel Hutchinson, Nottingham, 145
Commercial Inn, Beeston, 12
Coopers Arms, Bulwell, 19, 80
Coopers Arms, Nottingham, 80
Coopers, Mansfield, 61, *Plate VI*
Copper Beech, Bilsthorpe, 15
Corn Mill, Chilwell, 28
Court, Nottingham, 81, *81*
Cranmer Arms, Aslockton, 5, *5*
Cremorne, The Meadows, 68
Cricket Players and Tea Gardens, Hyson Green, 51
Cricket Players, Hyson Green, 50, *Plate VII*
Cricketers Arms, Kirkby-in-Ashfield, 53, *53, Plate VII*
Cricketer's Arms, Nottingham, 150
Crispin Arms, Newark, 74
Crocus, The Meadows, 151
Cross Keys, Arnold, 2
Cross Keys, Burton Joyce, 22, *22*
Cross Keys, Epperstone, 41, *41*
Cross Keys, Newark, 72
Cross Keys, Nottingham, 41, 81, 94
Cross Keys, Teversal, 126
Cross Keys, Upton, 129
Crown, Bathley, 15
Crown, Beeston, 12, *12*
Crown, Bingham, 15
Crown, East Markham, 15
Crown, Hucknall, 48
Crown, North Muskham, 15
Crown, Nottingham, 93
Crown, Rolleston, 106
Crown, Sturton-le-Steeple, 123
Crown, Tuxford, 128
Crown, West Stockwith, 135
Crown and Mitre, Newark, 71
Crown Hotel, Southwell, 114
Crusader, Clifton, 30
Crystal Palace, Nottingham, 144
Cuckoo Birch, Mansfield, 61
Cuckoo Bush, Gotham, 44, *44, 45*

Dame Agnes, St Anns, 117
Dame Agnes Mellers, St Anns, 117, 148
Deep Cellar, Wollaton, 139
Deerstalker, Bestwood, 14
Defatrons, Nottingham, 150
Denman's Head, Sutton-in-Ashfield, 124, 147
Devonshire Arms, Sutton-in-Ashfield, 124
Dial, Mansfield, 62
Dixies Arms, Lower Bagthorpe, 59, *Plate VIII*
Dog and Bear, Nottingham, 151
Dog and Duck, Clipstone, 31
Dog and Rabbit, Warsop, 130, *Plate V*
Double Top, Chilwell, 28
Dove and Rainbow, Nottingham, 151
Dovecote, Laxton, 56, *56*
Dover Castle, Radford, 144
Dragon, Nottingham, 80
Druid's Tavern, Arnold, 139
'Drum', Beeston, 13
Duke of Cambridge, Nottingham, 144
Duke of Cumberland, Newark, 144
Duke of Devonshire, Nottingham, 82, 144
Duke of Newcastle, Basford, 144
Duke of St Albans, Top Valley, 127, 144
Duke of Sussex, Fulwood, 65
Duke of Wellington, Hoveringham, 47
Duke of Wellington, Kirkby-in-Ashfield, 54, 144, *Plate I*
Duke William, Askham, 5, *5*
Dukeries, Edwinstowe, 40
Durham Ox, Beeston, 5, 12
Durham Ox, Orston, 12
Durham Ox, Wellow, 12, 131, *131*

Eagle, Arnold, 2, *2, Plate IV*
Earl Howe, Nottingham, 82, *82,* 144, *Plate I*
Earl Manvers, Sneinton, 111, *111*
Earl of Chesterfield, Carlton, 24, 144
Earl of Chesterfield Arms, Carlton, 24
Earl of Chesterfield Arms, Shelford, 43, 108, *108*
Early Bird, Bilborough, 14
Elm Tree, Forest Fields, 10
Elm Tree, Hoveringham, 47
Elton Arms, Elton, 41
Elwes Arms, Carlton, 25
Empire, Nottingham, 150
Empress Eugene, Nottingham, 143
Engine House, Carlton, 25
Exchange Hotel, Newark, 71
Exchange Hotel, Nottingham, 149
Eyre Arms, Rampton, 103

Fagins, Nottingham, 84
Fairway, Keyworth, 52

Feathers, Langar, 56
Feathers Tavern, Stapleford, 119
Fellows Morton and Clayton, Nottingham, 82, *82*
Ferry Boat, Laneham, 55, *55*
Ferry Boat, Stoke Bardolph, 122, *122*
Ferry House, Gunthorpe, 46
Ferry Inn, Wilford, 136, *Plate VII*
Festival Inn, Trowell, 128
Filho da Puta, Nottingham, 83
Filly and Firkin, Nottingham, 83, *83, Plate V*
Five Ways Hotel, Nottingham, 83
Flamingo, Worksop, 140, *Plate IV*
Fletcher and Firkin, Nottingham, 83, *Plate V*
Flying Bedstead, Hucknall, 48
Flying Horse, Arnold, 2
Flying Horse, Nottingham, 2
Flying Scotsman, Retford, 104
Forest, Bulwell, 19, *19, Plate VII*
Forest Folk, Blidworth, 16, *16*
Forest Inn, Nottingham, 111
Forest Tavern, Nottingham, 111
Foresters Arms, Nottingham, 81
Fountain, Nottingham, 83
Four Bells, Woodborough, 139, *140*
Fourways, Mansfield Woodhouse, 66, *66*
Fox, Basford, 9
Fox, Kelham, 52, *52*
Fox, Nottingham (Upper Parliament St.), 90
Fox, Nottingham (Valley Road), 83
Fox, Sneinton, 111, *Plate III*
Fox, Tuxford, 128
Fox and Crown, Basford, 9, *9*
Fox and Grapes, Sneinton, 153
Fox and Hounds, Blidworth Bottoms, 54
Fox and Hounds, Hucknall, 49
Fox and Hounds, Kirton, 54, *54*
Fox and Hounds, Netherfield, 70
Fox and Hounds, Sturton-le-Steeple, 123
Fox and Hounds, Walkeringham, 54
Fox and Owl, Nottingham, 90
Framesmiths Arms, Bulwell, 19, *19,* 81
Frank's Rest, Ragnall, 151
Freemans Arms, Normanton-on-Trent, 76
French Horn, Upton, 129, *129*
French Horn, Worksop, 140
Friar Tuck, Arnold, 2, 109, *Plate II*
Friendly Tavern, Arnold, 2
Frog and Nightgown, Worksop, 141
Full Moon, Morton, 38, 69

Garden Gate Inn, St Anns, 117
Gardeners, Cossall, 32
Gardeners, St Anns, 118, *118, Plate VI*
Garibaldi, St Anns, 146